THE VOICES OF
BRAVING THE FLAMES

"Fire is alive, there's no question about it. We call it 'the red devil' or 'the beast.' It breathes, it moves, it's your adversary. As a fire fighter your objective is to kill it . . ."

—DEPUTY CHIEF VINCENT DUNN,
Third Division Commander, Manhattan

"Everybody was screaming, 'Mayday! Collapse! Collapse!' What happened was that the top floor hesitated for just a minute and then started to pancake—floor upon floor—all the way down. Seven guys rode right down with the building . . . they were all buried."

—BATTALION CHIEF RICHARD FANNING,
Battalion 38, Brooklyn

"I had no desire to fight fires. However, after about four or five months in a very, very active tenement area, I began to really get caught up in the excitement and the challenge. Fighting fires was scary, but there was a real sense of accomplishment."

—LIEUTENANT ROBERT QUILTY,
Staff Psychologist, FDNY Counseling Unit

W9-AWB-434

BRAVING THE FLAMES

PETER A. MICHEELS

ibooks
new york
www.ibooksinc.com

ibooks, inc.
24 West 25th Street
New York, NY 10010

The ibooks World Wide Web Site Address is:
http://www.ibooksinc.com

ISBN 0-7434-5248-8
First ibooks, inc. printing February 2002
10 9 8 7 6 5 4 3

Cover photograph
copyright © 2001 by Matthew Daly

Cover design by carrie monaco

Printed in the U.S.A.

This book is dedicated to the more than 1,000 FDNY firefighters who have lost their lives in the line of duty. It is also dedicated to all those firemen whose lives have been cut short because of their exposure to the hazards of fire fighting.

This book is also dedicated to the memory of Battalion Chief Jack Fanning, firefighters Dan DeFranco, Jonathan Lee Ielpi, and John Vigiano II, and NYPD officer Joe Vigiano.

ACKNOWLEDGMENTS

At the time this book was originally written, it could not have been completed without the help of many terrific people. I first of all want to thank those generous men who, in addition to revealing their stories, allowed me to share in the humor, comradeship, and adventure of the fire service. I would also like to thank the following men who provided me with the background to understand what fire fighting is about: Dispatchers Dan Buckley (Supervisor, Manhattan), William Ladell (Manhattan), and Warren Fuchs (Brooklyn); Firemen John Driscoll (R1), David Gettens (L26), Ed Beban (L26), Richard Hannon (R3), John Romanelli (E282), Walter Fornes (Div3), Peter Riccardi (UFA), Robert Athanas (E217), Paul Hashagen (R1), Richard Evers (R2), Peter Martin (R2), and Dennis Conway (L111); Lieutenants John Scasny (E9), Sal Caliendo (E58), James Ellison (R1), Matty Shields (L26), Patrick Brown (Rescue Services), Steve Casani (R1), Gerry O'Donnell (HQ), and James Fitzgerald (L79); Captains Howard Kennedy (L4), Jack Boyle (E5), Brian O'Flaherty (R1), and Ray Downey (R2); Battalion Chiefs Robert Cantillo (B8), John O'Regan (retired), Bart Mitchell (retired), and John O'Rourke; Honorary Deputy Chief John Gill and FDNY Chaplain, Father Julian Deeken.

This book would have been only on audio cassettes had not Cecilia Anzalone meticulously transcribed the interviews and Kelly Steel retyped the manuscript. Special thanks to Hal and Barbara Freitag for the diagram of the tenement at the back of the book. The Bellevue Hospital crew: Susan Reed, MA; Louis Cuoco, ACSW; Stephen Siegman, CSW; Fred Covan, Ph.D.; Anne Hardesty, Ph.D.; Eugene Burdock, Ph.D.; Ed Robbins, M.D.; Bernard Salzman, M.D., and Robert Maslanski, M.D., get my gratitude for their help and support of this project.

Finally, I would like to thank five special women: Beth Waxse, my agent who deals with all those things I'm glad I don't have to; Adrian Ingrum, who believed in this book and originally acquired it for Putnam; Sallye Leventhal, who did a great job editing the manuscript; Trish Todd, my editor at Berkley who not only superbly brought this book to light, but made my role as an author a more pleasant one; and finally my mom, who kindled in me a love for books by taking me, as a young kid, to the Franklin Square Library.

FIRST WATCH

I'm no probie now
Today I turned fourth grade
Tonight I stand my first
Full watch alone, the three to six
It's a lonely lonesome watch
And sometimes very quiet
Except for those funny noises
Coming from the rig.

The lieutenant said it's just
That the rig is settling.
Nothing else!
Big Pat McDonough has
Another story, says he
It's the ghosts of firemen
Who've stood their last late
Watch long long ago
And come back and visit
In the wee small hours of morn
And climb up on the truck.

Bill Hyland, FR Fourth Grade
Ladder Company 10, FDNY 3-1-38

AUTHOR'S NOTE

Because I have allowed these men to speak in their own voices, there may be some terms with which the reader is not familiar. The glossary at the end of the book explains these terms.

CONTENTS

INTRODUCTION

There is nothing more formidable than fire. Its destructive power is awesome. Fire out of control is terrifying. And burns are the worst trauma a person can suffer. In the next 24 hours, there will be 80 fires in the city of New York. They may range from food burning on a stove to many city blocks going up in flames. The fire might be deep below ground or more than one hundred stories above the street. But whatever their magnitude or location, the members of the Fire Department of New York—the FDNY—will be there to fight them.

These fires kill. In October 1966, twelve firemen were thrust into their own funeral pyre when the floor they were standing on collapsed. Their bodies were carried out by their brother firefighters. In 1980, two hundred eighty-nine civilians lost their lives in fire, and their bodies, too, were carried out by firefighters. But the worst was yet to come. On the morning of September 11, 2001, two hijacked airliners were deliberately flown into the upper floors of the twin towers of the World Trade Center.

The FDNY, fully understanding the potential life hazard—since they had evacuated 40,000 people from the trade center after it was bombed in February 1993—within minutes dispatched a full five-alarm assignment to each building, along with every specialized rescue company the department has. The twin towers initially survived the plane crashes, but the resulting fires, raging at 2,000°, began destroying the integrity of the steel supports. All the while, the firefighters climbed up stairs on search and rescue missions as office workers and other occupants were climbing down. One witness who escaped from the 78th floor of one of the towers said later, "And the [firemen] had to go all the way up to the 90s—straight into hell. This was not lost on the crowd. We all broke into applause at one point." A woman with a broken leg, lying on a staircase landing, told several firefighters not to worry about her, but to save themselves. Their reply, as they carried her to safety, was, "We don't work that way."

But the buildings' steel skeletons could no longer do the work they were designed for. The one in the South tower failed first. The upper floors began pancaking down, one upon another, as if a giant piledriver was at work until, in a matter of seconds, the majestic building was reduced to a pile of rubble. Only to be followed in a short while by the collapse of the North tower.

That day at the World Trade Center, more than 4,000 people, including 343 of New York's Bravest, died. It was this city's and this fire department's darkest day. And to make matters worse, because of the incredible intensity of the destruction, there are relatively few bodies to be carried out by their brother firefighters.

If you are a firefighter in the FDNY, you have almost a fifty percent chance that in the next year you will be unable to complete your tour of duty because you have been hospitalized or sent home by the department's physician for an illness or injury you sustained on the job. Firefighting is the most hazardous peacetime occupation.

In the year 2000, the twelve thousand firefighters in New York City battled 29,891 fires. They responded to 31,058 fire emergencies and 174,620 non-fire emergencies which ranged from gas leaks to people trapped underwater in a helicopter. They also went to 58,806 false alarms. The FDNY is the busiest department in the world.

Like the city it serves, the FDNY has seen many changes over the past fifty years. In the 1950s, the two busiest companies were Ladder 26 and Engine 58 in Harlem, each of which did about two thousand runs a year. In the late 1960s and '70s, this dubious honor was given to companies in the South Bronx and Brooklyn as the wave of poor immigrants from the rule South and the Caribbean swelled the ghettos of these boroughs. During this time some companies were reaching the ten thousand runs a year level.

As the number of fires and runs escalated, new firefighting strategies were developed, new equipment was introduced, and the members of the FDNY rose to the challenge.

Although the people of the city of New York consistently give the fire department high marks for performance, the municipal government sometimes takes a punitive attitude against its firefighters. In July 1975, the city began laying off its firefighters—something that didn't happen even during the Great Depression. Though demoralized, those men who were still on the job continued to do their all in responding to fire alarms. But the worst was yet to come: 1976 was the busiest year for fires—153,263 of them. The high point for runs—472,405—was reached in 1978. The toll on men and equipment was enormous.

This was an incredible time to be a firefighter. The majority of firefighters love their work, and if there is a fire they want to fight it. In their own parlance, "to go to work" or "to catch a job" means only one thing: to fight a fire. Despite the hazards, there are numerous rewards to being a firefighter. Though no one ever made a fortune putting out fires, many have achieved richness in an existential sense. Simply put, for these men firefighting is not just a job, it is a vocation.

But the world of the New York City firefighter is one that few people outside of the fire service know very much about. The next time a news story about some heroic action by a member of the FDNY airs on television, take a good look. You will notice that most of the time the camera must be content with filming only the victims, the Emergency Medical Service personnel, or the cops who are present. On those rare occasions where a reporter manages to corner a firefighter you can tell by the look on the fireman's face that he can't wait for the interview to be over. The fire department has a public information department, run by Assistant Commissioner Frank Gribben and his two aides, that is smaller than the Brooklyn District Attorney's. The code of the firehouse dictates that you don't blow your own horn—at least not too loud. We all know the aura of bravery and romance surrounding firefighters, but when it comes to understanding what they experience, the public probably has a better knowledge of the ways of the Eskimos.

The world of these firefighters is closed, but it is not inaccessible. It is a place where strong bonds are formed out of mutual dependence in life-or-death situations. It is a world of high drama, an emotional rollercoaster that hurls you from deep tragedy to lofty excitement, then spins you through the spiral of terror into the loop of comedy.

When you get to know firefighters, you find out that their reasons for being "on the job" are varied, and in many ways they are just like us, but they do extraordinary things with great humility.

Unlike cops, who dream of retiring, most firefighters fantasize about "going to work."

To do that work, the FDNY fields 209 engines (also known as pumpers), 142 ladder trucks, 5 heavy rescues, 3 fireboats, one Hazardous Materials unit, and hundreds of support vehicles. The crew of each engine, truck, rescue, HAZMAT, and fireboat constitutes one company. These companies are organized into forty-nine Battalions and 11 divisions, which cover the five boroughs of the city.

Within the 312 square miles of the city there are over 825,000 buildings, more than 1,000 of which are high-rises. These high-rise structures have added a whole new dimension to the complexity of firefighting.

On February 27, 1975, a fire started in a high-rise building filled with switching equipment for the telephone company. When the fire was extinguished, fifteen hours later, the loss was put at $70 million, and phone service for 170,000 New Yorkers was cut off. Within the building were miles and miles of electrical wiring. The smoke from the burning insulation on those wires contained deadly PVC (polyvinyl chloride). One hundred and sixty firefighters and civilians were hurt at that fire. The number of firefighters who will subsequently develop cancer as a result of this operation remains to be tallied. The environmental effect on those firefighters who have been trying to find their fallen brothers in the debris of the World Trade Center also awaits its potentially gruesome accounting. But even those companies that lost almost half their men at the trade center were responding to alarms as they had replacements for their lost apparatus. The fact remains that firefighters love their work and have a tremendous sense of duty, and if there is a fire they want to battle it.

The hallmark of New York City is diversity. Each borough, for example, has its own character. The Bronx, which is the only part of the city that is on the mainland, is a mix of private homes, two- and three-story row houses, six-story tenements, H-type buildings—two tenements connected by a third, with courtyards in the front and back—and one- to six-story factories. It was the South Bronx that the nation saw burning down in the seventies, when TV cameras at Yankee Stadium would pan the surrounding neighborhood during televised games and catch the tenements blazing away.

Manhattan is the heart of the city. On the granite island that this borough occupies is a forest of high-rises surrounded by tenements. It is in Manhattan that the commuter rail lines terminate. It is where the poverty of Harlem and the Lower East Side coexists with the wealth of Wall Street and the glitter of Madison Avenue. It is where the World Trade Center was located.

Brooklyn is known as the Borough of Churches. It was an independent city until 1898, when it became part of New York City. Situated on Long Island, along with the Borough of Queens, Brooklyn covers 70.2 square miles. Brooklyn is home to over two and a half million people, most of whom live in three-story wood-frame row house and brownstones. In terms of population it is larger than Philadelphia. The many factories that once flourished along the waterfront from Red Hook to Williamsburg and Greenpoint are now being converted into loft apartments and artist studios as the New York economy continues to shift from manufacturing to service.

Death was no stranger in the ghettos of Brooklyn during the sixties and seventies. Williamsburg, Bushwick, Bedford-Stuyvesant, Crown Heights, Brownsville, and East New York were neighborhoods where children and adults died. But many were saved only because of the heroic actions of the firefighters—who bled and sometimes died themselves. Even today, companies in these neighborhoods are among the busiest in the city.

In area, Queens is the largest of the five boroughs, encompassing 118.6 square miles. Considered the "Bedroom Borough," it has 300,000 one- and two-family homes. It is the sixth most populous county in the United States. Queens is also considered the air crossroads of the world with over 30 million passengers passing through Kennedy and LaGuardia airports annually. In recent years, parts of Queens have seen an upturn in fire activity.

Staten Island is the least populous borough, with some 360,000 residents. Until the Verrazano-Narrows Bridge linked it to Brooklyn, most of the Island was covered with woods and marshland. But over the last 40 years it has seen an overdevelopment of private homes, and many civil servants have found it an affordable place to raise their families. In terms of structural fires—that is, fires in buildings—Staten Island has been at the bottom of the activity list. But it does lead the other boroughs in the number of cars that are torched for insurance fraud.

The diversity and complexity of the city are reflected in the demands placed upon its fire department. But along with these demands comes the opportunity for real adventure, not some contrived Hollywood or television nonsense. When you go to work as a firefighter, you do not know what catastrophe is waiting for you, nor do you know how it will turn out. But firefighters live their work and if some disaster occurs, they want to be there.

When I started writing this book, I made the decision to interview only seasoned firefighters. What follows is the result of a series of in-depth interviews with some of the best firefighters in the city of New York. Because they knew that their stories would be accurately told, these men opened themselves up to provide a rare look into their world. They have allowed us to vicariously experience their triumphs, and their defeats, their joys and their sorrows, their anger and their fears so that, in the end, we can be richer for knowing these heroic men. But because we will know just how truly outstanding they are, we will be further moved by the loss of so many, just like them, operating at Manhattan Box 5-5-8087 on September 11, 2001.

—Peter A. Micheels
November 2001

CHRONOLOGY

1958   Wooster Street collapse
1960   Grand Street collapse
1962   Training center opened on Welfare (Roosevelt) Island
        Telephone Company boiler explosion
1965   Blackout number one
1966   Twenty-third Street collapse
1968   Martin Luther King assassinated, riots occur
        Morgan Annex Building fire
1970   John T. O'Hagen becomes chief of department and
          commissioner
1973   The strike
1975   Telephone company fire
        The layoffs
1976   Busiest year for fires
        Training center opens on Randall's Island
1977   Blackout number two
1978   Augustus Beekman appointed fire commissioner
        Waldbaum's fire
1983   Chinatown fire
        Con Edison–Garment Center fire
1984   John O'Rourke appointed chief of department
1985   Grand Central Station fire
        Tenth Alarm fire on Forty-third Street

Chapter 1

Captain George Eysser
Ladder 6, Manhattan

We were sitting on the grass having our lunch at probie (probationary fire fighter) school on Welfare Island when we saw the Bellevue Hospital Disaster Unit going up the East River Drive. We knew something had happened. The instructor said, "Throw away your lunches. We are going." They loaded us on seven pumpers and we went in a convoy to the neighborhood where I lived in upper Manhattan. What had occurred was a boiler explosion in the telephone company building at 213th Street and Broadway. This was my first real disaster.

There was a boiler room in the basement, and adjoining the boiler room was a lunchroom. They'd had a problem with the safety valves on the boiler. And the pressure had just kept building up and building up until the boiler blew. The natural tendency was for the boiler to rise. It went up, hit the concrete ceiling, came back down, and rolled like a giant steamroller through the partition and into the lunchroom where over a hundred women employees were eating. It didn't stop until it hit the foundation wall on the other side. It killed eighteen of the women.

We went down into the basement to search for survivors and victims. It was filled with water and the water was red with blood. It was like a wine vat. It was unbelievable. We went up to the first floor to a desk that was right over where the boiler had hit the ceiling—it had come through the floor a little bit. There was a young woman who had evidently been pinned in her seat. She was directly above the spot where the boiler had hit. She was dead. Her guts were all in her lap.

An off-duty fireman from the neighborhood—not a good friend of mine then, but I got to know him much better later on—came to see if his fiancée, who worked there, was all right. He wound up identifying her body. That day I said to myself, "If this is for openers, I am going to have a very interesting twenty years."

I always wanted to be a fireman. My godfather was in the job years ago, and my father was in the Fire Patrol. They were hired by the local fire underwriters. The patrols responded to alarms very much the same way firemen do, but they performed strictly salvage work. My father put forty-two years in the Fire Patrol, and he kindled an interest in me to become a fireman. I came on the job when I was twenty-two, after I was discharged from the navy.

The first actual fire I went to was in the subcellar of one of those big apartment houses on West End Avenue in Manhattan. I had the can and the hook. I just followed the other firemen down. You couldn't see a blessed thing. We made our way downstairs, and once we got off the stairs I crawled along the floor with the others. It was hot. I began to have serious doubts if I wanted to be a fireman all my life. I said to myself, "Make the right choice, kiddo." Then I lost the other men. They had crawled ahead of me a little bit, maybe three or four feet, but as far as I was concerned they could have been in New Jersey. I was there by myself. The lieutenant crawled back and he asked if I was all right. I said, "I'm okay, I'm okay." I wasn't really sure that I was, but everything worked out fine. The fire was just burning rubbish in three or four garbage cans.

Since my appointment to the Fire Department I have mostly worked in ladder companies, which was also known as truck companies. What I enjoy about being in a truck company is forcing your way into an apartment under a heavy smoke condition and successfully searching the rooms, being in there with the fire actually burning and not being able to control it. Sometimes you're even able to pass that fire area to probe deeper into the apartment. I think it's a rather challenging assignment. It really does test your skills and ability every time you work in a fire.

My most challenging fire was back in 1966 when I was a

fireman in Ladder 4. We had a second alarm on Sixth Avenue in a pornographic bookstore. There were quite a few of these bookstores on Sixth Avenue at that time.

When we rolled in we had a very heavy fire condition in the first-floor bookstore. In the first minutes, as I recall, 65 Engine was almost unable to hook up their hard suction to the hydrant to get water. But they did and then did an extremely good job knocking the fire down and pursuing it back into the store. Unfortunately the fire had proceeded up to the second and third floor—it was a three-story building. Since the department had previously inspected this building, the men were familiar with its contents and layout. On the second floor there were old army officer overcoats from the Second World War. The third floor was actually cut off and vacant. The building was equipped with front fire escapes. So lines were stretched up the fire escapes and operated from them into the second and the third floors.

We were assigned the task of going down to the basement to secure the utilities—that is, the gas and electric lines. There was a rather eerie scene down there, the water was very high—in fact, it was up to my waist—and there were boxes floating around. We had brought a claw tool to shut off the gas key. For some strange reason, the fork on the tool would not go over the key. So John Cullinan went back up to the street to secure another tool. That left Lieutenant John O'Rourke, who would later become Chief of Department, and myself down in this dungeon. Since we were really wet, I suggested that we wait at the top of the stairs. Just as we were getting over to the entrance I heard this whistling sound like a rush of air. It caught my attention because it was so loud. But O'Rourke and I started to walk up the stairs, not really panicked because we weren't aware of what was occurring. Then, as I got up to eye level with the street I could see what was occurring: the building was collapsing. The sound was caused by the compression of the collapsing floors forcing the air out of the building. Running up, I saw this hose line stretched and snaked in the first floor. I knew that 54 Engine had relieved Engine 65 on the line. I said to Chief Wynne, "I'm pretty sure that 54 Engine is in there."

He said, "No, they're not! No, they're not!"

He knew they were, but he just didn't want it to be. So

a quick head count was taken and we realized that, in fact, 54 Engine *was* in there.

We had had a fatal collapse that killed twelve fire fighters in October of 1966. When this building collapsed, it was an instant replay of what had happened just two months earlier. Of course, we thought the worst initially. It was so hard for me to be positive and say that we would retrieve the seven of them alive.

We immediately began to remove the debris. It was all done by hand of course, because there was no other way of doing it. The task of tunneling into the store actually fell on Rescue Company One.

Some of us were redirected into exposure four, the building immediately to the right of the fire building. It was a Blarney Stone bar and grill. We came charging into the bar and began ripping the booths away from the wall. The fellow behind the bar was from Ireland, and I always remember him with the thickest Irish brogue saying, "My God, men, have you lost your minds?" He just absolutely couldn't believe it. He asked, "What's the matter? What's the matter?"

I said, "The building next door has collapsed and we have some men trapped inside."

We used a battering ram in an attempt to breach through the brick wall. All of a sudden there were about six of us totally encapsulated in black soot and smoke. We couldn't imagine what had happened—what had happened was we had breached through the wall into an old chimney, and three floors of soot had come down on us. The overall atmosphere was one of confusion. We abandoned that approach, because it was going to take us too long and we really needed power equipment.

I was told to take a portable ladder and go around the corner, where there was a one-story extension on the fire building. We had a difficult time getting the ladder around to the back, but once we got it raised, I climbed up. Just about as I made it to the roof, there was a secondary gas explosion and fire blew out at me. I never came down a ladder so fast in the whole of my life. I said to myself, "My God, if they weren't dead before, they're surely dead now!" I went right back up, but there really was nothing that could be done there. The building was sealed up there, and it would have taken a lot of time.

Fortunately the greatest Christmas present that we could ever receive occurred on that December 22: we were able to extricate all seven of those trapped fire fighters alive. A serious back injury was the worst of the injuries sustained by the men.

The last trapped fireman was removed around midnight—Harry Fay, from Engine 54. As he was removed, he wished the Fire Commissioner and the Chief of Department a merry Christmas. That was Fay's state of mind after being entombed on his back, unable to move, for four hours. I really complimented him.

Really the only thing that saved the lives of those men when it all came down was that the fluorescent fixtures braced the rubble, producing a lean-to effect so that they were able to breathe. Thank God, most of the fire had been extinguished and they weren't subjected to a lot of smoke.

My most tragic fire occurred in 1982 when I was a lieutenant assigned to Ladder 124 in the Bushwick section of Brooklyn. We responded to a fire on a Sunday evening around eight o'clock. Engine 237 was in there ahead of us. Their lieutenant was very excited on the radio. He transmitted a 10-75 radio signal indicating a working fire. As we approached, from a considerable distance, I could see that the fire was coming out of the roof of the building, which indicated to me that there was a heavy fire condition on the top floor—it was a four-story brick multiple dwelling.

What had happened was that a tenant had been evicted from that building several days prior to the fire, and he had vowed as he left that if he wasn't going to be able to live in that building, then nobody would. This individual returned and poured gasoline all over the interior walls in the stairway, right from the roof down to the first floor. In fact he used so much gas that the stone stoop in front of the building was on fire—that's how much gas he had used. And of course it created problems for us. We were the first due ladder company, and the entire interior hallway was heavily involved in fire. This denied us normal access to the building and forced us to go through a first-floor window. We went through the apartment to the rear, and we did all of our searches from the rear fire escape.

I split the company up. I sent two members ahead of me to the top floor. That is probably the most crucial area due to the mushroom effect. If the fire occurs on the lower floors, the superheated smoke and gases are tremendously buoyant, and they rise to the top floor. If there is no opening, it will make a mushroom effect—in other words, first the hallway will be filled with smoke; then, as the fire continues to burn it actually causes the smoke to move laterally across the entire top floor and eventually to drop into all the apartments below. So the top floor is always acknowledged to be the most critical spot that you must quickly get to.

As I was working my way up, I received a Handie-Talkie message from my outside vent man, who said he had two 1045 code 2's (two persons injured, not expected to live). So I immediately proceeded to the top floor.

When I got up there, I just really couldn't believe the sight I came upon. There were four children and two adults on the top floor. They had opened their apartment door and been confronted with this heavy smoke. The four children had started up the interior stairs to the roof. The mothers had started across the public hall to the adjoining apartment, which was vacant. The apartment door was open, so the mothers and the children were moving diagonally away from one another. The first child got up to the bulkhead door to the roof, got it open and escaped. But by opening the door she created a fire triangle. This gave the fire enough air, and the entire hallway exploded into flames, trapping the two women, setting their clothes on fire and critically burning them right in the hall. But they were able to get into the vacant apartment. However, three of the children were on fire on the stairs leading to the roof.

When I got into the apartment one of the members of my company was patting the fire out on one woman, but you could see that she was dead. We thought the other woman had a little life in her, so we immediately put her into our tower ladder bucket and removed her, but by the time we got her to the street, she had died as well.

But there was nothing we could do for the three children. They actually became part of the flame. All you could see were their bodies slumped on the stairs: one, two, three, going up to the roof. And until the engine company made their way up the stairs extinguishing the fire as they worked their way up, there was no way that we could even get to them. Of course, they were dead.

That probably was one of the worst fires I've ever gone to. To witness something like that—the impact of people actually burning in front of you—and the hopelessness of it . . . it was tragic, because there was really nothing that we could do for them. The entire hallway was lit up, and the only protection we had between ourselves and the fire was the apartment door. We had only cracked that open a little bit. There was no way that you could enter into that hall.

Ironically, when I first was assigned to that unit, about seven years earlier, one of the first fatal fires I had was in that same building, on the first floor.

There were three children and a mother involved in that earlier fire. The older boy had some mental problems. Somehow he had got his hands on some kerosene, spilled it around the living room, and set the apartment on fire. Fortunately, he and his mother were able to get out. But the two younger children were trapped in the apartment.

We were told that they were in there. But here again, the amount of fire that we encountered upon arrival was so awesome that we were unable to get into the apartment without the assistance of the hose line. One of the members of my company got in from the rear and made a search of the two back rooms, but the children, unfortunately, were in the front. There was so much fire that the plaster ceilings had fallen, along with the plaster off the walls. We had about two feet of debris on the floor. The kids actually had become part of the debris. We couldn't find them at first. In fact we were wondering if they really were in there. We were hoping that they weren't. A lot of times in those neighborhoods, people are found in a neighbor's apartment or in another building. But eventually, after digging and careful searching, we found their bodies.

In that one building, between the two fires, there were seven fatalities. In fact, in the seven years I was with that particular company I had twenty-five fire fatalities. It was a highly combustible area. It was a ghetto if ever there was a ghetto. Mostly frame buildings made entirely of wood.

In a lot of these fires gasoline was used. From time to time we would encounter revenge fires. There would be an argument between a fellow and his girl, and he would decide to settle the account with gasoline rather than with a gun or a knife. The buildings lent themselves to rapid burning, sometimes negating any possibility of any interior search without using a hose line, which costs precious time for us. I suppose that accounts for the high loss of life.

To some degree we take these fatalities as a personal loss. When we return to quarters I find the scene around the firehouse to be very . . . somber. I think that all of us in our own way probably reflect on our performance, wondering if we had done this, or if we had made that move, would it have made a difference?

I remember one particular fire that had somewhat of a humorous aspect to it. We used to interchange with a ladder company from the Woodside section of Queens. If your company worked in a very high activity area—this was in the seventies—the department would interchange you every other night with a slower company to give you some relief. Well, after we made the interchange, we had a major fire in a taxpayer—a row of stores—in Woodside. We were inside the building, pulling down the ceilings in this barbershop and waiting for the engine company to follow us into the store to extinguish the fire. The fire was in the cockloft, which is the space between the top of the ceiling and the underboards of the roof. Once we had pulled all the ceilings, the rooms lit up like it was daylight. Actually there was no smoke, it was a free-burning fire. We had this sea of fire rolling over our heads. The fellows, however, were fooling around sitting in the barber's chair, one of them pretending to be cutting the other's hair. I guess it just lends some insight about how nonchalant we can be about our predicament—sometimes.

Another time we were interchanged in Queens, and we responded as a second-due ladder company to a rather new multiple dwelling in a nice section of the borough. Prior to our arrival the battalion chief had transmitted a 1075, indicating to us that we did have a working fire.

As we got up on the fifth floor of the building, Ladder 154, the first due ladder company, was having some difficulty forcing the door of the apartment that was on fire and had taken quite a beating in the process. We were mask-equipped, and I suggested to the lieutenant of 154 that we relieve them and finish the job of taking the door. So my forcible-entry team and I made it down the hall to the apartment door and forced it open. We fully expected the door to open once we had disengaged all the locks on it, but that didn't happen. As we started to push the door inward we met resistance, and at first we really didn't understand what was happening. I said, "I wonder if there's someone behind the door." The door was ajar just about enough for me to put my arm inside and feel around. Someone was hanging by the neck from a piano wire tied around the doorknob on the inside of the door. It took the efforts of all three of us to push the door in, get this individual off the door, and pull him out into the hallway. To all outward indications it seemed that he was dead, and in fact he was.

We proceeded to make an interior search of the apartment. Normally you would just go straight in, but it was pitch black—there was zero visibility. I found the couch, and for some reason I just went along it and made my way to the window. I opened the window up and vented the apartment, and fortunately, the irons man, who was directly behind me, followed my path. We found out later that if we had gone straight across the room, we would have fallen through the floor into the apartment below. An accelerant had been used to start the fire. It had burned very rapidly, and it burned the floor away.

We made a complete search of the apartment and found a dead dog in there. As it turned out the fire involved two homosexuals who'd had a lovers' quarrel. The one had killed his lover, hung him on the door knob, killed his dog, and totally wrecked the apartment. He had literally pulled the kitchen cabinets right off the wall before setting the place on fire. It has to be one of the oddest fires I have responded to in my twenty-five years in the fire department.

Another unique fire that I went to as a fire fighter occurred in a fleabag hotel on the West Side of Manhattan in the mid-fifties. We responded one evening to a report of a fire in a room on the second floor. As we—the forcible-entry team with the officer—came up the stairs, we found the door slightly ajar. You could see that the entire room was fully involved with fire, and the flames were beginning to lap out into the public hall. We opened the door to use the extinguisher, and much to our amazement we saw a person inside the room who was actually on fire. He evidently had committed suicide by setting his room on fire. He was sitting on the sink totally engulfed by fire—it was just weird.

We extinguished the fire, but I'll always remember we had

had a tremendous amount of difficulty with the body. We had to throw sheets over him, lift him off the sink, and attempt to fit him into a body bag. Which was almost impossible, because the body has to be in a prone position to fit into the bag, and he was still in the sitting position; rigor mortis, or whatever, had already set in.

After the fire was extinguished we went into the overhauling phase and much to our amazement, we came across photos he had taken of Engine 54 and Ladder 4 responding to fires around the neighborhood. It seems he was a secret admirer of ours. We never knew the gentleman, or knew who he was. But it was rather strange that he should die like that and while evidently having at least some latent interest in the local fire companies.

It is kind of hard to imagine that someone would do that to himself. What would drive a person to end his life that way? It shocked me that someone would *choose* fire as a method of ending his life—and clearly that was no accidental fire. You would not sit up on a sink, right by the door, and purposely remain in a room until it became heavily involved in fire and make no attempt to escape.

I had a fire in another hotel—the Hotel Plymouth. The box came in at about four o'clock in the morning. When we pulled out of quarters we could smell the smoke, so we knew we had a job. When we arrived, people were coming down in the hotel elevators. One room on the tenth floor was fully involved, but there wasn't very much smoke in the hall. We received reports that some people were in trouble on the floor above the fire, so two of us went up to check on them.

We got into the room directly above the fire. We put our heads out the window and, to our amazement, we saw that the occupant of the fire room was clinging to the outside of the building. The rooms faced an interior courtyard, and next to the fire-room window was a duct that ran from a restaurant on the first floor all the way up to the roof. The occupant must have woken up, but was unable to get to the door to get out of the room. He had crawled out the window and was hanging on by his fingertips and toes to the flat bars that secured the duct to the wall. I don't think those brackets could have been more than two inches thick—he was like a human fly. And this was in the middle of winter, so all he had on was his undershorts.

While we were preparing to effect a roof-rope rescue, the men from Engine 65 stretched their line into the room and extinguished the fire. As soon as the flames stopped coming out of the room and only smoke was billowing out, the occupant disregarded our warnings to stay put and calmly stepped onto the windowsill of his room. Then he jumped into the room and landed on top of the men from Engine Company 65.

I spoke to the fellows in 65 later on. They said they almost had heart attacks when this guy jumped on top of them. They didn't know what happened. They thought the building had collapsed. Just visualize this: You're lying on the floor, there's zero visibility in this envelope of steam, and something heavy lands right on top of you.

Once we all got downstairs, I spoke to the human fly, who hadn't even gotten burned. He was shaking, but not from the fire. He was still in his undershorts, which had gotten wet. It was cold, and he was suffering from the effects of the water and the temperature.

Back at the firehouse when it was all over, we wondered if we would have had the coolness and presence of mind to do what he did. To cling to the outside of the building like that—it was one of the most amazing things I've ever seen a civilian do during a fire.

Just recently there was a fire in the Wall Street area where two men and a woman were trapped on the thirty-fifth floor in a corner office. One of the fellows climbed out on a ledge and lowered himself to the ledge outside the floor below. Then he stood there and allowed the woman and the other fellow to climb down his back to safety—just like Spiderman. If a fire fighter had accomplished that type of rescue he would probably be awarded a Class I—the highest award they give for bravery in this job. I really have to compliment that man. Some civilians under the threat from fire really surprise you at times. They keep their heads. Unfortunately, in most fires, panic is the killer.

Thinking about victims, I remember a fire we had right after that collapse on Sixth Avenue. Back in those days usually there wasn't any R&R given to a unit. When you took up from a fire, you could be soaking wet and it could be four degrees below zero, but if another alarm came in for your area you responded to it. We had gotten back to quarters after the collapse and needless to say we were really shaken up by the whole experience. We were upstairs putting dry clothes on when a box came in for the old Hotel America which has since been demolished.

The fire was reported in the penthouse. We'd had previous fires in that hotel, so when we got there, we were fairly familiar with where things were. We went up a stairway to the roof and crossed to a doorway which led into the hallway that serviced all the apartments of the penthouse area. When we opened the door we saw that the whole hallway was on fire—and there in the hall was a woman who was on fire.

Fortunately a fire fighter from Rescue 1 was able, with some degree of difficulty, to grab hold of her, pull her out of the hallway and get her to safety. After that, the line was stretched and the fire became rather routine. It was extinguished quickly.

Three or four months elapsed after that fire—we used to go to the Hotel America with quite a bit of frequency, mostly mattress fires and things of that nature. Then one afternoon we were called out to another fire in that hotel. We had gone through the halls and found a woman screaming uncontrollably, but there was no sign of any fire. She was just totally overcome by fear. Our presence had just caused her to flip out. After looking at her for a couple of minutes, I realized it was the woman who'd been on fire in the hall three or four months earlier.

A fire fighter from Ladder 4 put his arm around her to assure her that her life was not in jeopardy. Then she screamed out in pain. You could tell it was pain, because it was a different type of scream. So we took a closer look and found that her whole back was terribly scarred. I guess the skin was still so tender that just the mere fact of him laying his gloved hand on her shoulder to comfort her, caused additional pain.

I was really rather surprised to see the victim of one fire had come back to reside in the same hotel. I would have thought that someone who'd gone through what that woman had would never want to darken the door of that building again. But I guess her financial situation was such that she was forced to return and live there. It was really a substandard hotel, a down-and-outer, so to speak—I suppose that was what the poor lady was.

*   *   *

Fire fighters also experience fear. But I think that fire fighters just learn to control their fears—and their panic—and try not to let them get the best of them. Just the type of work that we do would put fear in anybody's heart. I mean we are not any different from anybody else. It is only through experience that we realize we are able to control the situation; we have the equipment to do it and the water to extinguish the fire. To the untrained eye the approach to extinguishment may seem rather chaotic, but really it's not, and knowing that keeps some of the fear in check.

I think, too, that the trust we have in one another keeps the fear factor down. The fellow next to me knows I am going to be there with him, and I know he will be there for me. In a sense, this trust has a calming effect on everyone there.

Also, some of the things that we become involved in, we figure we're never going to survive, and just the fact that we do survive helps to control our fear. We come to realize that we can control the fire. After a while we learn that one room of fire does not necessarily mean that we are going to lose the entire building. We become aware that there is a time factor and if we catch it right, even with the fire burning uncontrolled in an apartment, we still have a certain amount of time to search the remainder of the apartment without really jeopardizing our own lives. To the public it may seem that we are. And of course we know that occasionally it doesn't work out for us and we do sustain some fatalities and some injuries, but I would say for the most part we live a charmed life. We pull off a lot of things that probably shouldn't be pulled off; we depend a lot on sheer nerve. A lot of gutsy people seem to find their way into the fire service. I think we probably feed off one another.

The younger man coming into the job is unsure of himself, and that's understandable. He talks to the senior men and watches what they can do, and he begins to see that it's not insurmountable. The job can be done, and I think that knowledge has a calming effect on him. We try never to scream, because it is unnerving. Sometimes we would like to, but we just don't, because we know it would have a negative impact on the whole operation.

I've had the good fortune of working with a lot of first-class fire fighters—*thinking* fire fighters, as I like to call them. One of the men who impressed me the most as a young fire fighter was Bob Farrell. He was a lieutenant and later a captain in Ladder 31 in the Bronx at the time when the whole South Bronx was burning. He was probably one of the calmest, coolest fire fighters I've ever had the pleasure of working with. I always gravitated to that type of fireman. I always wanted to mold myself in the image of a person like Bob. Not only was he cool and calm, but everything he did was thought out. He didn't take many risks. When he did, they were calculated risks. He knew what he was doing.

He was awarded the James Gordon Bennett medal, the highest award given by the fire department. It was for a rescue on Third Avenue in Manhattan when a fire started in an antique shop on the first floor of an old tenement. It was in the wintertime and the fire had gained considerable headway prior to the arrival of the department.

Farrell and some other firemen were up on the roof. They had made the best search they could, under very trying conditions. The stairway had been lost, so the job of searching had to be done primarily from portable ladders and from the rear fire escapes. They pretty much thought they'd made a good search, but while they were looking through the rear of this tenement they heard this faint call, "Help! Help!" It was an elderly woman who was still in her apartment, and the fire was raging below her. It was one of those situations where time was just not on their side; every second counted.

The men tied Bob up in a bowline-on-a-bite—a series of knots forming a harness, which we use with the roof rope to lower one person to rescue another.

Bob was lowered down, and as he came in front of the window, he ran into some heavy smoke and realized that the fire was right behind the woman. He was extremely strong; with one arm he grabbed her, along with the venetian blind and the curtains, and pulled her out of the window. Somehow the other fire fighters were able to pull them away from the window and over to the fire escape. Just as they did, the fire blew right out of the window. If there had been any delay, the woman would have been forced to jump.

Now that I think about it, almost all the fellows that I worked with were first-class. What makes the fire service is the type of people that are drawn to it. They may come into this job average, but I think after they're in it awhile they turn out to be above average. It's back to that word—*com-*

mitment. Learning a job, becoming part of it, knowing what we're doing, what we're all about. But it's definitely the people, there's no doubt about it. That's the best part about the job—it gives you an opportunity to work with people who are a cut above the rest. It takes that type of person to do this job properly and to be successful.

Chapter 2

Lieutenant Robert Quilty
Staff Psychologist, FDNY Counseling Unit

I guess I joined the department because I wanted to finish my undergraduate degree and I knew the hours were conducive to being a student. I had no desire to fight fires. I was hoping I would get assigned to some relatively inactive area. However, after about four or five months in a very, very active tenement area I began to really get caught up in the excitement and the challenge of the job. It became contagious. The more fires I went to, the more I wanted to go.

The work fulfilled a lot of needs. I don't know how much of it was conscious or how much was unconscious, but I began to feel very good about myself physically and what I was capable of.

Fighting fires was scary, but there was a real sense of accomplishment. I began to feel good about being able to run into buildings that everybody else was running out of. Every fire I went to was different. There really are no two fires exactly the same, particularly when you are new in the job. The better trained I became, the more I wanted to use the skills I learned, and going to fires became something that I looked forward to, although in a kind of counterphobic way.

I was frightened a lot of the time. I think most of the guys, particularly when they are new, are more frightened than they realize. I don't think I would have admitted it during those years, but I know now that I was scared. But because I was in very busy areas, I was able to overcome some of the nervousness. I think most of the guys experience that early nervousness and some feelings of inadequacy. They see that the more experienced men have much better endurance because they know how to pace themselves. It's something that you just have to learn.

My first major fire was in the East Village, next door to the auditorium where they had rock concerts—the Fillmore East. It was a second alarm, and I couldn't get over the spectacle. It was larger than life. All multiple alarms are like that, where you see so much fire it's hard to realize that it's reality. You see four or five floors of fire, and these big black mushroom clouds, and you can see it from blocks away. While we were on our way there, the more senior men were pointing to the glow in the night sky and saying that we had a good job.

It was so huge. It was such a dramatic thing, seeing all this fire and then, as the fire developed, watching the many different units coming in and the lines being stretched. There were so many hose lines stretched into the fire, it was like spaghetti in the street. I just wondered how you'd be able to figure out whose line was whose and how you'd be able to get this mess untangled. Then they called for the searchlight units. It was like a Hollywood set. Most night fires are like that. There is something surreal about it.

It's so powerful. There is a temptation to withdraw, to step out of it and not really be in touch with the power of it. It's unpredictably wild, but somehow the assumption is made that a group of men are going to control it, and eventually they do. Sometimes it takes a lot longer than you expected, and other times it's over much more quickly.

It's fascinating how it happens; it's like a battlefield where every unit has its assignment. As more and more units come in, they report to the chief officer, and then they are sent off into different sectors of the building. Strategy and tactics are planned out, like you see in a good war movie.

At my first fire I didn't do very much until it was brought under control. We forced our way into a storefront and pulled some ceilings down. It was like working in a waterfall, because the water that was dumped on the fire on the upper floors was cascading down. The water's running down on you, while you are pulling the ceiling down, trying to get to fire that's burning between the ceiling and the floor above. It was hard, hard work, but I don't remember being in a particularly punishing part of that fire.

I do remember watching one of the men in my company go up the fire escape to the second floor, trying to get into an apartment to make a quick search. In every window you could see fire. I was impressed watching him and kind of afraid at the same time. I wondered, "Will I ever be able to do anything like that?"

I was a new fireman, what they call a Johnny, and being a little overly aggressive, at another fire, I found myself in a front room of a burning building with the door somehow closed behind me. There was no doorknob on it. The room got very hot. There was obviously a fire beneath me, or coming into that room. Feeling around, I couldn't find any doorknob. I couldn't feel any door. I just kept feeling walls as I was going around in circles. I thought I wasn't going to be able to get out of this building. Finally I got to a window. I yelled down, trying to show that I was calm, "Hey, could you please put a ladder up here?" Being very polite: "Could you please put a ladder up here? I can't get out." For a couple of months afterward, all I heard in the firehouse was, "Hey, could you please? I'm stuck up here. I can't get out. Could you please get a ladder up here?"

My first fifth alarm fire was in South Jamaica, Queens, in the middle of the afternoon. When we turned the corner about eight blocks away, I was up in the tiller seat (the rear steering position on a tractor-trailer type ladder truck), so I was much higher than anyone else. I could see this huge black mushroomlike cloud. It looked like an atom bomb had been dropped. It turned out to be a whole row of stores burning along Jamaica Avenue. I've never seen so much fire in one place.

I remember being up on the roof for a while. We should have been cutting with the saw. If I'd had more experience at the time I *would* have been doing that, but I really didn't know the job as well as I do now—I had only a couple of years in. The rescue company got up there and opened up the roof. Later I went into one of the stores with a lieutenant, and I remember being really frightened. The fire was rolling over our heads, and we had to get out quick. The smoke got so bad at one point that we had to get away from the storefronts. You couldn't even stand in the middle of the street, the smoke was so heavy.

Being in a fire is a really hard thing to imagine. I don't

think I can adequately describe it. The closest that I can come to is to think of yourself diving into a pool that is totally in darkness, totally black, without any air. If you have an air tank on your back, you can hear the air that you're sucking in and breathing. You hear muffled talking. If you don't have a mask on, you can hear shouting, but it's not all that clear. It's very black; if you see anything, it will be the glow of the fire. You can hear the crackle sometimes. If you take enough windows out, the room will brighten up.

When you see a lot of flame rolling along the ceiling, though it is very hot, you can sometimes breathe a little better. This is particularly important if your mask is out of air or if you don't have one on. But when the flames roll over your head, it's time to get out, because the fire will begin to drop lower and lower. It will be untenable after a while, and maybe that inch of oxygen that you have close to the floor will very quickly disappear. You try to look for windows where you can get some ventilation. You break the glass out. You don't have the time to look for window locks or try to open them. You want that whole area cleared out. Also, by just pulling a window up you still don't have that top area open, which is the most crucial, because that's initially where all the heat is—at the ceiling level—and you want it to get out. If you just pull the windows down, you don't have an area you might quickly get out through. It's important to take the glass out completely so you can get through the window if you have to; you're also letting a lot of that heat and smoke out.

What is it like? It's very painful; that is one way to describe being in a fire. A serious fire is very hot. It's like crawling into an oven. There's a lot of anxiety. I don't care how experienced you are, the anxiety is usually there. And it's different if you're an officer, because you've got not only yourself to worry about but the whole team of men you're supervising as well. You're concerned for the safety of all the men, but particularly the less experienced men. You are always concerned that they are with you; when they aren't, you're worrying about where they are. As an officer, you have that fear that an inexperienced man will get lost or fall through the floor because he doesn't know what to look for. With the more experienced men, you are worried that they are being a little too aggressive. You hope that they are not going to get themselves hurt.

The officer doesn't have to go through so much physical work; he's leading his men once he gets in there. The firemen not only has to go through the trouble of finding the fire and getting in there, but once he does, then he has got to physically operate. And it is dirty, bull work, opening up walls or opening up the line, which is under a lot of pressure, to get water on the fire. It is a difficult job, whether you're an officer or a fireman.

The more fires I went to, the better I got at it. I reached a point where the area I was working in wasn't active enough for me, and so I waited a year to get into a unit in Harlem, which had a very good reputation for turning out some really good firemen.

I have a feeling that most of the men think dying at a fire is something that might happen to the other guy but never to yours truly. You very seldom think, "I'm not going to make it." I've been trapped a few times in fires, and I've always figured, "I'll get off this roof, or I'll figure something out."

Being trapped, however, is probably the worst experience you can imagine. Usually the air is running out in your mask, or you're in a location that doesn't allow for wearing a mask—on a roof for example. That position is not conducive to wearing a tank on your back. Stumbling around on a roof, it's very easy to fall over the edge. Also, the mask cuts down your visibility even more.

I was up on a roof one time with another fireman. We went up on the aerial ladder because the interior stairway had already become involved. We had ventilated by forcing open the bulkhead door to the roof and taking out the skylight, and we had called for the saw to cut some holes in the roof. While we were waiting for that, we looked over the rear to check for victims, and we saw the fire blow out the windows. There was no way of getting down the rear fire escape—the fire blew out the bulkhead door that we had opened up. It got very, very dark on the roof—a lot of smoke. The fire was on the top floor, and the roof began to get spongy. Now there was fire in the cockloft, and we could feel it percolating under us. I thought that it might be time to get to the aerial ladder we had come up on. We could hear the men then down on the street yelling. They were warning the men, the deputy chief, everyone, to abandon the building: "Get off! Get out of the building!" We went toward the aerial, but by then we had a wall of flames across the front of the building. We couldn't get near the aerial ladder. All of our exits were cut off.

That particular building was vacant. That was one of the reasons the fire took off so quickly. And there was arson; gasoline was involved—suddenly everything just lit up.

Very often in a situation like that, you can go over to the adjoining roof. Even if the roofs aren't the same height, you can often just drop down. If it's just a one-story drop, it's not bad. You have to be very careful, though, because you lose your visibility very quickly if a fire breaks through. You have to be careful not to jump into a shaft or something.

This particular building, however, was isolated—the buildings on either side of it had been demolished, so there were no buildings onto which we could climb. It was six stories straight down on every side. Isolated buildings are dangerous, because if your escape is cut off from the front and back, and if it is impossible to get down the interior stairway, then shame on you, you're stuck.

I had the roof rope with me and a harness. I was trained to slide a rope, so I knew I could get off the roof but that's not the best way, especially if you have to do it under that kind of pressure. My company was in an early pilot program with the roof rope, because we were very active. The other company that responded didn't have the harness. The fireman I had with me was from the other company. I didn't have time to tie him up and lower him the way you would if you had all the time in the world, as in the training bulletins. So I tied the roof rope around a stanchion and threw it over the side. We had to get off very quickly, and the only way I could think of was to take him down on my back. It would be very tricky—we could topple or turn upside down, or the rope could snap. It was definitely not the best way to get off a roof.

All this happened within maybe the space of a minute. I straddled the parapet wall, told him to get on my back. He came over, began to do that, and in the process he spotted the aerial ladder on the corner of the building, just on the very edge. We could just see one rail of the ladder through the flame and the smoke. He said, "Come on, we can make it. Grab it!" Since that was a safer way to get down, I dropped the rope and ran. We were able to grab the outside rail of the aerial ladder. He got on; then I jumped on. The chauffeur, down on the turntable, rotated us away from the fire building; at first, we couldn't climb down because of all the fire coming up out of the windows. After he rotated us, the aerial ladder was whipping up and down because there was no support. We slowly climbed down to the turntable. I don't know what my friend did, but I kissed the chauffeur. My knees were knocking at that point—we were the last two men off the building; everyone else had been evacuated.

My lieutenant was looking for me. He thought I was still up there when the whole roof collapsed, but fortunately I had just gotten off. After the fire was over, we went back there, since my tools had disappeared in the ruins. It was pretty scary. I've been trapped in similar incidents, but that was one of the scarier ones.

Very often on a fire escape the fire will blow out underneath you. You have a choice of ducking into the nearest apartment—but it's horrible in there; it's very hot and smoky, plus you know that you can't get down the way you came in. You can stay out on the fire escape and try to get someone with a hose line to knock the fire down beneath you, and you can try to slide on the rope or have the men get the aerial ladder up to you. It can be a little tricky, a little anxiety-provoking. But you always figure you're going to get off. You never have the thought that this is it.

I know I've been afraid. But I've been optimistic, and I think there's the adaptive mechanism that allows you to keep looking—"There's got to be a door here somewhere. There's got to be a window here somewhere," a way out.

I've been trapped inside a building and above the fire, too. The fire came through the floor to an apartment that I was in, and that happened a couple of times. One time the air in my mask ran out. I was with another fireman, and his air also ran out. We couldn't get out of the apartment because we couldn't find the door. A table overturned while we were crawling around making a search, and it was in front of the doorway. Finally one of the firemen in our company knew we were in there and yelled in the doorway and guided us out. When we finally made it to the doorway, both of us ran once we saw his light and dove down the stairs. We both ended up in the hospital for about three days with carbon monoxide levels very, very high. They were afraid that we were going into pulmonary edema.

I think among the men, brute strength is thought of as an important asset. But also you've got to have a lot of endurance, and that may not always be connected with brute strength. The ability to tolerate pain and the ability to endure the heat and the smoke and the physical exhaustion and be able to keep going, keep crawling in one more room even though your legs are about to give in or your arms are ready to give out, to hang in there.

Very often the fire is behind a locked door, and the areas of the city where there are more fires are generally behind doors that have a lot of locks because they're run-down areas and there's a lot more crime. So you have to become somewhat of a second-story man; at least if you're in a truck company, you have to know about forcing entry.

You also have to be reasonably agile if you're negotiating fire escapes, particularly when you're the outside vent man or when you're by yourself. If you're in the rear of the building coming up the fire escape, you may fall off. Very often you go through a step because they're in disrepair or because a step is missing, and you better be holding on. Many times I was glad that I was hanging on; otherwise it would have been a long drop. You must be able to recognize the dangers in negotiating fire escapes and aerial ladders.

The ability to pace yourself is important, too, particularly in humping hose to the upper floors of the building—that is, taking a rolled-up length of hose on your shoulder, some tools or a nozzle in one hand, and some equipment in your other hand, with your air supply on your back, and climbing up to the fire floor. Very often you're exhausted by the time you get to the door of the apartment, and you haven't even begun to work.

A lot of physical skills are involved in operating on a roof: handling a very powerful circular saw, cutting a hole in the roof when very often the roof is vibrating underneath you. There's fire below you and you cut, and then you see the flames lap up around that saw blade, but you still hold on to that saw. Even with your gloves and your turnout coat on, you still expose a little gap of skin here and there, but you're able to get that hole in that roof. Then you have the men pull open the flap of tarpaper and let a lot of that smoke and heat out. And you have to be smart enough from experience to know when you've made enough holes in the roof and the roof is about to go, and that it's time to get off. You learn to recognize when it's time, by being on roofs where you've stayed a little too long and then maybe one foot will go through the tar and you'll say, "Thank God I wasn't farther out onto the roof."

You also learn the importance of being a team member by having a partner nearby. Frequently, particularly when there's fire beneath you, you'll find yourself going through a floor, holding on by your arms, with your feet dangling, yelling for somebody to pull you out. I had that experience in a tenement. The engine moved in with the line charged with the water. I was working in a truck company: I searched for victims and tried to get some ventilation by smashing windows. The other truckies were going straight ahead, but I went to the left into one room—and plunged right down through the floor. I was just holding on. I knew there was fire in the apartment below as well as in this apartment, because I could see the glow and I could feel the heat. But I just couldn't pull myself out. There was another fireman nearby, and I yelled out, "I'm caught. I'm going through the floor." At that very moment, the whole ceiling came down on the heads of another engine company below me. One of them looked up and was able to just see my legs dangling, and they opened up the water line. At first I couldn't understand why I got so wet all of a sudden. The men opened the line and bombed me with water from the floor below, because there was fire in the ceiling. They kept me from getting burned till my partner pulled me out.

It's a very punishing job. It's taken its toll. It ages you physically. I don't have the tolerance for the cold that I used to have. Also I have a lot of scars on my hands and legs from burns and cuts.

There's also something very special about it. I feel proud to be part of a special group of men. Not everyone can do it; not everyone would want to do it. Being close to other men, close in a very cohesive way, was something that I probably never would have experienced except in battling a fire. You're really dependent on the other firemen. Maybe you don't admit it, but you depend on them for your safety. I think the comradeship that results from that experience is really unique.

I can't imagine too many situations where you would have that kind of closeness. Something special comes out of knowing that you've been in these harrowing situations together and survived.

You also find out about the limits of your endurance. Knowing that physically you can just push yourself that extra distance. Ordinarily, you wouldn't stay in a room where you think if you don't get out the next second you're going to burn to death. But you learn that you *can* stay a little longer, even if you can't breathe. That's something that comes from experience. You learn that you can take an awful lot of punishment and survive and be effective in doing your job. I never would have thought that; I think most people would turn and run without that special training and experience. After several years of being in those situations you develop a tolerance for that kind of pain and fear, and it's a good feeling to know that about yourself—that you can come through it and survive. It is something I would never have known about if I hadn't been a fire fighter.

In South Jamaica we had a second or third alarm in a factory where they made corrugated cardboard. There was some fire behind a huge garage door, and there was talk of an employee being back there somewhere. They weren't sure if everyone was out. I remember having to go down a hallway and through an office—the area was filled with small office cubicles—to get into the garage and get that door open so they could get lines in. When we got into that truck bay, we couldn't really see, but we got behind that door and found out it was padlocked. I was with another fireman, another lieutenant, and all of a sudden we could feel the heat on the back of our necks. We knew the whole place was lighting up. He said, "Get out!" I didn't have to be told twice. I remember running—it was the first time I was really, really frightened. We got out. Then we worked on the door from the outside. We finally got it open, and one of the men jumped into this delivery truck that was inside the garage, because there was a lot of fire behind it. He pulled the truck out—the back of it was burning. He drove down the street and tried to stop the truck, but found out that with all the heat inside the building, the brake drums had burned or melted or something. He couldn't stop the truck and had to run it up on the sidewalk. I don't know what he hit, but he finally stopped it.

As a lieutenant in a ladder company, the first thing I do if I hear on the radio that I have a job is to let the men know. If I'm the first company on the scene, I have to get on the radio and let the dispatcher know that I want everyone assigned to come in on the box. While I'm doing that I'm thinking about whether the building will be occupied or deserted, depending on what time of day it is. If it's at night and it's an occupied building, there's a greater possibility of people being caught somewhere in it than if it is a daytime fire. If there's nothing showing or there's a lot of smoke all over the place, it will be harder for me to get a sense of just where the seat of the fire is. There's a lot going simultaneously: What is my water supply? Will there be a delay? Is there a possibility of a frozen hydrant? Will double-parked cars cause a problem in getting to a hydrant?

If you're an officer, you have to depend on the men and hope they'll in fact do what they're assigned to do. My experience is that the busier the area, the more fires they go to, the more you can depend on them. There's no waiting around to be ordered. If the fire's on the top floor, you don't have to turn around and order a man to get the saw up to the roof to cut the roof open. And you don't have to tell your chauffeur to raise the aerial in the front of the building. It's automatic—he knows. There's very little direction that you have to give as an officer in a busier area.

If you're a roof man, the first thing you do when you get to the fire is try to figure out how you are going to get to the roof. You're looking at the adjoining buildings to see if they are the same height. That's the safest way to go—up the stairs of the building next door, providing that's not also involved in the fire. Sometimes the front of the buildings may look equal, but if you step out to the middle of the street, you'll see that the windows aren't even. Though the parapet walls may be even in the front, there may be a story difference, resulting in a big drop on one side, so you might take the building on the other side. There may be a picket fence between the two buildings, or chain links and barbed wire, because of the burglaries. If you can't make it up the adjoining building, either, because the fire is in an isolated building, or because roofs are not the same height, then you'll think in terms of using the aerial ladder. But the aerial ladder might be involved in a rescue attempt, or the men could be using it to vent the fire by taking some glass out. In that case you use the third and the least recommended way: you take a fire escape up. It has to be the rear fire escape; that's the only one that goes to the roof. The front fire escape stops at the top floor. So you'd want to get to the rear of the building somehow. But that can be very tricky. It's okay if the fire is in the front of the building. But if the fire is in the rear of the building—or if it's in the front, but by the time you get halfway up it extends to the rear apartments—now you're cut off. If you pass the fire and then it blows out, you've cut off your means of escape.

I've learned that when I go up a fire escape I have to hold on with both hands. I keep my tools in one hand, but have both hands gripping the rail, particularly in vacant buildings, where very often you'll suddenly go through a stair or there'll be a missing stair and you won't see it. A couple of times I leaned on a railing as I made a turn to go up the next flight and the whole railing swung out. As long as you've got two hands on the fire escape, you're pretty safe. The chance that it will pull out is pretty remote. Usually it happens only when the building wall is beginning to collapse; that's when you lose your fire escape.

Once I'm on the roof, the first thing I do is get to the bulkhead door, which is the doorway that gives access to the interior stairs, and try to give it a quick force. More often than not it'll go pretty quickly if you're experienced in forcing doors. If there's any delay at all, I'll very quickly get to the rear of the building, especially if I've come up the interior of the building next door or via the aerial ladder and haven't checked the rear yard. That's the next thing I'll do, if the fire is in the front, because there will be people in the rear panicking if there's any kind of smoke condition.

If the fire is in the rear, there will be even more panic, because there's no aerial ladder access. So you want to check the rear for jumpers and for people on the fire escapes. Also to see if there is fire blowing out of the rear.

If there is fire in the rear apartments and people are caught above that fire, you get on the radio and notify your people that there are occupants trapped on whatever floor. Then, if you can get down to them from the rear fire escape, that's the preferred method; you get to them as quickly as you can. If they're in a room that's not close to a fire escape, you're going to have to use a roof-rope rescue: you'll throw a rope over the side of the building and slide down to them. In either case, you try to notify your unit of what is going on. But what I've found is that usually the worse the conditions are, the more crowded the radio traffic is. It never fails that when you want to get through, everybody else is on the radio. The reason you make the attempt is that you want to let them know what action you're taking, because if it doesn't work out and you're caught somewhere, they'll have an idea of your whereabouts. You'll get some help, and if you get trapped somewhere you'll get some backup. If you can't get through on the radio—and often I haven't been able to—then you have to make your move anyway. You can't spend more than a couple of seconds making that attempt to notify, and then you have to go into action and do your job.

You also have to check the shafts on either side of the building to see if people are at the shaft windows. There are no fire escapes in the shaft, so you'll use a roof rope to get down to them if you can't get down the interior stairs. It's very difficult to climb back up the rope once you reach an occupant in a shaft window. It's almost impossible. You'll go all the way down if you can, unless you're above a fire; then you'll either have to bypass it or try to get into a lower floor that's not passing fire. This can be very difficult and each situation is different.

After you've made sure there aren't any more victims, you have to see to it that the door to the roof is open. If there's any kind of delay with the bulkhead door, you have to get that information down to the men who are moving in with the hose, because if that door is closed it is going to make things a lot hotter on the fire floor. The men are not going to get any relief. You might get some help up at the roof level from somebody who's free in one of the incoming companies. Either way if there's any kind of a real delay with that bulkhead door you'll push yourself up onto the roof of that bulkhead and smash out the skylight. Leaving even one pane in can make a big difference in the amount of smoke that's relieved, so I always take the whole thing out.

When you're up on the roof, you get a lot of heat. You're right on top of a chimney. If it's a top-floor fire you might even have flame and smoke coming up at you, and it's very difficult to see where you are. You've got to be careful when you jump back down to the main roof or you could go right over the side of the building to the ground. Very often you can't see at all. The fire's burned through the roof now and you're jumping into that. I mean you've got to be really careful coming down. After you've opened the bulkhead door and the skylight, then you start thinking about the occupants on the top floor. You've got to try to get down to them either by the rear fire escape or by the interior stairs. The stairs are much riskier because all the heat and smoke are coming up that hallway and going out through the open bulkhead. The stairways in an old-law tenement are largely made of wood, which can burn. The fire can come up the stairwell at you. You can start down the interior and it can be very smoky and hot and you can't see very much, but you're thinking that you can make it. All of a sudden an apartment door in another fire area, which maybe was closed, keeping a lot of the heat and smoke in, now suddenly opens up and the fire blows out and up the stairs just as you're on your way down. You have no way of knowing that.

If there are no visible occupants in the top floor, then you reach over the edge of the roof and start taking the glass out of the top-floor windows. That's not really the roof man's job—it's the outside vent man's work for an upper-floor fire—but you can assist him in doing that. You tie a utility rope, which every truckie has to carry, to one of the forcible-entry tools. Then you reach over and swing it to smash out all of the windows of the apartment that's on fire. You get as much of that glass out as you can starting from where you figure the apartment entrance is. This can provide some relief for the company moving in on the fire. Generally you try to take out the glass on the hot spots. You want to give all that heat someplace to go.

If it's a top-floor fire, there's a good chance that you'll have fire in the cockloft. In that case if the outside vent man hasn't brought a saw up with him, you'll be calling for one. Most of the time, however, the outside vent man has been able to size the situation up and has brought the saw with him or called down for it himself. You'll be working with him to cut holes in the roof, starting with the hottest spot directly over the seat of the fire. After cutting with the saw, you'll have to put hooks into the tar and the roof boards and pull the flaps back. Then with your tools you will knock down through the ceiling of the top floor to get the fire to blow out.

If you've got any kind of real fire in that cockloft, the flames can lap up around the saw blade while you're cutting. That's very common and the saw gets very hot, but with experience you learn to hold on to the saw, and you know enough not to step on the piece that you're cutting, because as you cut, that spot becomes weaker and weaker. The roof gets smokier and smokier as you cut, because you're providing some oxygen to the fire. Very often before you even finish the cut, the fire begins to burn through the roof, and depending on where the wind is blowing, the flames could blow at you. You try to cut with your back to the wind if you can.

The can man has the fire extinguisher and a six-foot hook. He works with the officer and another fireman who has an ax and a Halligan tool. This fireman is called the iron's man. Together these two men are known as the forcible-entry team. On the fire floor they have to force open the apartment doors, because the men from the engine company are not carrying forcible-entry tools. In the process of opening the doors, if the fire's not too bad, the men will make an attempt to get into the apartments. They'll fan out and search room by room. They all know what they have to do. They also have a hand extinguisher with them, and the can man is usually able to keep the fire in check for a short period of time.

The second due truck will generally go to the floor above the fire. That's the most hazardous position to be in. The job of these men is to search for any trapped victims.

This whole fire fighting strategy was worked out some years ago by Captain John O'Regan of Ladder 26, and it's been found to be as valid now as it was then.

At a tenement fire the first due engine's assignment is to bring the hose line into the fire area with the intent of protecting the interior staircase, particularly if it's an occupied building. There will be people on the upper floors, and that stairway is their only means of getting out, especially if the fire is blowing out the windows onto the fire escape.

If people are caught out on a fire escape, it's like being on a barbecue grill: the fire is coming up underneath them. So anyone who's trapped up on that fire escape could be in a very nasty position. Ideally, we're supposed to get a line between any people and the fire to give them protection.

Just before I was promoted, there was a covering officer—an officer who doesn't have a regular assignment, because he's newly promoted—who went into a fire with a new probationary fireman and another fireman. My position was on the outside fire escape. The fire was in front of the building; it was actually in the store on the first floor. There was a lot of heavy, heavy smoke in that store, and it was clear that the fire was going to spread all the way up through the building. The fire came up through the floor into the apartment where these three men were working, and it separated the probationary fireman from the two experienced men. The officer and the other veteran fireman had to get out of the building very quickly. They came out into the street thinking that the probie was trapped inside. I was on the front fire escape at the third floor, and the fire started blowing up beneath me so I had to get out of there. The chauffeur threw an aerial ladder up to get me, because I couldn't come down the fire escape. The flame was lapping out of the storefront by now in front of the building, and out of the second-floor window as well. I was just about to climb onto the aerial ladder when I saw something. It was the probationary fireman in that front room. He had gotten to the window and broken out some of the glass, but his mask was caught in the sash of the window. I ran over to him and broke away the sash. Then we both got on the aerial ladder and made our escape. At the same time the covering officer and the other fireman came out of the building, obviously very anxious, figuring they had left that probie up there and needed to get him, but we were coming down the aerial ladder at that moment. That's the importance of every man being in position. Had I not been in that position, the probationary fireman might have had some difficulty finding that aerial ladder, or even knowing there was an aerial ladder up since he couldn't see very well.

That was a situation where I was on a fire escape—while working in my favorite position. That's called the outside vent man position. A lot of men don't like that because they think of it as sort of an outside position where you're not involved. However, if you're doing the job and doing it right, you are quickly inside. You're by yourself. Everyone else is coming in the opposite direction. But after venting, you go in and try to search at least one room. Then you have to get out, because they're pushing all the fire out in your direction. But it's a unique position for autonomy. You really have to act on your own and use your own judgment. It's a very dangerous position for the same reason—because you're very often on your own. Also, if you're on the rear of the building and you run into trouble, no one is going to see you. So I think it's a key position in a lot of ways. Also, although all the positions are dangerous, the outside vent man position is a particularly hazardous spot to be in.

During one fire, a citizen was trapped on the fifth floor, one window away from the fire escape. The fire was on the fourth floor; the smoke and heat had gotten up to his apartment, the fire was about to burn up through the floor. He couldn't stay in that apartment any longer; he had to get out of there. When I came around to the rear yard I looked up and saw him out on the ledge. I went up the fire escape and got to the fourth floor, which was the fire floor, but I couldn't get past the fire to the fifth floor, where this man was trapped. At that point I considered climbing up the outside of the fire escape and pulling myself up to the man. While I was considering that—it was only a couple of seconds—another fireman slid down with the roof rope. Now he's one floor above me and one window away from the fire escape to my right and there's fire to my left. The fireman and the civilian got on the rope together and slid down one floor, but then the civilian grabbed the rope, and that had a braking effect and stopped their descent. So they were now level with me at the fire floor. I was very close to the corner of the fire escape. I couldn't be anywhere else, because there was fire coming out of the window in the other corner. They were just hanging there, so the fireman yelled to him, "Let go of the rope. Grab on to me and let go of the rope!" The civilian let go of the rope and grabbed the fireman around the neck. But his body weight was up too high, and the imbalance turned them both upside down. Now the two of them were dangling upside down.

The fireman saw me and yelled, "Get me"—of course afterward I never let him hear the end of that—and I could just reach the toe of his boot. I thought for sure the civilian was going to fall off; I don't know how he held on. I pulled them into the fire escape, and we were able to pass the fire and go down to the ground. Again, that illustrates the importance of being in position. Had I not been in position, the civilian I'm sure would have fallen, he couldn't have hung on much longer. I also think the fireman very easily could have fallen; he said so himself.

There was one fire in Harlem that took the whole building. I remember five or six floors of fire. I was up on the roof for a while, making a trench cut—trying to cut the fire off—the whole back of the building was gone right up to the cockloft. We made the trench cut, but the fire jumped the trench. There was so much fire that we knew we weren't going to be able to stop it, so we went down into the front of the second floor or third floor. By then there were TV cameras there. German documentary people were making some films, and it was funny to see these guys in the hallway trying to get us on film—because once you got past the hallway you really couldn't see anything. They had lighting equipment with them, but the smoke was so thick they really couldn't get much on film. At one point I got to the top floor where the most fire was and tried to make a search of that front apartment. The fire had taken off by then. The rear apartments, as I said before, were gone from the first floor all the way up. Then the fire crossed over into the hallway where I was searching with a few other men, and we had to get out. The chief officer got on the radio and told all of us to evacuate the building, and almost everyone got out.

There was another chief officer in one of the top front apartments of the building with a fireman. I couldn't see them, because I was in the hallway. As it turned out, they couldn't get back to the hallway, so they went out the window into one of the tower ladder buckets and were taken out that way. I didn't know that they had gotten out, and I didn't want to go down the stairs without them. Also, it was hotter in the hallway. I mentioned this to the other fireman with me, so we ended up making a search of that front apartment, and then we couldn't get back down the hallway either. Finally we found a window and there was that tower ladder, so we ended up getting into the bucket. The fire was blowing out the windows right behind us as we were coming down. I was worried about the men who had gotten out ahead of us. There are lots of fires like that.

I remember one guy who was in a vacant building where the windows were all tinned up. I finally got the tin off a window, and right on the floor below the windowsill was the victim. He was dead, and it turned out there had been foul play. He'd been shot, but he was still alive when the gunman set fire to the building. He had crawled or run to the windows, but they were tinned. You could see his hand marks on the walls where he had clawed at the tin, trying to get out.

That kind of desperation . . . I've always wondered about the horror. It's one thing if a victim is asleep or unconscious during a fire, but it's more upsetting to realize that this person knew what was happening to him. It is for me; I always thought about that. When you find people with their coats on who died trying to get out of the fire, it's sad, it's upsetting. But if you're a fireman, you need a built-in mechanism—you have to distance yourself from the emotion; you try not to think of the people as individuals. I know that helps me; I try to do that. I think it's always upsetting, I don't care who you are. It's always upsetting for firemen to find someone injured or dead. The men show the strain, but they get over it and they function, because they have to. They develop emotional defenses; it's part of a system of organization, a system of mutual support, reliance on each other, and it works. It fits in with the system and it has evolved over a hundred or more years, this whole routine or ritual. You come back from a fire, and before you do any cleanup, you gravitate toward the kitchen and you all talk about what happened. This procedure is now recognized formally—it's known as a critique—but it's been going on a long time, and it's more than that. The department recognizes these discussions as a good management technique. You talk about what improvements could be made and what you could do differently, and the critique is very effective that way. But it also serves as an important emotional release mechanism. It allows you to unwind, and it provides important mutual recognition. There is a lot of emphasis on that kind of discussion. You get rid of some of your fear, and you have a place to put it, and you realize you're not the only one who's scared. These talks are important to us. They go on, not because they're encouraged or suggested, but because the men want to talk, and the men were talking about their experiences long before the hierarchy recognized the value of these discussions.

Two of the saddest things that ever happened to me in the department involved the death of friends and strangers. The first one was when Larry Fitzpatrick was killed in an accident during a fire. He slid down a rope to rescue another fireman who had passed out over a windowsill. The men could see the unconscious fireman from the roof, so Larry slid down the rope to where the man had collapsed. But after he lifted him and began to descend, the rope snapped and they both went down about six floors. Dear God . . . I wept about it for years. The shock, the disbelief. We all thought of Larry as indestructible. He had never even been injured, and he was a very, very tough guy, very strong. It was a real blow, a real shock to all of us.

I heard about it on a late night news broadcast. I was in bed and I called the firehouse. The members were out at a fire—I think they were at that fire—but another company was in quarters and I asked them, "Is it true?"

They said, "Yes."

I had been with Larry six days before, and he had talked about dying, and interestingly enough he talked about wanting to die in a fire. If he had to go, he said, that's how he would want to go. And that was six days before he died. And it was a real loss. He was a very colorful guy, very colorful. He had a presence about him. And the reunions we have every year, now he's not at them. There's a real gap, a real absence. Even though he and I didn't always agree—in fact, I can't think of too many things that we did agree on—in many ways I felt attached to him. You couldn't hate him, you couldn't dislike him; you could be angry with him, but to know him was to love him.

That probably made me realize—made a lot of us who worked with Larry realize—that it doesn't always happen to the other guy. Because that's part of the defense—we always figure that if someone's going to get hurt it'll be someone else. Larry's death made us realize how dangerous the job can be.

You always think you know for sure what you are doing. You might go through a roof with one foot or one leg, and you hang there for a while, but you always get pulled out or you pull yourself out. You always escape, so you always figure you'll get out some way. That's not to say you aren't scared, but your fear is the kind where you say, "I have got to find a way out soon," not the kind where you say, "I'm not going to get out." You're optimistic. But after Larry's death it was hard for us to keep our defenses working. Lots of us had been up on roofs lots of times. I had trained on a rope with him after we had that incident where the fireman turned upside down. Larry and I were experimenting with ways to prevent that from happening. I had him jump on me while I was hanging from the roof of the firehouse tower. We could have been killed very easily that day. But the rope didn't snap.

We had been trained on that same type of rope. We used to practice on it regularly at drill. I never had to use it at a fire, but quite a few of the guys did use it to make rescues. It was a good rope because it was lightweight enough that you could take it with you; you could carry it all the time. It was quick, and usually when things happen you need something very fast. That's the problem when you have to take the time to call for a bulky, heavy rope. When you've got something light that you can carry with you, you've got a personal rope for security, and you know you can escape. It was false security, though, in that it failed. But I still like to carry a light rope, because it sure beats a free fall. I might be inclined to wait for a more substantial rope, but if I couldn't wait, I wouldn't want to think that all I had left was to jump. That lightweight rope was a good tool, and if Larry were here today, I think he'd use it again if he had to. In a situation like that I'd use it. If I was at a fire right now, I'd use that rope. It works most of the time.

The loss that tops them all happened in February 1982. Things like this happen in Harlem or in the Bronx, but I was in an area in Queens that isn't particularly active. We responded to an alarm. On the radio the dispatcher notified me that they had a report of children trapped on the second floor, so I told the firemen, behind me in the truck, that we had a job. Before we even turned the corner, I could see people waving us in, and I could see the smoke. I gave the preliminary 1075 signal to the dispatcher to bring in all the units that are normally assigned on a first alarm. Well, there was an engine in before us, but they hadn't given the signal for some reason. They may have been too preoccupied with finding a hydrant.

I had been in enough fires to know we had a big job ahead of us. As soon as we got there I put my mask on. You could see a lot of fire on the second floor. It was two-story peaked frame house. The mother had been outside trying to scrape some ice off the sidewalk. She had left the children, a three-year-old and a one-year-old, asleep in the upstairs front bedroom. Suddenly she turned around and saw the house in smoke and flames. We later found that there was a break in the gas line, and it acted like a blowtorch. That's why the fire was so intense. There was so much heat and so much fire so quickly. As soon as the mother saw it she tried to run in, but she couldn't get in to the first floor. The neighbors tried, too. An off-duty fireman and an off-duty policeman also tried to get in but couldn't. They had tried putting a wooden ladder over in the corner, but it fell to the ground in the excitement.

We put our ladder up. I immediately got up to the second floor and onto the porch roof. I tried to reach in through the window, but it was like putting my hand into an oven. I burned my fingers just reaching in. During this time the engine company was trying to stretch their line. But during all this time they hadn't had any water. They had one hydrant, but it was frozen. That's why I tried to get in the second floor rather than go up the front stairs. Normally you'd go in the front door and up the stairs. But I could see that they had no water.

I was with one fireman I knew from working with him in Harlem. He was very experienced. This guy was good; I knew I could depend on him. And he said, "Forget it, we're not going to get in." And he was right. So I went down the ladder and got to the front door, and the engine still didn't have water. They were on a second hydrant by then, but for some reason they had trouble hooking up. So there was a delay of a few minutes. It seemed like a long time, but all this happened in only a few minutes. At that point I told the engine officer to get the booster turned on, at least give them something. He said he had called for that—but so far they still didn't have water.

I went up and touched the front door, but I couldn't put my hand inside the front door because it was so hot; the fire was right at the door. I knew that it was going to take too long to get up those stairs, so I went back up the ladder to the porch roof, and at that point it was like being inside a furnace; the porch roof was black with smoke and I could hardly breathe even though I had my air tank on.

I asked the fireman with me to clear the whole window, to take all the panes out and the sash, too, for a full opening. I knew we had to get out of there pretty quick. During that time while we were on the porch roof clearing the glass out, the room below us burst into flames. We were now surrounded by fire. The aluminum ladder that we came up was involved in flames at that point. Later it actually snapped in half. I thought we were probably going to have to jump off that roof, which was a long one-story drop.

I told the other fireman to stay at the window. I was going to take a look inside the room. It was very hot, but I went in onto the floor. I felt around and found what felt like a doll. And I knew—I knew that feeling: it was the three-year-old. I pulled him out onto the windowsill. He was like a rag doll. In that room it was very black—I couldn't see anything—and I knew I couldn't stay in there much longer. When I got to the window, the fireman was saying that we had to get off. At that point we were completely surrounded by a wall of flame. The wooden ladder that the civilian had thrown up was still on the ground, and one of us yelled down for the men to put that ladder up. There was only a small section by the building wall on the corner where there wasn't any fire, so they threw it up there. I handed the three-year-old to the other fireman, and he went down the ladder. I knew there was an infant on that second floor somewhere, but I didn't know where he was. At that point I couldn't stay in the room, and I couldn't stay on the porch roof much longer either, so I left.

I ran to the ambulance, knowing that infant was in there somewhere, and started working on the three-year-old. There was a pulse: the three-year-old was alive but he was really in bad shape. When the mother saw him, she became hysterical. They pulled her out of the ambulance. I was doing CPR on his chest when they slammed the doors and pulled off. When I walked into the hospital the three-year-old was alive, but while I was being treated for the burn on my hand, I heard from the nurse that he had died.

Much later on, they found the infant. It turned out that she was in that same room, probably only a few feet away from me. I didn't feel a crib—there was a crib in there somewhere—and it was very hot and the infant was probably dead, but I didn't know that, and it bothers me. I had a lot of thoughts about what might have happened if only I had stayed a few more minutes.

That was my most recent major fire, and I'll never forget

it. I don't know what that's done to my ability to do a good job, but it was one of the saddest things that ever happened to me. I know I tried—I know all that—but maybe if I had stayed a little longer, if I had looked a little more. The worst thing was seeing that. I've never been affected like this; I've never been involved with children in this way, where it was all me and no one else. I feel very responsible. It happened more than a year ago and I'm still in mourning. I don't care if I ever go to another fire because of that. That was the first time I ever broke down and really cried, really sobbed. I've cried before—I've been upset before—but working on that three-year-old, knowing the infant was still in there somewhere, and then the three-year-old died, too, that really affected me.

Chapter 3

Dispatcher Herb Eysser
Manhattan Communications Office

I've been a dispatcher for seventeen years. I came from a Fire Department family. My father was in the Fire Patrol for over forty years, and my brother is a fire fighter. Since I was about twelve years old I've been around firehouses. I always wanted to be in the Fire Department, but due to an injury I had in the military I couldn't become a fire fighter. So, when I came out of the army, I became a fire dispatcher.

Dispatchers are the middlemen between the public and the fire service. Our main function is the receipt of fire alarms from the public, which we retransmit to the various firehouses.

I consider myself fortunate because I came on the job at a time when it was very interesting to be a fire alarm dispatcher. I was appointed in 1967, just as the department started to fight a tremendous number of fires. We stayed extremely busy until 1977 or 1978, but I found the work very rewarding. Often, if we had busy nights here in the Manhattan office, the dispatchers who worked in the Bronx office or the Brooklyn office were even busier. They were almost up to a point where they really couldn't handle it.

I have worked on tours where we simply collapsed from the heavy workload. We'd have to ignore all alarms except telephone or voice alarms where they reported fire in a building. We couldn't take care of the car fires or the rubbish fires, and we couldn't respond to every alarm from the fire alarm boxes, because we just did not have the time or the resources.

There was no one available to count the alarms coming into the office, but there were so many that we would just get overwhelmed, especially during the summer months in the late sixties and early seventies.

I think what really started the trouble was civil unrest out in the streets, the kind of unrest that resulted in the burning of Watts and Chicago and Newark. The city of New York, except for the night that Martin Luther King got killed, never really experienced large-scale riots where whole areas were put to the torch on one evening or three or four evenings in a row. What New York experienced in Brooklyn, the Bronx, and Manhattan was a long-term type of thing where buildings would burn down night after night, but not block after block. There would be a building burning here and a building burning there. You can still see evidence of those fires on the Lower East Side and in central Harlem, the South Bronx, Brownsville, Bushwick, East New York. All those neighborhoods were systematically burned down over a ten-year period.

The department tried to fight the onrush of fires, but in those very busy years there were only sixty or so fire marshals, and they were so overwhelmed with work that they could not really handle it. Many, many, many times one building would be torched two and three times in the same night.

The fire marshals are now up to around a 300-man force, and I feel that they are a real deterrent. Now we have more fire marshals to get to these scenes quicker and prevent that second and third fire of the evening. I think another major reason for the decline in activity is the change in the welfare laws. They used to pay people to find a new apartment, and they gave them money for new furniture; people used to torch their own homes for the payment. This incentive has been eliminated. Also, the apartment vacancy rate in New York City has dropped very low. Nowadays people know that if they set their place on fire they will not wind up in a city housing project. They basically feel that what they have is better than living on the street.

The Manhattan Dispatchers Office is the oldest of the five communications offices. There is one in each borough. The Manhattan office has been part of the FDNY since 1865, when the paid department was first established. Since 1922 the office has been located on the Seventy-ninth Street Transverse Road in the middle of Central Park.

When I first came here we used to rely on the bells, and rolling the companies by phone. At that time, if a civilian went up and pulled a fire alarm box it would come in to us as a coded telegraph signal. For example, box 835 would be eight dashes, three dashes, five dashes. We would count the dashes, and then go over to a telegraph key and send out what they called strokes eight, three, and five to the fire houses. The signal would be sent out twice in succession. In the fire houses they would get two rounds of eight, three, and five bells. Then they would pull a card to see where box 835 was located and who should respond. Manhattan was divided into zones, so one third of the borough would get the alarm—unless it was a signal for a working fire, then the whole borough would get it.

In the intervening years this office has changed 100 percent. It is all due to the work load. We went from the bells and rolling the companies by telephone to the voice alarm, which was basically a public address system. We did that in 1970 or so. The work load kept going up, up, and up. After several years of working on it, they finally came through with a computerized dispatch system. It was created in 1977 in the Borough of Brooklyn. Now in 1984, it's throughout the five boroughs. It definitely is a plus in the receipt and transmission of alarms. It cuts down on the paperwork and the manual procedure of selecting box numbers and finding their location. Now it's all done by the machine. It has freed some of us up. We used to devote a lot of time to paperwork and recordkeeping. That has all been absorbed by the computer. I would say the computer took forty to fifty percent of our work from us. But it is a definite asset for us. It does work.

When these alarms come in, we type the information into the computer, and the assigned companies are automatically notified. A minute after the alarm is transmitted to the firehouse we are required to announce the alarm on the radio. We remain in radio contact with the companies and will pass on information while those companies are en route. We will report children or adults trapped. With fires in high-rise building we will get reports from several apartments or offices, so we let the companies know that we have multiple calls on this fire. We let them know we believe it's a working fire because people have told us that they could see flames coming out the windows or a lot of smoke coming out of the third or fourth floors. That information can be helpful, especially to the first due units.

While a fire or an operation, like a train accident, is under way, we continually take progress reports from the scene over the air. We end each of our transmissions with our badge number and the time, because all the radio messages are recorded in case they have to go back and reconstruct the incident for some reason.

When I first started we had only box alarms with the handle you pull down to activate it. If an alarm came in we would dispatch three engines, two ladder trucks, and a battalion chief. However, the false alarms became a severe problem, so they decided to go to an ERS box—where the person reporting an incident could speak directly to the dispatcher, and the alarms could be taped. When we used the box alarms a civilian would pull the handle, and you wouldn't know if a whole apartment house was on fire or if it was just an automobile or a rubbish fire. Now you can taper the alarm to what he tells you is on fire. And if he does not talk, we don't send anybody.

We had a policy from about 1970 to about 1977, if the citizen pulled the alarm box, but didn't talk we used to send an engine company to investigate. We found that that became a tremendous burden. Some of these companies were reaching the ten thousand runs-a-year level, and they were getting physically exhausted from responding to false alarms. In 1978, the department went to the modified response policy of not sending anybody if somebody didn't speak.

I think a lot of people initially did not like it. We always wanted to respond to everything, but I think it was a case of just giving up. We had tried and tried to provide that service, but we found out that it just wasn't working. The alarm boxes were being abused, and we had to do something to make the companies more rested and more available when it really counted. It led to an out-of-sight, out-of-mind type of thing. If we didn't come, after a while they would stop pulling the boxes. Some people would see an engine company respond to a box and would pull the boxes as they walked down the street. That was stopped, because the apparatus was not in the streets as much. It worked. Some companies cut their runs by fifty percent.

The telephone brings a dispatcher right to the scene. If callers are screaming and yelling that it's a big fire, and if they are from one of the poorer neighborhoods, then you know it really is a big fire. If you pay attention to them, you will know how extensive the fire is and what is burning. As an example, the other day this elderly woman called. She calmly told me her name and address and said that the building next door was on fire. Then she told me to wait a minute. When she came back on the line she said, "You'd better bring the mother-fuckin' cherry picker 'cause the flames are coming out the windows." It turned out that the fire went to a third alarm.

I have had more than a few occasions where people were screaming on the phone that they were trapped, and couldn't get out. When the companies got in, they found these people dead. You realize that you were the last one on this earth to speak with them.

I've worked a lot of interesting tours, and I've had to work under a lot of pressure. I worked the Martin Luther King riots on April 4, 1968, and I worked the blackout in the summer of 1977. In both instances we got completely swamped—there were so many major fires. During the blackout we also had all kinds of other problems—hospitals needing portable power and people trapped in elevators. I worked the day of the Macy's fire, too, and I've worked numerous fires where fire fighters have been killed. I really have had a cross section. I worked that fire in the office building on Fifth Avenue and Forty-eighth Street where eight people got killed in 1970. And I have worked five-alarm fires on the piers and in warehouses through the years. I've always considered myself fortunate, because you learn from those experiences, and in the end you become a far better dispatcher.

You sometimes have to run a little hard and not show your emotions. Otherwise you can lose control of what's going on. You can't get involved with the outside operation. You've got to dispatch the apparatus; you have to make sure that you have those empty firehouses covered. We have our own job here in the office.

When there's a big fire that requires a lot of ladder companies, we have to get ladder companies from the other boroughs to fill those empty houses and make sure we had companies available should someone ask for three or four more ladder companies. We couldn't just send three or four ladder companies from anywhere; we had to get them there quickly from as short a distance as possible.

We have a thing we call relocation—this means filling in the empty firehouses. I generally use the computer to do it, though sometimes I just use my personal preference to close the holes as I see fit. I've done it so many times in so many years that it comes as second nature to me.

It's like a chess game. You take companies from outside the immediate fire area and move them into the empty houses. In many other cities they would dispatch these relocated companies to the fire if they needed additional units. In New York, however, we seldom do that. We leave the relocated companies to cover any secondary fires in the neighborhood, because we sometimes have simultaneous fires. If necessary, we would send additional companies from a greater distance to answer a second or third alarm.

The Macy's fire was unique in that it occurred during the business day and there were about ten thousand people in the store. It was a serious fire that spread very quickly because the sprinklers had been shut off in the area of the fire while some work was being done there. The Fire Department was confronted with a major problem: the quick evacuation of all ten thousand shoppers under extremely serious and escalating fire conditions.

They were asking for a lot of ladder companies to remove all the people. We were calling Brooklyn and Queens to send the companies over the bridges and through the tunnels to fill up the empty firehouses. Then we got busy here with notifications to all the bosses in the department, because we had a report of a missing fireman. We later learned that he had died.

The night of Martin Luther King's death I remember getting out of the subway on Central Park West, and seeing all these police cars going north. When I came into the office they told me that there were two four-alarm fires across the street from each other at the corner of 125th Street and Seventh Avenue. From midnight until about seven o'clock the next morning, we had one major fire after another, maybe ten or twelve five-alarm fires going within a five-block area of

Harlem. We were bringing companies in from Staten Island and the farther reaches of Queens, trying to fill up the houses. Many times a chief would ask for a fourth-alarm response and we could only give him two engine companies. It was one of the few times we simply ran out of fire companies.

We had a similar situation the night of the blackout. All of a sudden our office went completely dark. It took us a while to get the system working—we didn't have the computer at that time. That was an extremely busy night where again we ran out of companies once we had a lot of fires in the ghetto areas.

As a result of two fatal high-rise fires in 1970—one at 909 Third Avenue, around Fifty-sixth Street, and the other at One New York Plaza—the City Council enacted Local Law 5, mandating that high-rise office buildings have private alarms that are transmitted to us. Basically it is a good idea, but it has caused a tremendous amount of work for fire companies in the Wall Street and Midtown areas. The companies seem to be constantly running to these buildings on account of defective alarms or alarms being activated by cigar smoke. But the buildings are complying with the law, and it's actually a law that we wanted. We forced them to put it in, because these buildings do have a large disaster potential should there be a major fire during the business day. A defective private fire alarm, however, could someday take the companies away from a real fire in the neighborhood. The city hasn't organized any new fire companies in Midtown since 1898, and those companies are handling a tremendous workload today.

I think that someday there could be a major high-rise fire with a large loss of life. I am more and more convinced of it when I walk around Midtown. You have so many high-rise buildings, and as the construction goes on, the odds of a fire go up. You could get a fire up on that thirtieth or thirty-fifth floor, and because of the traffic during the daytime the companies could be delayed in getting there. It might not be an accidental fire. If you ever had an arsonist who spread gasoline in an office on one of those upper floors you would really have a disaster. A fire that's set intentionally is a difficult fire to get ahead of, because the fire is already freely burning before the companies are even out the firehouse door. A heavy fire on one of those floors would have serious consequences for the people above it. You would have a major catastrophe with maybe forty or fifty or more people killed.

You would have to get a lot of ladder companies into that area. There are only two ladder companies to cover Midtown, and they were organized in 1865. There is one at Fifty-first Street on the East Side, and one at Forty-eighth Street on the West Side. I often sit down on a quiet day and look at the map showing the companies in Long Island City, and I think about bringing them across the Fifty-ninth Street Bridge or through the Queens-Midtown Tunnel. Then there are the companies from Yorkville and Harlem that I could bring down. I also would bring down the Bronx companies to fill up those empty houses. We could move the Brooklyn companies across the Williamsburg Bridge or the Manhattan Bridge. The key is to fill up those firehouses in Midtown as quickly as possible and to keep companies moving toward Midtown even from points as distant as Kingsbridge in the Bronx early on. The Macy's fire was proof that they could ask for five or six ladder companies, and that would leave you with empty firehouses almost into Harlem.

The dispatchers have a very close working relationship with the fire fighters in the field. A lot of us have brothers or other relatives in the department, and there is a lot of trust given to us. We have proven ourselves through the years, particularly those busy years in the sixties and seventies. They know that we know what to do; we will come through. There are no uniformed chiefs coming here to make decisions if we have a big fire. Some departments do that, but we make a lot of decisions ourselves.

For example, an alarm for a hotel fire came in earlier tonight. At 10:00 P.M. the hotel should be fully occupied. The chief asked for 32 Engine. We also gave them 32 Truck, and they used them. We gave them Rescue 1 on our own, just to give them more manpower. It's known that the first five or ten minutes is the most important time. In those minutes you're either going to get the fire or it's going to spiral out of control. We've always given a little more, and we've always found that it has been helpful, so we just continue to do it.

We have all kinds of other functions in addition to bringing in firemen. When the companies come on the scene of an accident they might request a public ambulance or a police response. If they report traffic lights that are out, or broken hydrants, we contact the appropriate agencies. We also get the police to secure someone's premises after fire fighters have forced entry. We have a lot of interrelationships with other city agencies, like the Sanitation Department for sand and salt in the winter, and the Transit Authority and the commuter railroads to cut the power when firemen are operating on the tracks. Also in the borough we get a lot of phone calls from the press, since they consider Manhattan the hub of the city. We take note of sprinkler systems in the buildings, whether they're in or out of service. We take complaints of overcrowding in nightclubs and cabarets, and we take reports of rubbish in public halls, blocked theater exits, and all kinds of conditions that could lead to fires. We pass this information on to the local fire companies so that they can investigate the situation.

After you get assigned to a borough, you should drive through the neighborhoods so that, as you are dispatching the alarms, you can have a mental picture of the buildings. You should definitely know where the companies are located, and after a while you should remember where the alarm boxes are located.

I was a buff in Engine 82 in the South Bronx, starting when I was twelve years old; I still am. That experience engendered in me a lot of respect for the men who work in those busy firehouses. I rode with them for almost fifteen years, and I saw an awful lot of heroic and dedicated action in that time.

I still read many of the Fire Department bulletins, and I listen to the guys in the field; I keep in the back of my mind, for future reference, the things that they tell me. Some of your best dispatchers are buffs. They know both the outside operation and the inside operation, and if you can mix them together, you become an excellent dispatcher.

While I was growing up I lived right by a firehouse, and I remember the old apparatus with the open cabs. The Fire Department did not replace a lot of those rigs because of the shortages during World War II, so a lot of the apparatus of the 1930s was still in service in the 1950s. You have to remember that back then the busy companies did maybe two thousand runs a year, and most companies did only five hundred to eight hundred runs a year. I guess the rigs weren't designed for the comfort and protection of the men because they did so little running.

The cabs were enclosed as a result of the civil unrest in the sixties. I can recall riding with Ladder 31 one night when we were firebombed on Kelly and 163rd Street in the Bronx. We answered a box alarm and got into the middle of a gypsy cabdrivers' demonstration. The demonstrators fired shots at the firemen and threw Molotov cocktails at the rig. By the time we got out of the block, every window in the rig was broken. All the guys were cut with flying glass. It was a major attack. They had set an abandoned car on fire and pulled the fire alarm, drawing us into the block. Then they just let go with everything. It was the worst incident that I have seen.

When I rode with Engine 82 they were the busiest engine company in the city. It was something to see the excitement of the South Bronx. People were getting shot, stabbed, and run over by cars—a hundred things like that. Many a time I saw a guy hanging on the alarm box with a bullet wound in his head or his chest. His last act, the pulling of the handle on the box to get help.

I remember getting off of Engine 82 and helping the MPO hook up. Meanwhile, there was a cop right behind us yelling at some guy to stop. The guy whizzed around, and they exchanged gunfire. The guy fell dead right at my feet. This was on Dawson Street. There was a period in the city in the sixties and seventies when many of those neighborhoods were almost lawless. Even with the best efforts of the police department they were out of control.

Now many people wonder where all those people went. We went from lawlessness and almost total anarchy in the streets to a relatively peaceful society between 1978 and 1980.

In the sixties and early seventies, however, especially in the South Bronx, I used to take politicians out on runs for the union. I never took a politician out and didn't catch a fire. It was almost impossible not to catch a fire. What was going on in the Bronx was being duplicated in other poor areas of the city. I rode with Bronx companies, but if I had chosen to be a buff with Engine 58 in Harlem or 28 Engine on the Lower East Side or Engine 231 in Brownsville, it would be the same.

I remember riding with Ladder 31 when they would average forty to fifty runs a night. I feel very strongly that all that activity, and all that heavy fire duty, caused a number of members of Engine 82 and Ladder 31 to die young. I think that if you don't go to too many fires, you can put in twenty or thirty years on the Fire Department. Many of those firemen in the South Bronx did in five years what they normally would do in thirty-five years in previous eras. If anything protected them it was the masks, though they didn't use them to the extent that they do now. Several friends of mine from Engine 82 and Ladder 31 died from heart attacks in their early forties. They endured prolonged warlike conditions during that time.

As a buff I was always very well received. I always knew my place, and I'd keep my mouth shut if I saw something I wasn't supposed to see. Also I would help the MPO to hook up the hoses, and I would aid in stretching and taking up the hose line. In 1975 I stopped riding because they laid a lot of guys off. I felt that if I helped them out, I was taking the place of a guy who was let go. Even today there are two thousand fewer fire fighters than there were before the layoffs.

One of the reasons that I got a side job working for the unions was because of the closing of some fire companies and the reduced manpower. I feel that I'm paying the guys back for being nice to me through the years. If I can be in a position to help fire fighters, then I will.

The manpower problem is universal in fire fighting. Many, many fire departments and fire alarm dispatching offices are severely undermanned. When an undermanned company rolls on an alarm, it's not only the public that's endangered; it's the firemen, too. They can get lost or trapped in a fire, and there is no one to come and get them out. In many places in the United States the men never really know if that second due truck or engine is going to come. That's why I think it is essential that the manpower of a truck or an engine company be kept up to a minimum of five.

As a fire alarm dispatcher, I saw many alarms seriously held up—I'm talking about five to ten minutes on busy nights—because we couldn't get the alarms out. When we did have serious consequences as a result of the delay, the top brass would come running in here screaming, "You killed this one or that one." Then we'd say, "Take a look at the manpower and what we were doing that night, and how we were doing it." In all cases, as quickly as they ran in here, they would run back out, because the administrators of the department soon realized that they had missed the boat in their manning.

I think that the blame for the manpower problem lies with the people who prepare the budget. You have to put up a sustained fight with the budget people, because these people are outsiders who have no knowledge of the fire service. I think the same goes for the police and the Emergency Medical Service. One of our greatest allies in this fight, believe it or not, is the press, because we can go to them, and they can expose the situation.

Fire activity has decreased to what it was in the early sixties, and a number of factors account for this other than those I mentioned earlier. The wide use of masks, the introduction of tower ladders, and the installation of alarms and sprinklers in a lot of the bigger buildings facilitate earlier containment of fires. Also the population of many areas has been thinned out. For example, where there used to be a row of fifteen wooden buildings, we now have a fire gap, because several of those structures have already been destroyed by fire. This reduces the likelihood of a five-alarm fire involving the whole block. Moreover, the fire fighters of the sixties and seventies became very, very good at their trade. I used to stand in the street and watch them pull up, hook up, stretch the line in, get water, and put the fire out. They were experts at it, and they seemed to do their job with such ease in many areas of New York. Many of the fire officers today were firemen during that time. Also, we are not getting as many big fires now, and so we have more companies available to respond to that initial alarm and control the fire in the early stages before it gets out of control.

The future of the NYFD will be very interesting. I feel that companies in the commercial areas will continue to face problems associated with fires in high-rises. As I travel around the Bronx and Manhattan, I find that some of the burned out ghetto areas are slowly but surely being rebuilt. In Brooklyn they have that Nehemian plan where they're putting up five thousand attached homes in the East New York section. These buildings are non-fireproof, so you are going to see a resurgence of fire in those areas—not of the magnitude of the sixties or seventies, maybe, but definitely a high level of activity.

Right now on any twelve-hour shift, we have two or three

working fires in Manhattan alone. Thirty years ago that would have been considered very, very busy. But those of us who were around in the sixties and seventies think of it as slow because we were used to having the town burning down around us every night, with four and five alarm fires. However, in areas like Washington Heights, Flatbush, and Corona in Queens, the companies are fighting more fires than before. Those neighborhoods will not be put to the torch or incinerated like Brownsville and Bushwick, but they will have a consistent and, I believe, a long-term fire problem.

Chapter 4

Fireman Lee Ielpi
Rescue 2, Brooklyn

As a little snot-nose I used to hear the whistle blow and ask what it was for. Then, as I got older, I used to follow the trucks with my bike. Once I started following them, it was exciting. I couldn't wait to join the volunteers, which I did when I was eighteen. Living on Long Island, close to the city, the next step, of course, was to get into the FDNY—just to get in there and see it firsthand. This was in the mid-1960s when we were having all that social turmoil. I was a buff in those days. I had my own fire radio, a scanner, and I would constantly hear that signal: "We've got a working fire. Transmit the all-hands." The amount of work at those fires was mind-boggling.

When I went to probie school, I spoke to some chiefs, and I asked them if I could go into a company that was busy. They said, "Sure, it's great to have guys who ask for that." Most probies are not buffs. So I spoke with the captain of 227 Engine in the Brownsville section of Brooklyn. He said, "Great," and I went to Brownsville.

On my first night tour we went to three fires. All three were vacants—vacant buildings—but they were three jobs. One fire was at Howard and Sterling, 1644 box—one of the busiest boxes. Yeah, that was the busiest time—a tremendous number of fire calls constantly coming in.

Howard and Sterling. I can remember the lieutenant asking, "Where's the probie? Where's the probie?" That's because as a lieutenant, he's always worried about the new guy.

That's one of his responsibilities. He's got to keep an eye on you, and if he doesn't see you, he gets plenty worried—which is good. Everybody has to watch a probie. I was just grabbing on to somebody. I was there wondering what the hell was going on. But I can remember him constantly asking the same question, "Where's the probie? Where's the probie?"

Once, after I'd been in that company about five years, I was working a fire with Frank Corcoran who's now a deputy in Manhattan. He was the captain then, a dynamite man. Jerry Dombrowski and Tom McMann were there, too. I had the nozzle. We were going up the stairs of a three-story frame building. The fire was on the top floor, but it wasn't a tremendous fire. I had another three steps to go to the third-floor landing when I saw something black coming at me from my left. That's the only thing I can remember. Something black—that was it. Then we fell down to the first floor. All the interior stairs and everything that was there just came down with us. I remember reaching for my head and wondering why I didn't have my helmet on. I don't know if it was knocked off when I landed or on the way down. But it turned out that my helmet was all crushed.

Maybe I was there a total of five minutes, if that. It wasn't a severe collapse, but I was very worried about what was coming down next. I don't know how many holes firemen go through. You have got to be very cautious at every fire. But at times, you just slip and you forget to be cautious for that split second, and then you find a hole and down you go, right through it. And you're wondering, "God, what's going to happen next? Is there a radiator following me down? A board or embers, or is there fire?" In this case there wasn't a lot of fire, but some embers were still coming down. So the first thing I was going for was my helmet. "I gotta find my helmet," I kept saying.

I was the easiest one to get out. Bill Ostrander dug me out in about five minutes, I'd say. It was a matter of lifting some two by fours off me. Getting the captain out took a little bit longer. He was next to me, but he had some big stuff on top of him and he was pinned. When Tom McMann hit the landing, he bounced right out the window. As he went out, the window beams came down behind him and caught his leg so he didn't get all the way out. He was hanging out the window with the beams pinning his leg.

I didn't see any of this because they dragged me out first and immediately put me in an ambulance. I didn't want to go, because I knew the other guys weren't out yet. They said to me, "You gotta go."

The ambulance rushed me to the hospital and once they got me there, the firemen with me were ready to return to the fire. Their adrenaline was still flowing. They rushed back to the scene. After they left, I jumped into a cab and went back to the fire, too. Later on, somebody went to the hospital looking for me, and I wasn't around and nobody knew where I was. But my place wasn't there. My place was with my guys because I didn't feel that I was hurt so bad I couldn't help out. I didn't know how bad off anybody else was going to be.

I could have stayed at the scene of the fire in the first place, I thought. It turned out that I was really not hurt too bad, just banged and bruised, as I said. You look a lot worse, you know, because you're covered with dirt. It's very dramatic. I'm a walking dirt pile.

The next fire I went to I had to say to myself, "You just gotta erase the memory of that fall. Just let it go." But it was there, the thought of it; it stayed. You're making a move and you keep asking yourself, "Is the floor solid?" Then you just have to say to yourself, "Hey, either you forget it or you're not going to do a good job anymore." So I made myself forget it. I really hadn't been in that long, and I fell three floors, got banged up from head to toe—nothing broken, just black-and-blue, little cuts, bruises and contusions. But I'd gotten in trouble.

That was a great house, 227 Engine and 123 Truck. Super companies, both of them. The truck did a lot of running, 7,500 runs in the first year I was with them, and 227 Engine did 5,500 runs. Engines usually are not as busy as trucks because trucks have more alarm boxes to cover.

I knew how the rescue worked and loved it, but I never thought I would have a chance to go into it. Rescue responded on all 1075s, the signal for a working fire. The first company in—that is, the first one to arrive at the fire—gives a 1075, which means "Give me my third due engine company and another truck." It doesn't mean you're going to use all hands; it just says, "Give them to me because I *might* need them." On a 1075, the rescue company automatically leaves quarters. Any place in Brooklyn. Captain Gallagher initiated that policy.

I spent seven years in Brownsville and worked with four captains of 227. They were super captains; there were a lot of dynamite guys working in the truck companies. Captain Gallagher, however, was super engine, super truck, super rescue. His attitude was very cut and dry. He'd say, "The fire's going to go out, and it's going to go out because we're going to put it out. And not because it burns itself out." Cut and dry. And that's the way he molded the rescue. He hand-picked the company.

The most significant event of my career was at a fire on Osborne Street right off Pitkin Avenue in Brownsville. It happened in a three-story row-frame building. I had been in the rescue company three years at the time. The way a row frame is built, the ends of the row hold everything in place. If a fire in one building in the row is so bad that the building is demolished, the house next to it is suddenly left unsupported. The buildings are going to stay up with one missing house, perhaps, but if there's a subsequent fire, the row is weakened very rapidly because it has already lost a main support. Well, some squatters were living in the building on Osborne Street. So naturally, you have to try to get into the building.

As it turned out, when we got to the box, we pulled up just in front of my old company, 227. Jerry Dombrowski, one dynamite fireman, was working.

"Hey, Lee, what are you doing?" he said to me. "You're in front of us, you know."

The chief said, "Hold it, give that hose line to 227." So we gave them the line.

Then, Lieutenant Connelly and I went through one building. There was a lot of water coming down on top of us. In fire fighting you've got to remember details. When you walk through a building and you see something funny, you don't just take it for granted. In that house the water was running right through the middle of the building like a waterfall. It just didn't look right. Normally, it would be more spread out.

We go outside and the chief says, "Come with me for a minute."

Meantime, 227 walks into the building. We walk along the yard next to the building. It's early in the morning, six or seven o'clock. We had just passed the main part of the fire building and were walking to the rear when we heard this rumble. We turned around and saw this big pile of dust—no more building. Totally collapsed. Our first thought was of 227; they'd walked right into that building as we went around to the side.

I said, "That's it."

It was a horrible, horrible feeling. I mean, I just pictured them all in there, and sure as shit, that's where they were.

They had heard the building crack, and something told them to get out. Truck 123 made it out. Jerry Dombrowski made it just out the front door as the building came crashing down. It crushed his left arm, almost severed it completely. John Kozack was at the door of the building with three stories of rubble just lying on—not crushing—his head. Now you have the picture—how they talk about lean-to collapse. But when that building came down, through the grace of God— and that's the *only* reason—it went as far as his head and then stopped. It never continued to the ground, but just pinned his head to the sidewalk. It was unbelievable.

Jerry Dombrowski was the first guy we got out, after picking up blocks, lifting the doors. It was just a matter of sheer strength. The first impulse of the guys was to hop on top of the pile. In fact, we had to yell at some of them to get off the pile because all they were doing was adding weight. As we got the stuff off of Jerry, I can still remember him saying, "My arm, my arm. Please don't let them take my arm."

We got him out and put him down as gently as possible in the stokes. Now, it would have been easy for me to stay with Jerry, because when he had the nozzle I backed him up when I was in 227. Or if I had the nozzle, he backed me up. They used to call us Starsky and Hutch 227. So it was tough to just let him go in the stokes basket and not go with him. But I couldn't go with him.

They told us that another fellow was trapped, so it was just a matter of crawling in after him. That was when I saw John Kozack with the whole building collapsed on top of his head. As far as I was concerned, he had to be dead because he had no helmet. He was totally black. At first I didn't know who the person was—and his head was just crushed into the sidewalk. I said, "Oh, God."

Then this pile of dirt said, "Hey, Lee, get me the fuck out of here."

Wow—I can still feel the tingle up my spine when I realized Kozack was actually alive. There he was, under that pile of building for a good fifteen minutes. It must be something to have this crushing weight on you and just be forced to lie there and not be able to do anything. Bill Hewitson, John Thomas, and I used a Hurst tool to get him out.

Meantime, Lieutenant Connelly got Chief Tuttlemondo out. But he was dead.

Then they got Lieutenant Ramos out. He was banged up from head to toe with multiple bruises but no broken bones.

Then another guy from 176 Truck came out. He knew me and John Thomas, and he said, "There's another guy in here." We followed him into this small opening with pieces of debris falling all around us. We were wondering where the hell we were going. We went back some fifteen feet maybe, and then the lean-to stopped. And here's this guy, Nick Vazigno, flat on the ground with three stories of building on him from head to toe. And he's alive. Alive. Through the grace of God—I really do think God watches over firemen—at times. Sometimes he slips, though, and lets one of the firemen die. But the number of times I've seen firemen in situations like this—and alive—well, I don't think luck has a thing to do with it. I really don't. It's gotta be the Lord watching over us. Maybe it's because we do a nice job for people and God takes care of us for that.

Now, John Thomas and Bill Hewitson and I, who are in the rescue, are all wondering, "How the hell do we get Nick Vazigno out of there?"

It was impossible to get him out from where we were. We had to cut. Three stories of building had collapsed on him, and he was all compressed. We had to go through the roof, through the floor, through the next floor, and so on, to get to the guy. Bill and I stayed there with him. We wanted to get his head to try to get him some air, but we didn't want to give him oxygen or anything because the fire was still burning in spots. Smoke was drifting in and out of the place. We did some shoring. We cut and we used the Hurst tool—the police had sent their Hurst tool in.

We cleared away as much debris as we could from his face

and used a blanket to cover his face and protect it from falling debris.

We had to coordinate where we were going to start cutting. You have to watch when you sink the saw in—you don't want to sink it into him. The ceiling was right on top of him. It was really horrendous. Nick was almost completely immobile. He could only move his head a quarter-turn. That was it. The weight of all that building was crushing down on him. It was a horrible thing.

They cut down and made a square opening and just took the roof off and the beams out. After they got into what had once been the third floor, they took it out. Then they went down to the second floor, under which he was pinned. I don't know how he lasted that long.

The fright alone was killing; I mean, look, he can't move. I kept talking to him the whole time, just trying to keep his mind active. By this time, Bill and I had done all the shoring and supporting we could possibly do. There was really nothing else we could do except stay there and guide them down from the top by telling them where to cut. When Nick got excited and began to scream, I got pissed off at him and said, "We're getting you out of here." I said a lot of things and I cursed a lot. He didn't answer me, but he calmed down.

Bill would talk to him and I would talk to him. We just kept it up.

We were very concerned about a further collapse, because there was a cellar in this building. As it turned out, some of the men were shoring it up underneath. All four rescues had come to the box and they were working on it from downstairs, too.

It was a good two-hour operation to get these men out and the last of all was Nick. They had all the rescues come in, but Bill and I never came out of that hole the entire operation.

We didn't have the vaguest idea what was happening in the other rescue company. We didn't know that the squatters we had originally gone in to rescue were dead. They had the other rescues on the radio every once in a while. But they switched channels on us because there was so much talk on the radio, which happens at these fires. It went to a third alarm.

Finally, they cut Nick out.

John Hines was in the collapse on Osborne Street but he

was in between some washing machines in the lean-to part. You have to see that building to really appreciate what I'm saying. Anyhow, John didn't get hurt. But he just felt—well, he felt very bad that he didn't get hurt and it just worked on him that way. You know, he stayed but he just wasn't himself anymore.

Jerry Dombrowski, whom I mentioned earlier, was the first guy we got out of the house on Osborne Street. They were going to cut his arm off, that's how bad it was. Then they said they'd try to do surgery. They put a plate in his arm and re-attached all the arteries and veins. The man is on full duty today, back in 227. He's one dynamite fireman, I tell you.

There've been a lot of smaller rescues, but I can't honestly think of the first one. And a lot that weren't successful, too. The ones that always stick out are the kids. Job in Bay Ridge. When we got to that job, the door was not forced yet, but just pried. You couldn't open it any farther, so I got my body up on it and I pushed. It turned out that there was a body behind the door and that's why I couldn't open it. We had to take the hinges off—it was the only way to open the door. It kind of fell in, and then we had to pull it back out. There was a decent smoke condition, and I got close enough to see the person on the floor. It was a male. As I went to move him, I saw a little baby next to him. I pulled the male out and grabbed the baby. The mother was also there. I handed out the baby and went back to grab the mother and found her holding another baby in her arms. They were all dead. They had panicked and couldn't get the door open before being overcome by the smoke. I think about them all the time. I can't forget it. I guess everybody feels the same way about children.

If only I had been there two minutes sooner, if only I had been there five minutes sooner, whatever. Or if they hadn't run down that hall and piled up on the door. You just keep thinking all these things. It's pretty bad.

At another fire off Flatbush Avenue I was going up the stairs, and some other firemen had a little guy out in the hall. A young fellow was doing mouth-to-mouth resuscitation on him. A probie. He was getting a little nervous and he wasn't really doing it correctly. I said, "Hey, babe, take a break and I'll give you a hand." He just stepped away. I started doing mouth-to-mouth and the lieutenant was doing compressions.

The lieutenant had taken a beating while he was getting the kid out, and he was falling to one side. The kid resembled my kid. I guess they all resemble my kid, but he did have a marked resemblance. It was so horrible. I worked on that kid a long time. I worked hard. It was bad. My lieutenant didn't know where I had gone. I should have told him. I went to Kings County Hospital. Called in ahead of time that we were coming with this kid. Now you're doing compressions on the kid, doing mouth-to-mouth, carrying him into Kings County emergency room. You put him on the damn bed, work on the kid, and he dies. It just pisses me off. But I was crying my eyes out. Just crying my eyes out. I can still remember just twiddling his toes before I had to go home. They were cold. The ones who don't live stand out in my mind like that, even more, it seems, than the ones who do.

We went to one fire that had nine D.O.A.'s. It was on Ellery Street in Brooklyn and nine was the most D.O.A.'s I ever had. It was a three-story frame building, a railroad flat building—front to rear is one apartment. The fire escape was at the rear of the apartment. Flat roof. Heavy fire on the first floor and they sent us out on the box because they got numerous phone calls. Oh, they attributed the fire to faulty gas heat or some other nonsense. The Stouffer's fire was going on while this one was going on. That got the big write-up, Stouffer's did. And this one also got a big write-up in the paper—nine people dead.

There was one woman who had a baby with her. She wasn't burned. She was more smoked than anything else. The occupants above the fire were burned. The fire fighters had tried to drag the woman out and found a small little teeny-weeny baby in her arms. After we took her body out, we went to the apartment next door, and there were bodies all over the place. After I handed the seventh person out the window to the guys in 111, I was standing by the window and the bed was right next to me. I think it was Jack Kleehaas who handed me the little people, and I handed them out the window. They were all in body bags. You stand there and you kind of say, "God, no more. We're finished."

I looked down and right by the bed was just a teeny little hand sticking out. I'll never forget it. Dead. Horrible. I wasn't ready for that. I always try to be ready for things, but I really wasn't ready for that. Number eight. The ninth body was found by an engine company lieutenant.

Firemen don't like to show emotion. Firemen would rather hold it in and just go do their own thing in the corner someplace, maybe driving home or maybe when they go to bed at night, if they can't go to sleep. Firemen just do not like to show emotion.

I can think of a bunch of shit fires that were unusual. I got lost in a building once due to my own stupidity. It was a furniture showroom, a second alarm had already been transmitted for the building next door—the fire building. The buildings were attached and there were fire doors, so the chief wanted us to check the exposure between them for extension of fire. We went in—total blackness and a large, open floor space. Lieutenant Vigiano said, "I'm going to follow this wall." You should always have a plan of what you're going to do. If you don't have a plan, one mistake in this business, one mistake—and that's all there is. For some reason, I said, "Lou, I'm going to walk straight in and find the far wall." I really feel that I do very well in dark conditions. I can sense where I've been. I started walking straight in, figuring that if I didn't find anything, I'd make an about-face and come back. I thought I would hit the front wall. I might not hit the door, but I'd surely hit that wall. I didn't find anything in there. I should have stopped right then and there, in those ten paces—I was counting my paces—but I had the time and there was no rush, nothing there. Eleven paces, twelve, thirteen, fourteen. Now I'm being stupid. I'm going in a little bit more and I'm going to stop. I went in some more and I didn't find shit. Here I am, now, I don't know how far in I've come. Twenty paces, twenty-five paces? Whatever—no objects, nothing—just total blackness, a black mass and a lot of yelling on the radio. The fire's burning like mad and now I'm saying to myself, "I've got to turn around and go back." I make a turn and I start walking. Twenty-one, twenty-two . . . twenty-five, twenty-six . . . twenty-nine, thirty. Thirty paces, but no wall. No door, nothing. Now I can hear the fire extending. I had my radio on and I said, "Aw, shit, c'mon, you've gotta be kidding. I'm lost and the fire's extending. This is really great."

Two things can happen with fire fighting. One: I panic and possibly die, depending on what happens with the fire. Or two: I don't panic; I say, "Well, let me think of what I'm going to do."

I'm not praising myself, because there are thousands of firemen who do the same thing every day, but there are also firemen you read about who don't. A fireman will be found without air in his mask in a small building. How can you run out of air in a small building and not find a way out? Well, by banging around and getting all excited and not knowing what you're doing. Panic, in other words. Winding up in a closet and spending five minutes in there trying to get out. That sounds silly, perhaps, but believe me, I've spent time in bathrooms that weren't very big, saying to myself all the time, "Where's the damn window in this bathroom?"

You can get disoriented in a fire. If you don't maintain your cool, if you don't say to yourself, "Okay, stop it. Get control," you're going to get into trouble. I stopped and lifted my mask and said, "Hey, Vig." He answered me way off in the distance.

Then I said, "Where are you?"

I thought I heard him say, "I'm trying to find the door."

And I'm thinking, "Aw, shit, he's trying to find the door; I'm trying to find the door."

I lift my mask up again and say, "Okay, Vig, look, I'll find the door and call you."

But I didn't realize what he had said. He had said, "I'm *at* the door."

I kept walking, but I couldn't find that wall.

"Forget it," I said. "This is the pits." Then I yelled to him, "Vig, where are you?"

Now he's moving closer and I said it again.

"Where are you, Vig?"

"I'm at the door."

"Keep talking," I said, and put my mask back on.

I managed to find him, but I was totally lost. It was a horrible, horrible feeling. I mean, there was no fire in there yet, no heat, but it was pitch black and I could just about see my light. But I'm lost, and I don't care if there's no fire in there because just the same, it's a hostile environment. I'm lost in a hostile atmosphere, breathing air out of a bottle, and I know that eventually the air is going to run out. If I don't find my way out of here and I run out of air, well, now I've got to take off my mask and hope I can keep my nose close enough to the floor and keep on crawling.

This is where I made a mistake. I went the first ten steps and didn't find anything. I should have said to myself, "Okay, stupid. Go on back." I should have known better than to make a stupid move. I was lucky, though, and I got away with it that time. The fire never came in.

I carry a fifty-foot rope in my pocket. Vigiano and I went back in and I tied it to a door. We had a probie from the engines working with us, a sharp kid named Steve. All right, we thought, and we went back in and got to the end of the rope and I said to Steve, "Here, put your hand through that loop and keep that rope taut. Don't leave this room."

Now we went off, but Steve could call out and we had a reference point to come back to. Sure as shit, we had to get out again. The men outside started yelling at us, "Hurry up, something's coming up."

"Steve, where are you?" I called.

"Okay, over here. I'm over here."

We easily got to him and that's how simple it was. But the first time I went in without a rope—well, that's all it takes.

People think I'm crazy because I like going to work. I don't tell them I'm going to work. I never tell anybody I'm going to work. I go to play. Some people don't like that word, because fire fighting is tough; it's people's homes burning down, it's people dying. But I take it as if I am going to play. When I go to play, I'm going to do the best job I can. When I go fishing, which I enjoy, I do the best I can to catch those fish. When I have to fight a fire, I fight it as best I can. I try to ensure that the fire is not going to extend beyond the point where we hit it when we get there. So, I go to play. That's how I look at it.

We had this scuba job once. It was in January of 1983. I got the Dr. Albert Cinelli medal for that job. Three boys were fooling around in a van, and they drove off a pier into the East River. The van landed upright on its wheels on the bottom and they sent us in there on the box. But it was a little bit of a ride from where we were. In the meantime, the engine and truck had made an attempt to go in the water. Firemen will do these things. It's great. The van was in about twelve feet of water. You could actually stand on the top of the van, and the water would be up to your chest. Two of the kids managed to get out of the van. They said their friend was still inside.

We put on wet suits on the way to a job to save time. The truck company was super; they had everything set up. They had a big light shining into the water. It was around six o'clock in the evening, but it was dark because it was winter.

They had a ladder in the water where they had tried to reach the kid in the van. This was in Greenpoint, 106 Truck. Jack Pitchard, the lieutenant, said to me, "You and Dave DeFranco go in." Going in involved nothing more than climbing down the ladder. I was first and Dave followed. The van was two feet to the right of the ladder, so I took a rope underwater with me as a guideline. We tied it to the van. Then we went to the surface to tell the others we'd found the van and were going to make the search. We went back down—all this only took fifteen or twenty seconds. Underwater visibility was about six inches. It was totally the pits. I opened the door of the van, which was unlocked, but I had to brace one foot against the van to pull the door open because the vehicle was sinking in the mud. I swam maybe three or four feet inside the van. The kid's hand was suddenly hanging in my face.

It was interesting—the first time I was involved in finding somebody underwater. It was a completely different kind of experience, not like a fire where you could yell through your face piece, "Hey, Dave, I got him. He's over here." There's nobody to talk to underwater. If you need help, you bang your bottle, but sound travels crazy in water, so you can't reply on it.

The kid was just floating near the ceiling of the van. The van was full of water. So I grabbed his arm, and of course, being in the water, he floated very easily out the door.

I towed him right up to the surface. The other guys in the rescue took him right away, but I was sure the boy was dead.

We went back down. Dave went in this time and made a search. I stayed down by the door for a while. Our lights were just about useless now. I went up and stood on top of the van while Dave made a perimeter search of the van. That was the whole operation, and the whole time I was sure that kid was dead.

When we came out, they told us that the ambulance people said they've got something on the scope. He was alive, but as it turned out, sad to say, he died two days later. I don't know how they treated him. That was our mistake; we should have gone and seen how they were doing it. I don't know why we didn't; we normally do. Maybe because we were cold and the other men were worried about getting us back, or whatever. I guess it had to be something—but we didn't go.

The kid died and I feel bad about that.

I can remember some funny things about my experiences—funny things that aren't really funny. Like going down a hall and it gets so hot you get blown down the stairs and you're laughing. You say, "Wow. Where did that come from? Holy shit." And you just say, "Well, let's try it again and see what happens." Then you laugh.

One time we caught a parasite while scuba diving. We all had to go to this laboratory in Manhattan to give stool samples. They gave us times to go there. "Lee, you go at eight o'clock; Bill, you go at eight-thirty; and Jack, you go at nine," and so on. So we wouldn't go as a group. We all said, "Well, look, let's meet at the firehouse and go in two or three cars. This way everybody doesn't have to use his own car."

So fifteen or sixteen of us showed up at once to give stool samples in this laboratory. That's all they did in this laboratory—stool samples. If you can picture all of us walking into this place with nothing but stool samples—well, I'll tell you it was unbelievable. There's an odor right off the bat when you open the door. It's an odor of Lysol.

I don't know how they stay there all day long, but I guess you can live with it. We all went in and they didn't like us right away. They said, "Okay, we'll explain to you what you have to do, where you go. First, you have to drink this little vial of laxative, and then you go out to have breakfast. Spend about an hour having breakfast. Then come back and we'll show you the bathrooms. Here's two bathrooms, one here, and one here."

The toilet seats had the ultraviolet lights around them to kill any germs on the seat. There are also stacks of cups like you get at McDonald's, thick malted cups. Piles of them with covers. The tops have slices in them for the straw. The girl was saying, "Now, when you come back from your breakfast and you have to go to the bathroom, put your stool into this cup. Put the cover on it and bring it over here to this office."

So, you walk into the office and there's a microscope there and this little horseshoe-shaped desk, and you give the sample to the person in the office.

Now, fifteen guys are drinking laxatives. Fifteen guys now go out and have breakfast. The laxative worked pretty quick for some people. Some people ordered breakfast but they couldn't wait for it. They had to get right back to the laboratory. Now, as the guys started going back, the last guy is stuck with the bill. But there's only two bathrooms in the laboratory.

When I walked back in there, there was a Hasidic family sitting there—husband, wife, and three kids. There's also a young couple sitting there and a lady and man on the other side of the room. And there are fifteen or sixteen firemen who tend to be, you know, a little carried away at times. And everybody has to take a shit, and there's two bathrooms.

You had to see it. Somebody asked the girl, in the beginning, "How much do you want in the cup?"

She said, "You have to put all of it in the cup."

"All of it?"

"Yes," she said, "all of it. We want the very last drop, as well, because that may be where we find the germs, not in the beginning. We don't know, so we want it all whether it's one, two, or three cups."

"You gotta be joking," he said.

"No, all of it," she said.

She wasn't joking.

So here we are and everybody's going into the bathrooms. Of course, being firemen, we're going to have a contest to see who's going to fill up the most cups. You had to see it. Here's the contest going on. First of all, Larry Gray goes in. He's going in his cup, and he can't stop when his cup is filled. And his cup overflows. It covers his hands. He goes all over the floor. He's in there yelling, "Who's at the door banging?"

"Let me in, let me in."

The nurse said, "Use our bathroom. Use our bathroom." Their own private bathroom. They're shuttling guys down the hall, and they're coming out of the bathroom with these cups, big malted cups. You had to see it. The guys are coming out and holding up their cup. "Look at me."

You can see the line of shit through the cups, and they're

walking past all these people there. We laughed so hard they called up the department brass at the medical office.

The families would put the newspapers up closer to their faces. You had to see, I mean, to see this shit wobbling in the cup back and forth as they ran through the place.

Then it's my turn to go in, but the laxative isn't working. The girl says, "The stool has to be soft for the girl to do the test."

So I go to the bathroom and sure enough, my stool is not soft. I had corn the night before, and you know how that shows up in your stool. So I'm saying, "Man, this is the pits. It's downright degrading." Thank God we went with fifteen guys. We could make a joke out of it. Otherwise, it's really degrading.

There's a girl constantly going around with a Lysol can, spraying everywhere. It was the pits. All you heard was the girl or the banging on the door, "Let me in. Let me in." And the answer, "I'm not finished."

Some people got up and left. I come out with my little cup. I couldn't even put half an inch in my cup and they said, "That's not enough. You're going to have to stay here or come back again."

So I take my little cup and I go through the crowd and of course, I didn't win the contest. One guy had three and a half cups—three and a half!—and I'm talking about filling these cups up. It was the pits. So I take my cup and here's this Oriental girl; it turns out she's the doctor who examines the stool. She's sitting at this horseshoe desk. There's shit from one end of the curve all the way around to the other end. She had fifteen guys who are filling up one, two, three, cups with shit, and the cups were all around and in front of her—cups full of shit. I said, "Oh, Christ, I honestly don't know if this is enough."

"Well, let me have it," she says and takes it with a big smile. She pops open my cup and says, "Oh, that's good. That's plenty. That's just fine." She puts the cover back on and puts it down.

I said, "Let me out of this place. You have got to be kidding." She really loved her work. Smiling half a mile and surrounded by shit. I just couldn't get over it. What a day that was. Well, they called up the city immediately: "You will never send guys here again."

Boy, did they get teed off.

While this whole shit thing was going on, the brass said, "Well, let's also test the guys from the engine to get a comparison because you can contract this parasite from not properly cleaning the dishes and cups. To get a sample, we'll test guys from Engine 210."

It turned out that one or two guys did have the parasite. They told this one probie that he had to go the next morning to the city laboratory with this other fireman.

We handed them each a paper cup and told them to shit in it. We told them that they had to take the shit into the lab, but the cups could not be covered.

The next morning they set off in this one guy's car. They had these cups balanced on the back seat, and they had all of the windows rolled down.

When they arrived at the lab, they set the two cups down on the counter. The people in the lab were not too pleased. They screamed at them, "Never again! Never come back here again!"

Chapter 5

Lieutenant Gene Dowling
Ladder 22, Manhattan

The most rewarding part of this job is saving someone's life. That may sound corny, but I don't think there is any greater high than knowing that the only reason some people are alive is because you made an effort, and you were able to extricate them from a tough situation.

I was involved with the Morgan Annex Post Office fire on West Thirtieth Street in Manhattan in 1968. I was a fireman at the time. We weren't supposed to be at that fire, but we were sent to cover for another company that was already there. When we got into their quarters, the dispatcher's office wouldn't take our taps—at that time we used a telegraph key to tell the dispatcher that we were in service. The lieutenant then called the dispatcher, and the dispatcher told us to go over to the fire.

When we pulled around the corner, I thought that all the lights were on in the building—just about every window was lit up. It never entered my mind that this building was totally consumed in fire. It went to ten alarms. The entire square block was on fire.

When we got closer to the fire, we could see that a command center had been set up, and the lieutenant had to report in. I was in absolute awe. This was the biggest fire I had ever seen. I have yet to see one bigger.

I said to one of the other firemen, "If the lieutenant is looking for me, tell him I'm just walking down the block. I want to see what's going on here." I'd walked maybe a hundred feet when somebody yelled, "There's someone up there." The smoke was obscuring our view, but every now and then you could see this one person up in a window. I yelled for the chauffeur in my company, Dick Chase, to bring the aerial ladder, and for someone to tell the lieutenant we had somebody trapped on the sixth floor.

Another company, however, beat us in—7 Truck, manned only by the chauffeur and tiller man. I grabbed a scaling ladder off their rig. Since somebody had to stay down on the platform at the controls of the aerial ladder, I told their tiller man, "Come on, you and I will do it." But as they started to put up their ladder, I could see that it would be way too short. This was a huge commercial loft-type building, so the height between each floor was almost double. So I handed the scaling ladder back to them and jumped down to the street.

I then told Dick to put 25 Truck up on the sidewalk, between 7 Truck and the building. Because of the steeper angle, our aerial ladder would extend farther up. After Dick raised the aerial, another fireman, Clyde Williams, and I went up. When we got to the top of the hundred-foot ladder, it was still too short to reach the window, but in anticipation of that I had brought along our scaling ladder, or Pompier ladder. This is an eighteen-foot pipe with short rungs sticking out on either side. At the top of this ladder is a hook with sawteeth that can be hung over a windowsill.

I got this scaling ladder hooked on the window where we'd spotted the guy, and I started to climb up. But I really couldn't see where I was going because all this smoke was billowing out the lower windows.

I was about halfway up when I felt it begin to pull out of the window. Chances were it only pulled away one inch— from one sawtooth to the next—but I saw my life pass before me. I climbed back down to the top of the aerial ladder. I took the Pompier and smashed it through the bottom half of the window to secure it better. Then I climbed back up.

Instead of one person being up there, it turned out there were three. I brought them out one at a time onto the scaling ladder. I went first and held them on the ladder.

One was an elderly man. He was scared, very scared, and he froze on the ladder. His name was Garrett O'Leary. I'll never forget his name. I talked to him and tried to reassure him. I was afraid I was going to end up on the street with this guy. I made a conscious decision not to let that happen. I had detected a brogue, so I asked what part of Ireland he was from. I wanted to gain his confidence, so I told him, "Listen, we're going to get out of here. Don't worry about it."

I can honestly say that I wasn't scared until it was all over. Firemen don't like to talk about fear. But it's there. I was under a tremendous amount of pressure. I knew O'Hagen, the chief of the department, was downstairs with Lowery, the commissioner, and I didn't want to screw up. When I got down to the ground, O'Hagen came over and told me it was one of the greatest things he'd ever seen. He told me "You have a Class I on the books." That's the highest award there is. It was a super feeling, absolutely super. I was even interviewed on the radio. It was quite a high, I was on springs that night. It's probably the most gratifying feeling to save somebody's life.

I had another rescue one night. It was a fire in a multiple dwelling, on the eleventh floor. There was talk on the way up that somebody was in there. When we first went in, I couldn't find the person. Another truck company had preceded us to the alarm, so I went into the back of the apartment and got past the fire. On my way into the bedroom, my foot got caught on something. It was a woman who was propped up between a two-foot wall and a chest. It was part of the entrance. I learned later that she had a walker, but she must have left the walker in the room because it wasn't in the corridor where she had fallen down. I remember grabbing her. I couldn't see anything in the room.

The heat was tremendous, and there was fire coming out of the room I had just passed. I wanted to get her out as quickly as I could. When I grabbed her under the arms, I could feel her flesh coming off in my hands. She was burned badly. But she was a feisty old lady. She turned out to be seventy-seven years old. She'd just bought another apartment in the building, and was taking care of her mother, who had to be up in her nineties. Her name was Xiphora Spiro. She died forty days after the blaze. I felt bad about that. Maybe it would have been better if I had left her in there. I'm sure she suffered a lot between the time I rescued her and the day she died.

I had an incident where we lost a five-year-old kid in a brownstone. We got there about six-thirty in the morning and there was the mother of the child at a window, and she was on fire. Literally. Her hair was burning. She was in a basement apartment with bars on the windows, but we were able to get the bars off the windows and get her out. This was one in a million. Usually the bars on a basement apartment in a brownstone are embedded in the stone sill of the window. You can't get them off. This time we were lucky. These bars happened to be anchored into the frame of the window, so they came off fairly readily.

She was screaming, "My baby, my baby—he's in the back. He's in the back." We interpreted that to mean the child was in the back of the apartment, but that was a mistake. She meant he was in back of her, and when we found the kid, he was dead.

The boy was only five years old. I remember seeing a bicycle, some trains, and finally . . . I don't like to think about it. When you lose somebody, particularly kids, you don't want to start thinking. You know how old they are and you start comparing them to your own children. But because you have to maintain a certain composure, that curtain comes down. Otherwise, it will really bother you. The guys really felt terrible, absolutely terrible.

After a fire, you're always a Monday morning quarterback, especially when you lose somebody. I think most firemen feel even worse about children, since it's not the children who cause the fires; it's the adults. Maybe some guy downstairs came in drunk and fell asleep in bed while smoking. Innocent people die as a result. I feel bad about it. I'm sure that I echo the sentiments of most fellows on the job.

Aside from the rescues, what is it about truck work that I like?

I don't think it's as routine as when you're with an engine company where you're very, very confined to a specific area. When you're with a truck company, your field of endeavor is greater. You're thinking of trapped occupants, how the fire is extending, how you can gain access into the building. There's a lot of things to think of. I'm not taking anything away from the engines. A truck company never put a fire out yet.

I have never been *at* a fire where a fireman was killed. When I first came on the job, six firemen were killed in Maspeth, Queens. This was in October or November of 1962.

I was a pallbearer at the funeral. Francis X. Egan was the fellow that I helped carry. I remember kneeling in the church.

It was a Catholic church. His family was behind me. I cried, and I had never laid eyes on this man. I felt I would never want to be a pallbearer again. You try to hold back the tears, but you feel a lump in your throat the size of a football.

I've had friends who've died on the job. I remember when twelve firemen were killed in 1966 in the Twenty-third Street collapse. I woke up the next morning and heard a newscaster announce that twelve firemen had been killed in New York, and I thought it was a mistake, because sometimes the press gets things wrong. Then the impact of what might actually have happened hit me. I said, "I can't believe twelve firemen were killed."

They were. I knew two of them—Rudy Kaminski and Jimmy Gallanaugh. I was absolutely devastated. Not only because I happened to know these two guys, but the thought of twelve firemen in New York City being killed was, to me, absolutely incredible. When I first heard the newscast, it seemed so outrageous—*twelve* firemen—that I thought the guy was making an error. As it turned out, he was telling the truth.

About a month after this, at about five minutes to eleven at night, they broke into a television program. They said that six firemen were trapped somewhere in the city. I tried to call another friend of mine, who was also a firemen, while he was trying to call me. We finally reached each other, and we made it down to Forty-eighth or Fiftieth Street and Eighth Avenue in about half an hour from suburban New York.

It felt good to be a fireman that night. The camaraderie on this job is incredible. I saw helmets with numbers on them, numbers that I had never seen before. Triple numbers. Generally, in that area there are only two numbers—22 Truck, 76 Engine, 21 Truck, 34 Engine. But that night it was one big family of firemen working together to dig their brothers out.

In that case, thank God, we got all six of them out. Rescue 1 and 2 and some of the other rescues went into the cellar of the adjoining building, and tunneled through the wall. It was amazing. When it was over, I looked at the place where the building had been and if I hadn't known it had been a building, I would have thought somebody had put a big pile of garbage into a vacant lot. I couldn't believe they got them out.

But there were *hundreds* of firemen in the street that night just milling around waiting, ready to do anything they could to help. It's hard to explain—there's such a tremendous bond among firemen that outsiders can never fully appreciate.

I think it comes from the hardships that you face on the job, the tragedies you experience, the common economic problems. I got my introduction to that camaraderie one time when I was coming home from probie school. I was walking down the street, maybe about a block and a half from where I lived at the time, carrying a big bag over my shoulder, and I heard a horn honking behind me. It was a chief's car driven by a fireman. He wanted to know if I wanted a ride. I had my probie uniform on and I said, "No, it's just a short distance to my house." That was really nice of him, though, to stop and ask me if I wanted a ride. Now I realize that it's part of the bond—recognizing each other, being ready to pitch in and help out.

A lot of the guys don't like to talk about the sentimental aspects of the job. Firemen put up a big facade at times, but they're very, very kind people.

At my first multiple alarm, the only thing I remember was being extremely nervous. Firemen are always out to prove themselves. When you go into a fire as a probie, you don't know how you're going to react. You're uncertain as to whether you can do the job or not. And firemen don't want to admit fear. When firemen come back from a job, they talk about the fire, about the building, but they never give any indication that they were afraid. They never talk about fear, but most firemen experience it—and they go on despite it.

If you have faith in the guys you're working with, you won't feel so much fear. When you're with somebody else—someone you trust—it's not as bad as when you're alone.

I don't want to sound like I'm trying to be macho or anything like that, but there is something in me that enjoys fear. I enjoyed it as a kid. I liked to see who could climb highest on a tree or who could climb highest on a building. There's something about overcoming fear. It's there and you feel it. But you also have the presence of mind to overcome it. There have been times, though, when I have really been afraid on this job. Fear is a very restricting feeling and there is a point where you say, "Time out." You're not going to push any further. It would be bordering on insanity to continue further.

I am convinced that there are a few guys on this job who have a death wish. I don't think there's many, but I have seen and I have worked with firemen who had a death wish. They would push to where there was no rhyme or reason to what they were doing. It was just them against the big red devil.

I worked with a fireman once who pushed right into a vacant building. I couldn't understand it. The violence of the fire was incredible. This was a vacant tenement, and he just kept pushing right in.

You have to evaluate everything you do on this job, what the risk factor is, and what rewards you hope to gain by accepting this risk. If you are in a vacant building, or if you're in a cellar fire, where you know nobody is trapped inside, and you're pushing in, and you're way ahead of everybody else, you have to understand what your goal is. And if I see a guy pushing to a point where there's nothing to be gained from it, I would say the guy has a death wish. It goes beyond the point of being a good fireman . . . you begin to question the guy's sanity.

I think a good fireman is somebody you can depend on, somebody who has control over himself, over his emotions, somebody who is physically capable, somebody with endurance who won't lose his cool very readily.

There are guys on this job who are cut out for it. They have the moxie when they need it. They have the reserve when they need it. They have control of themselves. They seem to know where they'll find people. They have a sixth sense about that. Tom Neary is one of them; he's got the Gordon Bennett medal *twice*.

Sometimes the tenants do things that make it harder for us to fight a fire. We were in an apartment a couple of years back, and the level of heat was incredible. We had two or three rooms burning in the rear of this tenement. I told the guys to back out. I no sooner said that when the plastic covers on the furniture ignited like Christmas bulbs. And when we came out, the flashlight on one fireman's helmet was melted.

I found out later on the reason for the intensity of the heat was that the tenants had nailed plywood over the windows. Generally, with that much heat, the windows will blow. They didn't blow because of the plywood. All I could figure was that these people must have been broken into on a number of occasions, and they'd put up the plywood to keep burglars out.

There are other situations: I remember going to an apartment on the thirty-fifth floor of the Hampshire House. I was a young fireman and we were forcing the door and the paint was blistering on the door and I remember being scared. But the lieutenant, Joe Gorton, I would follow anywhere. We went into this apartment, and some paint must have dripped off the ceiling onto my coat. A guy was hitting me on the back saying, "Hey, your coat's on fire." I thought it was a joke. He wasn't joking; my coat *was* on fire. I'd felt heat but thought it was the ambient temperature that we were in. That was a tough fire.

We had a fire one night, above a paint store in a tenement, and it went to a second or third alarm. We were second due. I went up above the fire to force a door. Then I moved on into the apartment, taking a tremendous beating. I was absolutely positive—it was two or three o'clock in the morning—that I was going to find somebody in that apartment. There was no doubt in my mind.

The smoke was down to the floor. The heat level was rising in the apartment, and I remember thinking I knew my way out. I went under and over every bed in that apartment, and I'm getting my balls beat in. I didn't find anybody, and after a while I lost my bearings. Where I thought was a door, there wasn't any door. I ended up in a small bathroom, not being able to get out for a while. I felt that my number might be up. But I was able to take a blow of fresh air at the narrow bathroom window, and I eventually found a door to get out of the apartment.

There wasn't anybody in that apartment. That's another thing. When you get to a fire, someone will tell you that people are in there, but there's nobody in here. A lot of firemen will say, "Oh, that jerk, why is he telling me that people are in there?" Because they believe it—they know somebody lives there and chances are they're home.

What goes through my mind before we leave quarters is what kind of a building we're headed for and which side of the street it's on. You try to visualize what you're going to. When you get off the truck, you'll look to see if there is any visible fire and what kind of building it is. The more you know about a building before going in, the better position you are in to perform more efficiently. If you know the way it is laid out and where the fire is, you can decide what action you will take. Obviously, there is more to consider if you pull up to an old age home as compared to a vacant building, or if you pull up to a heavily occupied building at four or five o'clock in the morning when people are asleep. There are many, many details that you have to consider.

I am sure people sometimes think we're crazy for doing this job at all, but there's nothing like walking down a long hall and seeing a wall on fire. There's something captivating about it. I don't know what it is, but there is something about it . . . When the post office burned, I was in absolute awe. I have never seen anything like it. There's an exhilaration, a feeling of we're-going-to-get-it. The elements roar against you, but we're gonna get it—*pow!* When two fighters confront each other in the ring, they fight fiercely, and yet when it's all over, they embrace. The harder they fought, the more respect they will have for each other. It's the same with firemen. The harder they fight, the more difficult the fire, the more exhilarating the feelings. And in a fire, you really feel the contest, it's you against the red devil.

The big red devil. Sometimes when you go into a job, you don't see the fire. When you *can* see the fire, you know where your enemy is. But when you see this black smoke pushing out and you feel the heat, but you don't know where the fire is, that's where your mettle is tested.

How far into the building will you go, maybe without a line? How far should you go? How far do you want to take your guys? This is where your experience comes into play. It's not something you can learn from books.

In June of 1974 there was a fire in my mother's building. I'd been on the job probably for twelve years by then, and I'd seen a lot of fire, but I never really appreciated the tragedy of fire until then. I had to go in and pull all the ceilings down in my mother's apartment. Fortunately she was okay. It was absolutely incredible. I think you never *truly* appreciate fire until it happens to you.

Not long ago we had a fifth alarm at six o'clock in the morning in the Grace United Methodist Church at 131 West

104th Street, 1294 box. There was a fire showing on the side of the church when we arrived.

We were first due, so we cut the chains on the gate in the front of the church. The engine men saw the fire first. The chief sent an "all hands" right away. Then the fire went to a second alarm and from a second to a fifth within twenty minutes. It was incredible. Anyway, we cut the chains on the gate, and we got up to the front doors of the church. There was tremendous heat, but I felt that we might have a shot at it. When we popped the front door and opened it, the smoke just billowed out. And I go in about five feet, and I hear *crrrr*—as the smoke pulls back into the church. This is an indication that we are going to have a backdraft. That means the whole building is gonna go up in flames, and that is exactly what it did. Before long, the choir loft fell and all we had was a sea of fire.

The backdraft is the fire sucking oxygen. The fire has consumed all the oxygen inside the structure and there's a lot of heat. When you open a door in this situation, you all of a sudden face the smoke, which has been under pressure pushing out. But now that the door's open, the fire has more oxygen, and it just sucks it in. It's an absolutely incredible phenomenon—you can *feel* it happening.

What you want to do when you start to experience a backdraft is get out fast, if you can't control the situation. But if you have a hose line, you immediately open it up and try to push the fire back. Here's what I mean when I talk about control. An apartment door in a fireproof, concrete building for example, will hold the heat because fireproofs are very tight. The fire can burn inside that door for a long time because there are combustibles in the apartment to feed the fire. When you come to the door, you feel the door is very, very hot. You force the door, but you also *control* the door—that is, you don't open fully all of a sudden. You open the door gradually until you see what's going to happen. If the smoke starts coming out and then starts sucking back in, you want to do one of two things. You either close the door—and make sure the engine has water. Or, if you have to get into the apartment right away, you get somebody to vent the fire from the other end. This way, if the fire's gonna blow, it will blow the other way first, and then you can go in.

These are things you have to learn. They are learned from

experience and from talking to other guys. But you can't actually appreciate a backdraft until you see it. When you do, it will make a lasting impression on you, and you will be very, very conscious of it.

But, to get back to the church fire. The men were there until six o'clock the following night. The building was totaled—it was sad, really sad. I had to break some stained-glass windows—if you have to do it, you have to do it. I thought about it later on. I wish I could have done something else to vent the fire, but there's wasn't anything else I could have done. It was just too late.

When you get that volume of fire, it has to be one of two things. There has to be either a delayed alarm—in other words, it's been cooking for quite a while—or it's been helped along. This church had a lot of programs for the elderly, they had Boy Scout troops, they had a band. Two pastors ran the church. Woodrow Wilson used to go to church there. They were very community oriented, very involved with the youth. I imagine they were trying to prevent people from being involved with drugs. Apparently the cops had made a drug raid on the building behind the church at about 3:00 A.M.; they cleaned the building out. There was talk that the drug dealers started the fire in retaliation for the pastors informing the police about them. But whether there's any validity to that story, I don't know.

Sometimes there is a conflict between the firemen and the residents of a firehouse's neighborhood, especially in the poorer areas. Generally, the trouble stems from the firemen's parked cars. People sit on the cars or tear them apart or steal things from the firemen's cars—there's retaliation. Then the neighbors retaliate. It can develop into a very, very nasty situation. But I think overwhelmingly, people in the ghettos of the city like firemen. They call us for everything, because they know that within two minutes or so somebody will respond to their plea for help, whatever the reason is. I've responded to situations where we were called because the man downstairs was beating his wife. The neighbor calls the Fire Department because she knows we are going to be there in two minutes. The Police Department? Maybe not at all.

We got a call one day for a fire in a vacant building. When we arrived, there were two police sergeants standing on the stoop. They said, "There's a fire up on the third floor." We got to the third floor and there was a little smoke in the hall. It was a vacant single-room-occupancy hotel. One of the firemen went to the right. I went to the left. He said, "I think it's down here." So we went to this room. There was a pile of rubbish burning on the floor, or so we thought. The smoke was banked down. I said, "Get the extinguisher." He extinguished the flames, and another fireman knocked the window out. The pile of rubbish turned out to be a young woman, twenty-five years old. She'd been murdered. Some guy had taken all her clothes off and put them over her body and set her on fire either before or after he'd shot her twice in the head.

The whole thing was absolutely devastating. It was the most distressing thing I have ever experienced in my life. It was the day after Thanksgiving five years ago, Friday, and when we came back to the firehouse, nobody talked about it. Usually, when we get back after a fire, you talk about everything that happened. But that day everybody sat down to lunch and nobody even mentioned it, like it never happened. Then one of the firemen said to me about eight or nine months later, maybe even a year, "Remember that thing we had on 102nd Street? What did you think? How did you react to it?" And I told him, "It absolutely destroyed me, Jimmy." And he said, "You know, I felt the same way." He said he didn't want to talk about it either. A lot of guys felt terrible. The fireman who was with me when we found her later quit the job. I don't know if this was the reason why he quit, but I'm certain it was a contributing factor.

I dreamed about it for months afterward—eight, nine, ten months, maybe a year—and I'd wake up at night. It really blew my mind. The day it happened, I went home and talked about it with my wife. I remember I didn't want to eat. I went upstairs and I hammered away at the typewriter. I must have written and then torn up six or seven letters to Governor Carey, because I felt we should reinstate capital punishment. Carey was against it.

I was outraged beyond belief. I shouldn't have torn up those letters. I should have kept them, but they sounded like maniac writing. However, I finally sent him one, and I know he personally got it. I'll tell you what I did. I thought, am I going to write to the Albany campus or the Avenue of the Americas building, waste my time, and have some clerk read this letter from some maniac lieutenant of the Fire Department and throw it in the garbage can? So I got Carey's home address. I made a lot of calls and eventually one nice man gave it to me. I called up the Hotel Des Artistes, and I asked for Hugh Carey. They said, "Just a minute, please."

And I said to myself, "Okay, I got it," and hung up.

One West 67 Street, I believe was the address. I sent the letter registered mail; it cost me three dollars. He sent me back a bullshit letter that had no bearing on the letter I wrote to him. It was a waste of time, like barking at the moon. His letter made me want to write to him again.

I know he personally got it. Then I thought, What am I wasting my time for? This man is an asshole. He has no feeling for what's going on in our society.

They caught the guy who murdered that girl. I testified at the trial, and the assistant district attorney, Robert Warren, a very nice guy, wanted a conviction in this case—I think more than he ever wanted anything in his life—because of the circumstances that surrounded it.

The killer pulled this girl into a vacant building. What a terrible feeling of futility she must have had, screaming and nobody would help her. I talked to a fellow who was involved in the case. A fellow who, if I'm not mistaken, worked for the Housing Authority at the time.

This girl ran over to him for help, and he said, "I can't help you." She told him the guy had a gun. I have my doubts that she told him that, but he's gonna live with that guilt for the rest of his life for not helping that girl. There was also a guy driving a bread truck who closed the door on her. Nobody would help her.

It was bizarre, absolutely bizarre, that series of events. The police sergeants' test was that day—the day of the murder—and most of the cops walking the streets were rookies. The cops got a lot of bad press over it, and I have to admit that I sort of indicted them also.

What I found incredible was that the original call came into the police department at 8:04 A.M. I was unaware of this at the time. I think we responded at 9:21. I said to myself, "How long was this girl in the building?" I mean, she had to have been there for a long time, and the terror she must have experienced. . . . He dragged her into one building, they assume, and then took her to an adjoining building, probably by way of the fire escape in the rear. He had a .9mm automatic, and he had a full view of anybody entering the building and coming up to that floor. There's no doubt in my mind that if two cops had responded to the first call, you would have had two dead cops. But how many other people didn't help her?

I listened to the 911 operator tapes at the trial. Before I even heard them, I knew what happened and where it happened. I knew the building, too. The woman who took the calls had me confused, even though I knew what happened. The only thing consistent for all the calls was "Black man, leather jacket. White girl." The calls gave the location as 104th Street, 102nd Street, 101st Street. It was very, very sad.

It absolutely blew my mind that a human being could do this to another human being. I said to somebody one night, "He's an animal." And then I thought, no, he's not an animal. Animals don't do this to each other. He was something all by himself and this was his second murder. He had done seventeen or eighteen years in prison for killing an elderly woman with a screwdriver. And he had only been out on the streets for a few months.

Robert Warren, the assistant district attorney, wanted me to be explicit about what I saw, what I heard, what I smelled, and what it did to me. He told me of a way I could remember everything I saw and heard. But her parents were in court every day—the victim's parents—and I said, "Bob, I'm never going to be able to give the testimony that you want unless you get them out of the courtroom." He kept on saying to me, "Don't worry, don't worry, Gene, I'll get them out of the courtroom." Then eventually it came my turn to go on the stand. I said, "Bob, you're not listening to me. I want you to get them out of the courtroom. I will not testify if you don't get them out of the courtroom."

Finally he realized this was a threat, and he said, "Gene, I've worked it out. I've talked to her parents and they won't be there."

I said, "Promise me, Bob," and he answered me, "Yeah." So I said, "Okay."

It turned out that I wasn't going to be on the stand that morning. When I went out to the elevator, I was the only fireman in the criminal court, so it was pretty obvious who I was if you had any familiarity with the case.

Her father came up to me and said, "You're the fireman who's going to testify this afternoon, aren't you?"

"Yes, I am," I said. "I want to tell you something," I said to him. "I didn't know your daughter, but it really upset me."

He said, "It upsets us, too." Then he said, "I won't be in court today. Bob doesn't want me there."

I said, "Well, it'll be a lot easier on me if you're not."

"Thank you," he said, and turned away. He went into the elevator, and he wasn't in the court when I testified against this man.

I remember testifying in that courtroom. A couple of jurors were crying, and my voice cracked a few times. Maybe I identified with this case. I don't know. My wife is a nurse and I found out that the dead girl was a nurse, too. Paradoxically, here's a nurse who worked in obstetrics in Mount Sinai Hospital, bringing life into the world, and her life gets snuffed out by somebody who should never have been walking the streets.

When I came out of the courtroom that day, I went into the anteroom off to the side. The judge, Burton Roberts, came over to me and said, "You're married, Lieutenant, aren't you?"

"Yeah," I said.

"I bet you have a daughter, don't you?"

"Yes, I do."

"Well, you did a good job. You came across well," he said.

How could any lawyer defend that guy in all good conscience? They did it, though, and the defense attorney tried to confuse me on the stand.

It's a big game.

Lawyers are interested in principles, not in justice.

It's sad.

Chapter 6

Captain Joseph Nardone
Ladder 27, Bronx

I joined the New York City Fire Department in 1967. I had taken the test in 1964, but it took me three years to get appointed. I came to New York because it was *the* place to be a fireman. I had left a small department in the suburbs, where we had oil burners, electric doors, and nice bunk rooms in the firehouse. I also had a degree of respect there; I was on a rescue unit and had made a lot of friends. When I came to New York it was like going back to the Dark Ages. They hadn't yet upgraded any of their equipment. We had coal for heat in the firehouse. We had old bunk rooms in old buildings. The medical office looked like a dungeon with peeling paint. When I looked around I said, "Oh, my God, what did I do?"

One of my first fires in the city was in December 1967, just after getting out of probie school. It was a bitter cold night. The fire was on Third Avenue and 162nd Street, under the El. We put the fire out about two or three o'clock in the morning. I was soaking wet. It was the first time I'd heard the expressions "watch line"—"we're going to need a watch line." I had no idea what that meant. It means that somebody has got to stay at this fire with a protective line and hose down the remains of the fire. The company gets together, and they have to pick one man. "You have got the six-by; you have got the nine-by; who's got the open watch?" I had the open watch, so I had to stay there without changing into dry clothes. I sat in a car across the street from the fire with another guy for a while, but the chief chased us out of the car. Now, the first consideration in most cities would be to get the firemen into dry clothes, or get another company to perform this function. That was an eye opener, and that was my initiation into the Fire Department.

As a New York probie, I had a captain who had lost a few men at the Grand Street collapse seven years earlier, and he was well aware of the department-wide fear of losing more men in another fire. At that time we had a job in a corner building. The Fire Department people would always tell you that the corner building was a hairy situation, because the layout is always different. I was a probie, and I had the can—the fire extinguisher—but don't forget that I'd had four years in another fire department, so I wasn't really too naive. When we pulled up I looked at the building. I saw where the entrance was. I watched my whole company go into the wrong building. I said, "Hey, you're going into the wrong building." But who the hell pays attention to a probie? They all just went right off. So for right or for wrong, I went to the fire by way of the side entrance.

When I got to the apartment I passed a lieutenant coming out. He said, "The fire is in there," but he didn't say where it was, specifically. I went into the apartment and found a small fire in the kitchen, so I began extinguishing it. But the smoke is starting to bank down, and it's getting worse and worse. I use the extinguisher to take the window out in the kitchen. I now realize that there is something else going on. I turn around and the doorway that I passed through is fully involved with fire, right down to the floor. What had happened was there were two separate fires. When he said, "It's in there," he probably meant the larger fire. But I didn't see the larger fire; I just saw the smaller fire in the kitchen.

Now the only option left to me was to close the kitchen door, but there was none. So I sat on the kitchen windowsill—this was on the third floor—and who was looking out of the building across the shaftway? My captain. I swear to God his eyes came out of his head. I calmly said, "Cap, I'm cut off here." Then I took a hose strap out of my pocket, and I hung it on a spike. The window gutter had one of those spikes that hold it to the brick. I knew the strap would pull the spike right out of the brick, but still I hung it there, and I just sat waiting.

One of the guys from Rescue 3 was in a window above me, and he hung a hook out to me to swing on and climb up. I chose not to use it that way. I took his hook and passed it down to where the guys had brought a ladder to the back yard. I hooked the ladder, brought it up, put it on the windowsill, and climbed down. I found out later that fire was coming out of every window except the one I was sitting in, which was in the third floor rear. When I got out I was embarrassed. I apologized for causing such a problem, being a probationary fireman. To this day, when I see that captain he remembers that. All I can remember him saying was "I'm glad you kept your cool. I'm glad you didn't jump out of that window." Later at that fire the captain went up to a chief and said, "Hey, this guy used to be in another fire department." I found that telling somebody from New York that you belong to another department didn't really dazzle them too much. But during those four years in the suburbs, I saw a lot of loss of life.

In the suburbs they have lots of wood frame houses, and the people use the attics of these houses for bedrooms. Often it's just a death trap up there if a fire should break out. I saw whole families burned to death. It was really an eye opener. You can't locate a body after a fire when it's been badly burned. You have to really slow down. When it's still smoking, you have to bring the light as close as possible and go inch by inch, because you can go right by the bodies. They look just like everything else in a room that is incinerated. It's really an unpleasant task. Thank God, I never had to identify a fireman like that, but many guys have.

There was this one fire in the suburbs where the entire top floor was lit up. It was a private house, a frame dwelling. A bunch of us in the rescue team made repeated attempts to get up the stairs. It looked easy, because there was no smoke, just pure fire. But we failed to make the stairway. The father jumped out the window, but his three children burned to death.

After the fire was out, we went into the bedroom where the kids were supposed to be, and I asked, "Where are they?"

Somebody said to me, "You're standing on them."

I stepped on their bodies, and to this day I remember that feeling. It felt like stepping on three pillows bunched together. That bothered me a lot. I can still feel it, and that was seventeen years ago. I also remember feeling stupid about it. Why didn't I watch out? Why did I stand on them? You can't identify them. You can't find them.

In taking up from that fire this guy, Eddie Dunlea, and I were putting the tools back in the truck. He put his hand up and I slammed the door. I almost caught his finger. The two of us just looked at each other with all this frustration. No words were spoken, but we both had that look in our eyes and both of us smacked each other. Him being pissed off at me for almost catching his hand and me being annoyed at him for having it there. But we had nothing to do with it, it was really those kids dying.

There was another fire, back in 1968, that was my first loss of life in the FDNY. I'll tell you that it bothers me to this day. I was a probie. We were first due, and we didn't get the kids. Dick Hurst of Rescue 3 got to the kids but they were overcome by smoke. I often ask myself, "Why didn't we get those kids?" We didn't have an engine at the time, and maybe that had something to do with it. I can look at a picture of that fire and be bothered by it. I wanted to get those kids.

Also, it is a reflection on your fire company. The pride you have about your company is a big thing in the fire service. Being part of a good company is what motivates this whole department. To be put down as a bad company, if you have any pride, is a blow. Those are fighting words.

Looking back on that fire, I ask myself, did we really do our job? I don't know. At the time, I didn't even realize that there were kids in there. But it was probably a reflection on our company that the Rescue got to the kids and we didn't. I wish I had that one to do over again.

One time I got trapped on the floor above a fire. Well "trapped" is too strong a word. I got lost on the floor above, and it was a weird situation. A woman was believed to be trapped there. I went searching for her by myself, which happens a lot in a truck company. I got lost and all I kept finding was doors. I couldn't find a window. And after the fire was extinguished and I could see again, I knew what the situation was—every window had a door nailed over it. It was like one of those playland mazes. Imagine trying to find your way out of a place with doors everywhere and they're all nailed shut. That's a terrible feeling, being lost, and then put a little heat on your tail and it really is a lousy feeling.

Searching on the floor above a fire is another dangerous thing that you have to do. But there are certain sounds that encourage you on, like when you hear the engine operating a line from underneath. You hear the water striking the ceiling, and you know you're pretty safe: the most that could happen if you should fall through the floor is you're going to get hurt from the fall, but you're not going to fall into a fire. When you're searching and the fire is out of control, it's a whole 'nother ball game and you have to conduct yourself differently. You're not as quick to make certain moves. You're a little more cautious, and all of that works well as long as you're perceiving danger. But it's always the unforeseeable danger that gets guys in trouble.

I don't know if it happens to all guys, but I'll come back from a run and it will just stay on my mind as to what I should have done. Some guys perhaps can just put it out of their minds. I can't. I have a need to continually prove myself. I don't know if it's a reflection of insecurity or security, but I like being in busy units, and I continually feel the need to achieve some sort of satisfaction from doing a daring deed. And yet I'm not looking to get hurt.

There's a lot of satisfaction in saving somebody. Although I've never really had a clean, clear-cut rescue, I've been involved in a few things. But I have yet to have that one rescue that I really want. I don't know if I'll be up to it when the moment comes. But I get a lot of satisfaction out of the job.

One of the problems is that fire fighting is really a young man's job. I'm having great difficulty with my physical ability to keep up. I work out, but I have a philosophical belief that somewhere in the chain of all those fire trucks and tools that I've worn out is me. You just can't keep wearing out equipment without you wearing out. Somewhere along the line you've got to let go. I've only got fifteen years on this job, but I can feel it already. I was hoping to do about twenty-five or thirty, but I don't really know if I'm going to be able to. I could hang it up and say, "Give me a slow fire company," but I don't know if I'm ready to do that mentally. I like working with the young guys. The young guys keep up a better attitude. Some of your outlying companies are manned with guys who used to be in busy companies, and they realize that, hey, now, we earned our rest, yet still keep up a good attitude. They're okay to work in, but if I hit an outlying company that's always been slow, and that only has guys in there who take their money and run, well, I think I'd rather be out of a job than work in an outfit like that.

I've had some trouble with carbon monoxide. It was a fire on the top floor of a very large building. When we arrived we saw smoke coming out of the newel post in the downstairs lobby, and the mailboxes, and I knew right from that point on that it was going to be a smoky fire when we got up there. The fire was in the cockloft, and the rooms to the right were on fire. There was plenty of companies in there pulling ceilings. The apartment to the left was a no-man's-land. It was pitch black and nobody was in there.

I was in the rescue. I thought we were supposed to search as a team, but I couldn't locate one of my guys. I started to do a lot of overbreathing. You have to keep yourself under control, and I felt myself losing that control trying to locate this guy. I went up onto the roof. I told the guys in the tower ladder bucket to get the windows out, because I thought I had a guy in there. I went back down and proceeded to go through this apartment and still didn't locate the guy. Then I located him. He was in no trouble at all.

I went out onto the fire escape, and companies that were behind us in the hallway were hollering, "Hey, you can't get back out." Now the apartment was ready to light on fire. But at that point I didn't want to let my crew know that I was finished. My legs were wobbly. I said, "Let's go down the fire escape and through the apartment below, and we'll come up the interior stairs again and we'll be back to square one. We'll start searching for possible occupants all over again and we'll be fine."

And one guy said to me, "No, we can't go because Larry's in there. He went back out the other way. We can't go this way when he went that way. He could be in trouble."

So now we had to go back through the apartment again, and at that point I was finished. The fire was put out by then. It was all over, but I felt as though my legs had turned to rubber and that I couldn't continue the rest of the tour with this particular company, knowing that you could easily go to another fire again. So I went to the hospital. I had nineteen percent carbon monoxide in my blood, and it was all due to a little overbreathing and a lot of smoke.

I had a very scary incident with PVC gas, too. A bulldozer was making an excavation hole, and by accident it grabbed the wires leading into a factory building. We're talking about big underground conductors. The bulldozer pulled them in such a manner as to short them out. There was a great amount of sparking and popping. This happened long before PVC really came into the limelight and it wasn't so well understood.

I was new on the Fire Department. I followed this officer to the side of the factory and we looked in the window. I would never approach a building this way now that I have more experience. At that time this officer probably knew what he was doing, but I didn't. We had what they called an all-service mask. That was the mask we used before we got self-contained breathing apparatus. All it did was filter out smoke. It didn't filter out any other gases at all.

We jumped into the factory from the window and dropped down about ten feet. Instantly it was as if someone garroted my throat. I could not breathe. My throat had shut down completely. Now I didn't know where the officer went and I couldn't get back up to the window. I tried putting my face piece back on, but it was useless at that point. I couldn't breathe. The only thing that saved me was that that type of smoke is very light, so you can see through it. That's also what enticed us to jump in, because we could see and it didn't look dangerous. Now I'm in a factory, I don't know my way out and I can't breathe. But I found my way out, though I was still quite unable to breathe, and I sat on the opposite side of the rig so no one would see me until I recovered. I never told anyone. I knew that I had done damage to myself at that time.

I've gotten numerous small burns and one good burn on my wrist that was pretty painful and took about a month to heal. At my very next fire after I got that burn, I was certain to wear my gloves, but it was a very hot room, and even with my glove on the whole thing just blistered up right under the glove. That was pretty painful and it gave me a lot of respect for burns. I got that by trying to get into a doorway of an apartment that was burning, and I didn't have my gloves on. There was a dog chained right behind the door, and the dog was on fire and yelping away. I was trying to smack the chain that was restraining the dog with the tool I had in my hand. Some paint came down and landed on my hand. I got it off as quick as I could. About five minutes, ten minutes later, after I broke the chain and the dog ran away, I put water on it, but the damage was done. I put Silvadene on it. When I would clean it and wash it off, I couldn't wait to put the Silvadene back on. So that was an eye opener.

Then I got a nice scar on my shinbone from stepping off a fire escape. I actually was pretty lucky I didn't fall five stories. It was on an old-law tenement, top floor, rear fire escape, and I was looking in the window. I saw what I wanted to see, and I turned and walked right off the landing. I was so used to more modern fire escapes having that guard rail that I just wasn't accustomed to an open well on a fire escape with no guard rail. I caught myself with my two arms, but my leg went back and dug a good hole in one. And rather than appear foolish I made up a story that the fire escape had a hole in it and I stepped through the hole.

I have had a lot of conjunctivitis from the smoke. So much so that now when I get a smoky fire, my eyes go right away. Evidently there's no coating or whatever protects your eyes—they just close right up.

But all in all, I would say I've been lucky. And I use that word "lucky" with great care. As much as we'd all like to think we are all heads-up firemen, the heads-up part comes with experience. You learn by getting past some silly mistakes, such as when you're a new fire fighter and they make you the roof man. You have all this pressure that's been put upon being the roof man. You must get to the roof. I've seen myself and other guys take some pretty foolish risks trying to get to that roof. I've seen myself hang off the backs of buildings and climb the gutter pipe to try and get up there. If I fell into the rear yard, nobody would even know the difference. Cutting the roof is probably one of the most dangerous things we do. The whole purpose of cutting the roof is to ventilate the building. We direct the fire to where we want it to go, which is out through the roof, and by cutting the roof, we enable the troops to come in from underneath and extinguish the fire. But it's a ballet, I swear to God. If it isn't done just right and at the right time, it can go wrong. A guy has to read those conditions. What happens in the fire department is that guys will stay on that roof and push themselves right to the brink, and if you take one step over the edge you'll die, and if you take one step back from the edge you're a coward. That's basically how they size things up.

A belief I have is that one heads-up guy is worth about ten guys with their heads in the sand. Because a guy just saying, "Hey, watch out for that," can save your life. I worked with Johnnie Williams and Russell Winoball. They were in my groups, but I transferred out shortly before they were electrocuted in the Mott Haven rail yards, on Brook Avenue. They had put up an aluminum ladder earlier at a fire, and they were in the process of taking it down when the order was given over the air to turn the power back on. The ladder touched the wires, and 11,000 volts went into them. If one heads-up guy had been there to say, "Hey, watch the wires," maybe it would have turned out differently.

You have to be aware, because every incident you go to is different from all the previous ones. The most bizarre fire I was at was in a funeral parlor. We arrived on the scene early in the morning, and there was a police car in front of the building. The bottom panel of the front door was broken. It was sort of a subdued operation, because there was no outwardly observable fire on arrival. What we found was a light smoke condition throughout the funeral parlor and a sort of calm demeanor about the police officer and the owner, who were already on the scene. We proceeded to search the building to find the fire. I remember coming upon a child in a coffin, in a room, by myself. The child was all dressed, with this little cap on, and I felt very uncomfortable being in that room. I remember saying to myself, "Well, that's it! There's no fire in here. I'm getting out of this room." I felt a little spooky.

But before we can leave, one of the fellows calls from upstairs to say that he's found the fire. We go up to the floor that the fire is on, and the smoke is heavier there. It was banked down around shoulder height.

Visualize a long room such as you'd find in a funeral parlor with the casket all the way at the end of the room. I remember the vision to this day: it was like a funeral pyre. You could look down the room and see the casket, on a platform, being consumed by the fire. The hands of the corpse were up in the air and you could see just the glow of the body burning, enough so you knew what you were looking at. The rest of the room was enveloped in smoke. It was a weird vision.

We went in and actually used our extinguisher on the body. The side burst open, where I guess they had done the autopsy and the hands were up in the air, because of the natural muscle contortion, like a boxer's stance. We extinguished the body and that was basically the fire.

Now it got to be about eight o'clock in the morning and we all sat around downstairs in the funeral parlor such as the family would do. We're talking—about twelve or fifteen fire fighters sitting around—and now we start finding some gallows humor in the situation. A couple of us pretended to be the undertakers. How were we going to break the news to this family as they arrive? They're going upstairs. "Not so fast, sir, we got a little something to tell you." We kind of got through that okay.

Now, one thing leads me to believe that there was a little hanky-panky going on there. The official story was that someone this particular person—this dead person—knew when he was alive came in and torched the body, because all that was burning was the casket, the body, and perhaps some drapery behind it. But I have never seen the classic burn pattern in more clearer detail than I did at this fire. Right behind the casket was a perfect V of charred wall paper down to the electrical outlet with all the wires sticking out of it. The initial story on arrival was that the cop had kicked in the door. Very shortly after we got there they changed the story to "someone came by, a burglar, or someone out to torch this body, kicked in the door and set the body on fire." I think it was a quick arrangement between the owner and the police on the scene to come up with an insurance steal rather than a lawsuit.

When the fire marshals try to ascertain how a fire started, they look for the V pattern. Fire and heat travel naturally upward and out. Well, if you trace it back from the natural path you got to come to the point of origin of a fire. You'll see in certain fires if the fire started down low enough, you'll have a perfect V right to the ignition point. Well, the burn and char mark led right down to the electrical outlet. If a person uses a flammable liquid such as gasoline, you could have a lot of these patterns, because the fire would be spread across the floor.

Another incident that I remember involved a Mrs. Rizzo. She was a bag lady down in Midtown Manhattan, and all she had was one of these carts that they use to transport fabric and clothing in the garment district. Well, anyway, she had all her possessions in that thing and kids were going by tormenting her. They kept throwing matches until finally they got her cart to catch on fire. Here she was all bundled up, and her husband happened to be lying on the sidewalk. This was a one-unit operation, a special call for an engine. We pulled up and we extinguished her cart. She was standing there watching us. After we put out the fire and we put the hose back on the rig, we were standing around for a few minutes. Mrs. Rizzo came up to me and stretched out her hand. Her hand was wrapped in a glove with no fingers, and in that was thirty-seven cents, and she said to me, "Buy the boys some coffee." I'll never forget that. We didn't take the thirty-seven cents, by the way.

But some of the best rewards I have had were with kids. One of them involved a fire on the second floor. The mother reported it to me. She couldn't get back in the building, and she had left her kids on the top floor.

The hallway was really charged with smoke, and I went up to the top floor wearing a mask, because I couldn't see and I had to feel for the doors. I opened the door to the apartment, and it was filled with kids—about eight kids of various ages. They've been left alone by their mother and they hear sirens, shouting, and banging, and now I appear on the scene with this damn mask on like some sort of Martian. The apartment was pretty clear, and my intention at that time was to just stabilize them and stay there. But the fire is gaining headway downstairs and I'm starting to get concerned. Then it started to get comical. I'm trying to arrange all these kids to get their clothes on, and we're like shopping for shoes. "Who's got what shoe? Get Jimmy's shoe."

And I'm saying, "The hell with the shoes. Let's get him out of here!" But finally the fire was brought under control downstairs and we did not have to get the kids out. But it was a rewarding feeling to be with those kids, even though they were scared and crying, to know that you could get them out of there.

Another time in Harlem, and this was pretty recent, we had to evacuate a building rapidly because it was about to fall down. We discovered that on a routine stop to buy a meal. One of the guys went next door to a bodega to buy a pack of cigarettes, and he happened to see that the soda refrigerator was leaning to one side. As you walk to the back of the store the floor just sloped right down. We found the stairs to be pulling away from the wall upstairs. After examining the basement we could see all the supporting beams were rotted and just ready to give way. I went down to the cellar with the deputy chief. As soon as he took a look, he said, "Vacate the building!" So now we proceeded upstairs. One apartment had a child in it, and she wouldn't answer the door, and again I empathize with these kids, but now we're beating on the door, yelling, "Get out of the building! Get out of the building! You have to get out of the building!"

The kid is on the other side crying, "My mommy told me not to open the door."

She won't open the door. So we had to send a fireman out on the fire escape to break the window, and now you could hear the kid go completely hysterical. You can imagine what's going through her head. The fire fighter got inside and opened the door. Then we went in. There was a nine-year-old girl baby-sitting for an infant, and she was crying. We had to get her out, and we had to get the baby dressed. So she places the baby down on the bed, and she is still crying and trying to find clothes, and now the baby is hysterical. I thought about it for about twenty seconds or so, and nobody was making a move, so I scooped up the baby. I'm sort of cradling the baby, and then the girl brings out some formula, and now I have a bottle in the baby's mouth and I'm wondering what the hell are the guys thinking, looking at me and I'm doing this? I think of my own kids in a situation like that. I think of the responsibility that nine-year-old had. I have a seven-year-old, and I would never trust him with that responsibility.

After we got outside, the mother came running up and told the nine-year-old to go get Grandma. I'll tell you the kid hesitated for a second, and the mother shouted at her. That kid turned around and was gone. She just was disciplined as far as the mother was concerned. Then the mother carried on about how the city owns the building and this and that and the other thing.

That was on 125th Street next to 37 Engine and 40 Truck. The building didn't fall down, but it was definitely vacated.

The Building Department came up and cut off the gas in the street, and then the community board came and the guys with the clipboards came. Usually the Fire Department doesn't like to vacate a building, because it means a lot of paperwork and most of the time we don't like to override the Building Department.

One thing about our job, we get into people's homes where a lot of other people don't. Where even cops don't. They have difficulty; they need warrants and so forth. We see how people actually live. We see the city from one point of view, cops see it from another. I remember one Christmas Eve coming in off the fire escape to search an apartment and not seeing one thing about Christmas in that apartment. And again you can't help but think of your own family and what's going on: the shopping, the anticipation, and the thrill of it all. Then you go in and see these black kids sitting around with nothing for Christmas.

I remember often looking around and seeing people living in actual hovels. I always say I'd rather live in a cave than live in some of these unheated apartments. You go in and there's ice inside. Then you have places like the Trump Tower downtown, the Hyatt Regency, and condominiums selling at a million and a half dollars, and in the same city we have people living in dung heaps. It just makes me wonder. It really does.

Then there was my friend Leroy in the Grant Avenue fire brigade. Grant Avenue was a street right behind our firehouse. During the time I was assigned to that area I saw Grant Avenue go from fully occupied to fully vacant. It's in the southwest Bronx. It was probably our worst block at the time. Now it's totally vacant like a lot of other streets in the Bronx.

On one particular night I was driving the tower ladder. As I was approaching the corner where the fire was, I heard the chief say, "Get the tower ladder in front of the building." So I knew pretty much right away what he had in mind. He needed the bucket on the tower ladder. And I pulled up. There's a certain procedure with the tower ladder for efficiency of motion: you want to have that bucket right under the person or the objective so that you're not really requiring a lot of moving. But I wasn't able to get in that position because of the double-parked cars. I had to be where I really didn't want to be, but I could still reach the guy. I could see three people on the windowsill on the top floor, and they were actually outside. Now as I'm setting up the tower ladder, lowering the jacks, I'm looking over my shoulder. I see them drop someone out of the window. It turned out that it was a small girl. Then what I call "the Grant Avenue fire brigade" caught her in a blanket. The two remaining adults are still on the windowsill. I was the chauffeur, so I raised the bucket with Gerry Madill in it. He gets this woman in the bucket. But now the guy, who we later found out was named Leroy, starts punching Gerry. With that, I know Gerry needs help. On the tower ladder boom there's an escape ladder, I used to dash up that thing quite regularly; it's a little hairy because the sections can shift without the bucket dropping down. The ladder can actually pinch you, but if you move fast, take a little chance, you can make it. So I scurry up there, and I sort of stand on Leroy's head. Gerry's trying to wrestle him down. We get him inside the bucket and down on the floor. Now we lower ourselves to the street. Leroy, however, decides to run back into the building. He hits the street, and boom he's back in the building and up inside the apartment making quite a nuisance of himself. Of course I followed him. Now we're trying to dissuade him from staying in the apartment by standing in his way and nudging him around. One of the firemen pulled the ceiling over his head, and it came crashing down on him. But Leroy's standing there in red shorts with nothing else on. To get him out of there we said, "Come, get dressed, get dressed." He wouldn't get dressed. So we brought him over to his closet. You have to visualize a closet in a room that's been totally burned away. There's hangers with just inches of fabric left on them fully charred. Leroy is going through these like he's down in Barney's looking for a $400 suit. With that a cop comes in. He's got a pair of checkered white pants over his arms and he says, "Here, wear these." Leroy turns to the cop and says, "Man, you want me to look like a fool?" I couldn't get over that. But with that, everybody's rage just broke out. We grabbed him and threw him out of the apartment. Here's a guy who's particular about what he's going to put on, standing in his apartment with everything else destroyed.

•   •   •

A lieutenant of mine was severely burned one time. I wasn't at the fire. He fell through the roof and he was removed to Jacobi Burn Center. One of the guys that witnessed it said he looked like a charred marshmallow when they brought him in there. But he was fortunate in that even though he fell through the roof into the fire apartment, he was able to jump through a hole in the floor into the apartment below. And the way they got him out of there was that a fireman in the shaft across from where he was threw him a rope and the lieutenant swung across. He knew he was running out of time. The fireman was fumbling with the rope to get the right knot. But the lieutenant said, "Give me the rope!" He didn't even care about a knot.

I went to see him in the hospital about two days later. When I came out of there, if I could have retired at that moment, I would have. Because being burned is no fun. His head was the size of a pumpkin. You just swell up. It was all red and he was eating feverishly and he was drooling. He said, "You have to forgive me, just forgive me. I know that I have to eat; a friend of mine just went through this. I have to move and I have to eat." He kept moving his legs under the sheets. His friend happened to be this officer in 91 Engine who was badly burned. I just couldn't get over the panic he had to eat, because he knew that's what he had to do to get better. He said to us, "You don't really want to see my legs." He never did show us his legs, but just looking at his face was enough for me, although I knew that he would get better. His face wasn't burned to the degree that he'd be deformed, but if I could have quit that night I would have quit. That was probably the first time that somebody I knew was burned badly.

There's a few fears on this job. I think the biggest fear is of not doing your job, or not being able to do your job. It seems to be like a ghost that follows you around just waiting for that incident that you're going to have to measure up to.

I have this scenario in my head of the most extreme situation I could think of: a fireman falling into a fire. Now it's either go in and get him or write him off. I guess when that moment comes you have to make a quick determination of whether he's lost or you have a shot at saving him or you're going to die with him, one or another. Dying with him is not such a foreign thought.

A situation occurred where an officer and a fireman fell into a burning basement. I really think that if they hadn't been in that particular area with such good, aggressive companies, they would have died. The men didn't give up on them, though. They lowered a ladder to them and Lieutenant Howard Kennedy went down, found and carried fireman John Masterson out. One of the rescue companies breached the wall and pulled the officer out. Both of the guys who fell into the basement were badly burned.

As an officer, there's also a fear of looking bad in front of the men by making a wrong decision. There's a tremendous pressure on an officer to make snap decisions. As hard as snap decisions are, if you should hesitate for a second to make a size-up, well, the other men will come right around you and somebody else will make the decision. They want you to make a snap decision, and yet snap decisions in this business are pretty dangerous. I have an electrical background. If I come upon an electrical problem, as an electrician I would never just jump in there and start taking wires apart. I would stop for a second, take a look, and see what I have. If we pull up in front of a building and fire's coming out the second and third floor, there's pressure on the officer to do something. Well, there's a need also to stop and take a look and see where the fire's at and what floor it's on in relation to the remainder of the building, and so forth. It's difficult because you have to make this quick decision, and God forbid you make the wrong decision. There's a lot of Monday morning quarterbacks.

There is a fear of getting hurt, too. I think the more time you got in this job, the more times you visit the burn center. One thing we all tend to forget about in this job of fighting fires is that it is a brutalizing job. There's a lot of glamour to it. We ride around on our apparatus and blow the horn, the kids wave to us. Most of the time the runs are bullshit runs or they're emergencies or gas leaks, water leaks, people stuck in elevators. But when the right situation comes along it's a brutalizing, grinding, dirty, nasty job—those nights when you're soaking wet in a dank, smelly hallway and you're filthy. After a smoky fire it takes me about a week to get that smell out of my skin. It just stays in your pores, and you wash your hair and you smell it. After every shower you smell it until it's finally out of your system. During a fire, you get soaking wet right down to your underwear. You pour the water right out of your boots.

There's one expression I use—"Winter hurts." In the heat you can take your coat off, but in the wintertime the cold physically hurts you. Once you're wet under your coat, it's the most miserable feeling in the world. Especially if you know you can't get back to the firehouse for another three or four hours.

I remember the two coldest winters in my entire time on the job. In the winter of 1981 we were special-called on a fourth alarm to a renovated building on Rosedale Avenue. Most renovated buildings have been constructed so that they burn faster than we can put them out—as opposed to old buildings, where we really have a shot at getting the fire under control.

When apartment houses are renovated, large voids are left for the pipes and the wires to run through. Now the fire can spread from apartment to apartment right up to the roof so fast and through so many different channels that we have a very limited chance of putting it out. Once the fire gets inside the wall—or the skin, as we call it—it goes right up through the building. And people who have been relocated to a renovated building after being burned out of an old building are now being burned out all over again—only this time it's worse.

Anyway, to get back to the Rosedale Avenue fire: it was about six degrees outside, dead of winter, two or three o'clock in the morning. We were ordered to the floor above the fire and were told to go through the interior. The sprinklers were going off and the noise of the fire gong was unnerving. When we got up to our assigned floor, the sprinkler heads hadn't gone off there yet. Our job was to force the doors open and search the apartments above the fire. Well, when we opened the first door, fire came out and set off two deluge sprinkler heads right over us. We were being drowned. Now, think about this: we can't see because the smoke is right down on the floor; we can't hear because that damn bell is ringing; the water is just cascading all over us; it's about six degrees out; we're not even inside the apartment yet; and we have to get the other doors open. Well, we got them open, but by then the fire was all over the building. We put out the fire in that apartment, but then we sat around in another wing of the unheated building in that six degree weather for about two hours. By the time we went outside we had expended ourselves. We had done all we could. We were told to take a break. The fire was still breaking out in different pockets of the building, but for the most part it was pretty much under control.

The Fire Department doesn't have a clear procedure for sending the companies back to get changed and then getting them back to the fire. At a smaller fire it's easier for the chief to turn around and say, "Okay these two units go back and change and come back in an hour." But at this large fire, on that particular night, they were already short of units, because there were a couple of major fires going elsewhere in the city. We had units at this Bronx fire from as far away as Queens and Brooklyn. So it's not that easy for the chief to say, "Okay the first alarm assignment, go back." We were there for a couple of hours in that cold trying to keep warm. Finally the chief called us to the street and I approached him for our orders. By then I was in the first stage of hypothermia. I could not stop shaking. If he had said anything to us but go back, I would have had to say, "Chief, it's all over. I can't do anymore. I'm going to have to report sick."

With that he said, "Go back."

We went to move the rig out of the block. There was a sheet of ice all over the place. But at this point I was determined to get us out of there. I was almost into self-preservation. We had to move our rig out of the block, but it was blocked in by a city transit bus that the Fire Department had called for the members to sit in and stay warm. The guy couldn't move the bus; it was skidding on the ice. I got to the driver and told him to back up the bus, step on the gas as fast as he could, and get off the ice. He did that and he went speeding down the block and pulled a hose right off the goddamn pumper. I couldn't have cared less. I got on the truck and off we went. The loss of that hose would have been very serious if the men had needed it to protect themselves from fire, but at that point the fire was pretty much out. I didn't even look back, that's how much I wanted to get out of there. And that was probably the coldest I've ever been on the Fire Department.

The winter before that, on a just plain cold night, we had a fire in a frame building in upper Harlem. This guy Ronnie

Lepper from the Sixteenth Battalion and I took a hose line into the building. The other companies couldn't put this fire out. This one company in particular had spent themselves. It was the dead of winter again. The water was cascading through the building. We got to the fire. There was a minor collapse in there and stuff came down on top of me. But we put this pocket fire out.

I went outside, and my men were complaining to me that they were soaking wet and cold. Again it was a busy night with a lot of fires around, but the chief, I guess, didn't want to send us back and call another unit. I approached the chief; I really didn't like doing it, but I did.

Finally the chief turned to me and said, "I'm cold and wet, too." I had to go to my men with the bad news. My gloves were soaking wet. The cold from the wet gloves was just killing my hands, so I took the gloves off rather than have them on, that's how cold it was. That was a real miserable night, too.

Those are moments that the public really doesn't see. The pictures of the fire fighters with the ice all over the mustache— that's baloney. That guy is nice and snug and dry underneath. It's those nights that nobody sees when you're soaking wet and the cold goes right through your bones. While you're young you recoup fast, but as you get a little older it's pretty tough to get over that and you could have another fire that same night. The end of one fire doesn't mean the night's over. Winter's tough.

You also have all the hazards of skidding. I was driving the tower ladder one night. We came over to High Bridge, in the Bronx, and we're up on top of a hill, but to get to this response area you have to come up a hill. It started to snow and freeze on the streets, and another alarm came in from the same area, then another one and another one. We couldn't get off that hill. To show you how slippery it was: I was sitting in traffic with the apparatus perfectly still; the lieutenant blew the siren and the vibration made the rig slide over to the side of the road. Then I was driving the rig real slow and I started hearing this high-pitched screeching noise. I thought, "My God, what did I do, run over a kid or a dog?" Everybody on the right-hand side of the apparatus was doing a lot of hollering. It turned out that a small sports car was trying to pass me and our tire was rubbing his fender. If I had just cut the wheel to the right we would have squashed him into another car.

In winter you have all the hazards—the driving hazards, the accidents, the chance of not being able to get a hose line into position, not being able to get the apparatus into the street because of double parkers and all that, but mostly it's the debilitating effect of the cold upon the men. Winter's tough.

There used to be a lot of resentment against the chiefs drivers, for the fact that they were sitting in the car and we were out doing our thing, but that doesn't happen so much anymore. Some of those guys put in years in the busy companies before they became chiefs' aides—and rightfully so, because the unique thing about this job is that it's a young man's job. It's a physical job. As a fireman, where do you go after your twenty years on the job? You have a family, maybe kids in college, and you want to stay in the department. It's tough to stay on that back step or stand on the side of a truck. You have to become a driver of an engine or a chief's aide or find a slower area.

The Fire Department has affected me tremendously. It's been my life, there's no doubt about it. I think I've grown into manhood on this job. I came in as a boy and it matured me. For a while I really had a hard time making friends off the job. It was tough to go home, socialize with people, and talk about a lawn mower when I had just fought a major fire. And back in those days people really didn't appreciate how busy we were. The media didn't pick it up much. I would play down anybody else's job as opposed to mine, but it wasn't all braggadocio. I just couldn't see how any of my functions compared with theirs. To this day most of my friends are still firemen, but I do appreciate other people's careers now more than I did then. There's also a degree of withdrawing from people, though, because people don't appreciate our jobs or they play down the civil service role or feel as though it's a job for guys looking to duck rather than compete in the business world. But the job has been good to me, it really has.

Chapter 7

Battalion Chief Richard Fanning
Battalion 38, Brooklyn

I was in the job I guess about three or four months, and I was assigned to a very busy company—19 Truck, up on 166th Street in the Bronx. I was dying to get my first job, and have it done with. Everybody had their own opinion about whether it is best to start off at a big fire or a small fire. All the experienced old-timers said, "Don't worry, it'll come, it'll come." They knew we were champing at the bit.

"Come on," I said, "I've got to get a job. I've got to get a job."

The winter I was assigned to 19 Truck was busy. I used to come in at nine in the morning, and I'd smell smoke, and everybody's coats would be wet. The place would be dirty, and the saws would be lying on the floor. They would have had a big fire the night before. But I was outside the cycle of work for that whole winter, because every time I worked there were no fires.

I guess it was late March or early April when we got a job on Clinton Avenue. A roarer. It was in a three-story frame building attached to sixteen other buildings. We came out of the firehouse, turned the corner, and you could see that mother blowing in the sky. It looked like sunrise. I had the can. The officer we had was relatively inexperienced, but he took us up to the fire floor. There was so much fire, though, that we really couldn't do much with the can. We just got into searching the exposures—the sides of the fire building—and then operating up on the roof for a while.

It really wasn't as scary as one might believe. I was surrounded by talent, and they watch out for you when you're a probie. They keep a grip on you, and you just feel confident. For a long time I operated with an aura of invulnerability. As an inexperienced fireman, when you hear about somebody getting killed or severely injured, you rationalize it—"Well, that guy doesn't pay attention," or "He's always screwing around, and it's not going to happen to me." I think I pretty much felt that way until the Jennings Street collapse.

We were in a vacant six-story new-law tenement on Jennings and Wilkins in the Bronx. It was June 6; I had celebrated my wedding anniversary the night before. The night of the fire was super busy. Normally we would not have responded on the initial alarm, but Engine 82 and Ladder 31 were already out. We wound up getting special-called.

It was a good job. There was fire in the stores on the first floor, which had extended into the second and third floors. We'd started to initiate an outside attack when we got reports that kids were playing in the building. So we had to get a search under way. I went up the aerial to the roof in order to open the bulkhead and the skylight. After I did that, I was able to drop down into the top floor. I had started a search when they called everybody out of the building. The deputy had arrived and he went back to an exterior attack. It had been determined that the kids weren't in the building, and the intensity of the fire made it too dangerous for us to be in the building.

After that it was a piece of cake. We stood there for a couple of hours, pouring water on everything, and controlled the major portion of the fire, except on the top floor in the vicinity of the bulkhead and in the cockloft. We were all down on the street, but the next thing we saw was the rescue up there pulling ceilings. We told our officer, "If they're up there we should be up there, too."

He went to the chief: "Hey, Chief, let us go up and give them a hand. We'll be careful."

The next thing I knew there were five or six companies in the building. Just to give you a sense of the scene, it was a kind of fire we had done a thousand times before. Most of the troops were operating on the sixth floor. I was on the fifth floor pulling ceilings. This guy Dennis, of 19 Truck, said, "Hey, Richie, Richie, look at this." He pointed out the window. There was a woman across the street changing her clothes. We stood there watching and had a cigarette. Then we went back to work. It was a pretty relaxed state of affairs.

We were overhauling—this is pulling ceilings and getting at exposed pockets of fire. I was in the bathroom area. There was a fellow John Pierno. John was a pretty big guy, quite muscular, assigned to 19 Truck, but that night he was working a detail in an engine. I was pulling ceilings for a long time and I was really getting tired. He said something like, "Give me the hook and let me pull for a while." I told him something classy like "Fuck you, get your own hook."

I no sooner finished those words when I could feel myself falling. All the books you read tell you that you'll hear sliding plaster and creaking beams before you drop, but I heard nothing. Whether I shut it out or not, I don't know. I remember the thought that flashed in my mind: a common vacant-building injury involved stepping in a hole or a damaged portion of the floor; the boards would collapse and you would get a beam in the crotch. And all I could think of was, Aww, shit, I'm going to land on my nuts.

All of a sudden, I realized I was up to about my nipple line. Then I said, "Wow, I'm in here." But I couldn't put it all together. Somehow I lost my tools, and I grabbed at a sill, but Pierno had ahold of me. I used to carry a flashlight tied on by a piece of rawhide. He grabbed me by that, but it broke. He then grabbed me by the coat collar and just held me.

What flashed through my mind was Gee, I know what I'm doing, or I think I do. I've been studying like a son of a gun. I have a mastery of the technical knowledge, the book knowledge. I feel I have decent instincts and I don't drink when I'm working. All of this, and look at where I am—hanging in this hole with some guy holding me by my coat collar. The realization of how easily it could happen really rattled me. Fortunately a couple of other guys grabbed me, too, and I was able to get back up on the other side of the sill, which was still secure. Suddenly, everybody was screaming, "Mayday! Collapse! Collapse!"

What happened was that the top floor hesitated for just a minute and then started to pancake—floor upon floor—all the way down. As each floor gave way, the impact of the load coming down took larger and larger sections of the lower floors with it. All in all, seven guys rode right down with the building. They were all buried upside down with a lot of serious traumatic injuries, but nothing fatal, no limbs amputated or anything like that. Nobody was killed, but the last guy, Harry Mitchell, was down there for about three hours before they got him out. It was a bad, bad night.

One thing that helped me was knowing that you never go into a bathroom in a vacant building, because over the years the water splashing out of the tubs and the sinks and the overflows of toilet bowls could have created dry rot. In the old tenements, ashes were used underneath the tile as a form of insulation. The ashes also add a tremendous amount of weight, in addition to the plumbing fixtures. Also, when the junkies come in to strip the buildings, they sometimes cut away portions of the beams to get at the copper pipes. As a result, the bathroom floors are quite frequently weakened and always an area of fire extension, since ripping the pipes out leaves open holes from floor to floor. So although I was operating in the bathroom, I knew enough to put one foot over the sill.

When it was all over, I just sat and cried. I couldn't believe what had happened. I've always been a very aggressive fire fighter. I didn't even go sick that night. I was hot to stay. I know, in retrospect, though, that I was really keyed up; I was afraid to stop working for fear I'd lose control. I came to work the next night, too, but my confidence had really been shaken. It took me a long time to get back to a state where I would call myself confident, and in an honest analysis of myself I don't know if I'll ever reach that peak that I had before.

That doubt probably has a lot to do with physical limitations; then I was twenty-seven; now I'm forty. At that time I knew I was fast, I was good, I was hot, I was there. Now I find that being an officer, being responsible for the other guys, is really tough. I feel a tremendous ambivalence about pulling them back from what I used to do.

You do what you are capable of. I was never a strong guy, and I am not a weightlifter, so I try to master the skill of picking locks, instead of being the door killer and breaking them down. I used my own techniques to overcome my lack of strength. When I first went to 19 Truck the men all looked like Terry and the Pirates—I mean eye patches, earrings, and bandannas. It was a real heavy-hitting place, a real animal house, and I was a kind of baby-faced 150-pound guy who was put in this super truck. The captain used to break my balls: "Where did you come from, fucking ballet school?" So I always felt a need to work two and a half times as hard as the next guy just to stay even.

There was a guy up there—Bob Foley. He was a big gorilla who loved to fight, but he kind of took me under his wing. He showed me how to stay in the smoke. He took me into places where I would have never gone by myself. I developed to a point where I know he really tipped his hat at me, and that gave me a tremendous sense of accomplishment.

I remember one night when 31 Truck was out at a box and we got special-called over to Southern Boulevard and Freeman Street. We come in as the second due truck. At that time, Bob Foley was training me to be a roof man, and I was then what they call a secondary roof man. I was just to go with him and follow his orders. The roof is a tough position. Because a man is usually alone and a lot of decisions have to be made, they really try to work you gradually into that. We got up there and we did what we had to do—open the bulkhead and smash the skylights. Everything was pretty good.

I found a fire escape that went down into the top floor, which was the floor above the fire. I said, "Here's a fire escape should we get down?" His attitude was always Get the fuck down there! I mean, he was a very gruff, aggressive guy. He practically walked through walls and never wore a turnout coat, just a denim jacket and a helmet.

My initial goal was just to be able to keep up with him. Once I accomplished that, I was able to make my own decisions. He would go into a place and make a thorough search, and there would be nothing more that we could do until the engine came up or until the smoke lifted, but he wouldn't leave. He would find a corner, curl up, and just stay there. His thing was to be as tough as he could possibly be in the smoke. The longer he stayed there, the tougher he thought he was. In the beginning that was how he got me started, but eventually we kind of hit the switch in the tracks and parted ways in operational techniques.

Smoke is tough to operate in. Your nose, your eyes, your lungs burn, it just burns inside, it hurts. In those days nobody wore a mask. One night I remember we broke the windows in a fire building, and the smoke was almost solid. It was falling out like big balls of cotton. In Foley went. I knew I either had to go in with him and hope to hang tough, or sissy around. But you're always looking for that acceptance by your peers. Peer recognition is so much stronger than any awards or medals they can give you. So in I went, and I thought I was going to die—I really thought I was going to die. He of course had a few shots of anti-freeze in him, and he was going to buzz along at nine thousand feet.

"You all right?" he asked me.

"Yeah, I'm all right."

"Are you kidding me?"

"I'm all right."

I wasn't blindly thrust into this job. I knew I wanted to be a fireman and that this was what I had to do to be one. I was a transit cop before I came to the FDNY, and one of the problems on that job was that I was almost always alone. I didn't like it. I really didn't like hassling with the people. I was never a big barroom fighter, nor was I a fighter as a kid. Some guys are always hassling—bug tusslers. I found myself one night, with another cop, dangling a guy over the side of an elevated subway platform telling him we were going to drop him on his head over some bullshit. I said, "I got to get out of here."

At that time I was debating whether or not to leave the transit police and become a fire fighter. I'd already invested two years in that job, and I was studying for the sergeants' exam, but it was going to make me insane. I guess different people can stand up to different pressures. I had people there tell me, "You're crazy to go to the Fire Department. No way would I go into a house on fire." But I felt I didn't want to spend twenty years hassling with those nuts on the Seventh Avenue train. I'd rather go into burning buildings.

I like calling myself a fire fighter; I identify with it strongly. The pleasure for me is in going into a fire over which I have some *control*. An example of such a fire is where you have two or three rooms of fire going, but the hydrant is in service, the truck is there, the roof is vented, and it is easy. Some fires are easier to put out than others. You get to do this great job, and you come out of it and feel good—nobody got hurt and nobody got killed. The job just went super, super smooth.

The guys just feel tremendously cohesive, a lot of punching on the arm and ball-breaking. On the other hand, there are those situations when things get away from you, you just don't have enough resources to control everything, and you know you've done what could be done, but it's not enough—those times are not so pleasant.

Some jobs are frightening. I got stuck one night in a six-story building in the Bronx around 163rd Street. We were the second due truck. The fire was on the third floor, and it had extended into the upper floors. We were delayed in responding because we were coming from way over by the Concourse. By the time we got in there, the operation was well under way, but the extension of the fire had been quite severe.

We started working our way above the fire. The captain and the can man got to the floor above. I told them I was going to try to get to the next floor above that. I got in, and it was pretty shitty up there. I started crawling. In a situation like that, you're by yourself. You're always a little hesitant, but you're moving, moving, moving, getting to the back of the building. I vented the windows in the rear apartment. I checked the bedroom; it was empty. As I started to work my way out I could hear the firemen on the roof with the saws. They were having a tough time getting the roof open. I realized that the fire must be in the cockloft above me by now. I could feel the heat in the walls of the kitchen and bathroom. I knew the fire was over my head. I turned around, and on the way out I spotted a door. I said, "Oh, shit, there's another room." I just knew if I opened that door it was going to light up. But I kept going, saying to myself, "Naw, don't exaggerate, don't exaggerate." But I was reluctant to leave the apartment without checking that room for fear that there'd be somebody in there.

I guess I should have just stopped and vented the window and if it lit up, it lit up, if it didn't then I'd go in and search it. But I didn't. I just opened the door. I tell you, they heard me scream up on the roof. I guess I had built up in my mind that the fire was going to flash over, but all it did was start to roll along the ceiling. However, I got the impression that the whole place was going to light up and I yelled, "Ahhhhh!" I started to crawl. I didn't lose my tools. I don't know why, but I just built it up in my mind that a fireball would come rolling through the place and I would not be able to get away from it.

Afterward, a guy from 59 said, "Jesus, I was crawling in and I heard you scream. I didn't know what happened. I rolled into a room on the side, expecting to see this big ball of fire." Then he said, "I never saw anybody crawl so fast."

My first fire as an officer in an engine company responsible for the operation was in Flatbush, Brooklyn. I had never been to a fire in a private house before. Coming down the block, I told this dispatcher, "Ten-seventy-five—give me a full assignment. I got a fire on the second floor." I told my crew to start the line. I went upstairs and it wasn't all that bad. I could see the fire down at the end of the hall, and I tried to get down there to get the door closed. I figured I'd contain it to the room. We would have vented the windows by the time they got the line up. It would be a piece of cake. But I just couldn't get down there. The ceiling started to fall; it was all on fire. I got chased back downstairs. On the way down I vented a window, which just drew the fire farther down the hall, so in essence, I extended the fire.

My MPO—motor pump operator—had trouble getting water, so now the line was delayed. The fire was starting to burn down the stairs, and we were making progress in reverse. And I had all these young kids with me and one guy with about twenty-two years on the job who I thought was pretty good, but I wasn't sure yet. As it turned out he was the savior of the day.

We finally got water. Now, though, instead of starting from right outside the room, we're a floor down and we're going to have to fight our way uphill. The kid on the knob— the nozzle of the hose—did a good job. He pushed the fire up and we made the turn. Well, I'll tell you, the smoke banked down on me. I didn't have my mask on. I was from the Bronx, I was tough, but I couldn't handle it. I had to dive in the side room and try to get my mask on. You're the officer, you want to stay with them, I thought. But this old-timer Pauly DiLeo came up, and they actually did the job without me. By the time I got my mask on, the fire was out.

I felt like a dope. I owed those men an explanation. They did a credible job, although maybe if we had gotten water right away we wouldn't have those problems, but still I realized that I should have had my mask on. That fire wasn't so pleasurable.

Another fire I took them to was in a taxpayer—a row of low-rise stores. It was mostly fire; the smoke condition wasn't bad. They were hitting it with water, but you have to keep that hose line moving—unless you're going to have a collapse or something, and then you're going to be on the defensive. The quicker that line gets in there the quicker it's going out. The young kids just didn't have much experience yet, and they were kind of stalling. I said, "Come on, we can do this one." I made them take a two-and-a-half-inch line. (Usually they take an inch and three-quarters.) We got in there and went right past the first due engine, they were dilly-dicking around the door. We pushed that line right through there and knocked the fire down in minutes. That fire was great, because we didn't take a beating. We came out, we felt good. We did a good job and built a lot of confidence in the kids by bringing them through that.

Sometimes we'd go to four fires a night in Flatbush. Sometimes it was fun, other times it wasn't. I find that the older I get, the harder the work has gotten; my body doesn't take the beating as well. I feel that firemen are too modest about the amount of punishment they take. You watch them come out of a fire, and some reporter walks up to them and asks, "Well, how was it in there?"

The guy's eyes are hanging out, they've got blisters on their ears, they've got snot from their noses to their belly buttons, and they say, "Uh, it wasn't too bad." Well, bullshit! It was extremely bad. Otherwise everybody from the neighborhood would be in there, not just us. It was terrible in there and that's why these guys looks like they do. That's why tomorrow when they wake up they probably won't be able to get their eyes open, or they're going to go home and puke for two days. But most fire fighters are not braggarts. I guess that's a quality that I do admire in them as a group, yet I feel that we've been short-changed in recognition because of that quality. It's a paradox. I wouldn't want to see us lose that quality, however, like the police emergency services have. They come within a block of a burning building, and if you can believe the stories they tell, they have saved people who were overcome by smoke, they've rescued nine hundred little babies, and they've done a hundred other heroic things.

We had a fire one night on St. Ann's Avenue in the Bronx. We used to go to this box—2314—all the time. On the way the dispatcher said he'd had a phone call reporting a fire on the top floor. It was a fairly cool night, and as we approached the site, we saw nothing. Then all of a sudden the officer of the engine, Frankie Barry, spotted what he thought was a glimmer in a window on the top floor of a building around the corner, so we took the rigs over there. At first we thought it was just a candle in the window, but we went up to check it out anyway. I took it real nice and easy. I had the irons, and John Pierno had the can; we were the forcible entry team. It seemed like every call in those days was the top floor.

By the time we got upstairs we could see that it was a job. In other words, it wasn't just a candle in the window. (What I pieced together afterward was that this fire had burned in an unusually tightly secured apartment—for a tenement. It must have used up the available oxygen and brought itself down to the smoldering phase.)

We got the door of the fire apartment open. Then, a minute later, the engine officer came falling out of the place and said, "It looks like just a pile of rags, but the air is rotten in there." We were going to need the engine to get the line up. So John and I went in along the floor with the can. We could see something glowing, and I was using the can on it. I was thinking to myself, "This ain't a pile of rags; this is a couch. Boy, something *is* rotten in here." And the next thing I knew there are pieces of flaming something dropping in front of me. I said, "Where is that coming from? Maybe there's drapes here." I was throwing some water up in the air. However, there's only two and a half gallons of water in the can. I figured we weren't going to put out a lot of fire until we got the hose up, but we'd do what we could. I put my hand up and I got burned. We must have been just crawling underneath the fire. I remember saying to John, "Let's get out of here." At that point, we were just a little over fifteen feet inside the apartment. So we turned around, scooted out, and closed the door behind us. We were the last two people to get in that apartment. The fire was up in the cockloft burning over our heads, and what was dropping down was pieces of oil-based paint. By the time they got the hose up there, the whole place was lit up.

I remember there were some tough guys working that

night—Emil Marotta and Joe Minarik. Emil was real tough, and he thought 50 Engine was the greatest in the world. He said, "I am able to stand the heat on my ears, and with the mask I can stay in there forever; I just can't stay on my knees that long." Emil was always getting his knees burned. He used to have his wife sew these pads of rags in the knees of his pants just to give him a little more insulation, but he was getting the shit beat out of him trying to get in there.

We had the fire well vented; we'd opened the roof. It was just that the fire had gone throughout the entire cockloft.

Joe Rio, another tough guy, was also working, but Joe had a little carbon monoxide in him. He was completely knocked on his back. We dragged him downstairs and stuck him in a corner. Everybody got beat up; guys were in the hospital.

Fires like that, you go home and the next day your throat is all closed. Your eyes, your nose, everything in your respiratory system hurts. *That* would be a tough fire. At the time we would say, "What a bitch! What a bitch!" In retrospect, all the fires that were well vented—blowing out the windows—they looked dramatic, but you'd move right in, force the door, and go in with the line. Those fires were great. They were textbook cases. Everything fell right into place and you just knew you'd made good moves, and everything came out right.

We did most of our fire fighting in non-fireproof Class III brick buildings. On a national basis they call it "ordinary construction." They were anywhere from three to seven stories in height with brick bearing walls and wood beams. The roofs were wood-joisted with tongue-in-groove roofing boards, with a top layer of tin and tar paper. The beams were spaced about sixteen inches apart in the center, and they were very solid—three inches by eleven inches. It took a long time for that roof to collapse under fire conditions. Unless it was an unusual situation, we could spend a good while up there operating. I was the roof man a lot. I think they used to park me up there because I was a little light in the ass and not so big on forcing the doors.

I think the scariest and most unusual thing that ever happened to me was at a vacant building on Melrose Avenue in the Bronx. I climbed the aerial to the roof because it was an isolated building. But when I got up there, the bulkhead and the skylight were already open. I went to the soil pipe and I felt it—it was hot. So I called the outside vent man. I said, "Get the saw up here, because we're going to get fire in the cockloft." I knew it was going to move up through the bathrooms.

He came up with the saw, and I started cutting a hole. I'll tell you this roof was exceptionally thick; it had a lot of roofing materials on it. It was kind of tough to open, but I got a fairly good hole cut and started to pull it open. Well, something came flying out of there with such pressure that it hit me in the face. I thought that they had a hose line operating on the top floor and that I must have just opened the flap at the time they were sweeping the ceiling, so I was getting hit in the face with the stream of water—there's a tremendous amount of force behind that water. I fell backwards onto the roof and dropped the saw, and the guy behind me kind of grabbed me.

We were experimenting then with the prototype of the mask the department now uses. The interface between our helmet and the face piece, however, was no good, so they provided us with a different type of helmet. It looked like a German army helmet and it had a full face shield. I had this full face shield down, so when this blast of fire—which is what it turned out to be—came flying out of that hole and hit me in the face, I didn't get a burn. It was like a punch; it actually knocked me on my back. But I was okay. The guy who was behind me got his eyebrows burned off, and he was all singed around the ears. He took a shot of superheated air in the throat, and he had to go to the hospital. I stayed at that fire. Thank God I had that helmet on.

One of my first D.O.A.'s was a kid. Irony strikes again. That time 31 Truck was out—31 Truck was always out—and we were special-called. It was an H-type building, a big six-story residential building, up around Crotona Park East and Charlotte, and it was in fairly good condition. Like almost all the buildings we went to, it was occupied by poor people. The living conditions inside were not great, but this building itself was not in bad shape. We got in there first-due. But 85 Engine was in by themselves and they were stretching the lines. I had the irons. It was a first-floor fire, and in we went. It was only a one-room fire. A hysterical woman was in the hallway screaming that there was a kid inside. The engine officer, Rudy Bilsik, had already been in about a minute or two before us. He came and said, "There's no kid in there." I then made a search. The woman was still screaming, "There's a kid in there! There's a kid in there," so in we went again. It was uncomfortable, but we had been in worse smoke conditions, and we stayed. We searched, we tore everything apart.

The only room we didn't enter was the room that was actually involved in fire. The engine had the line and they were putting the fire out; it only took a minute and a half for them to knock that fire down. Then we went into the room and made a quick search, but we still didn't see this kid. We continued to search, though, because this woman swore there was a kid in there. By now we were five to seven minutes into the operation. We were going through closets and pulling furniture away from the walls, asking ourselves, "Where is this kid?" The couch was still against the wall.

I remember pulling that couch out. When I first saw the child, I thought it was a doll. I kicked it out of the way and as an arm fell off I could see it was real. The kid must have crawled behind the couch when the fire started. I gave her mouth-to-mouth. I remember her skin was stuck to my face, she was so badly burned. I remember trying to count the sequence of breaths and compressions.

There was a guy in the company, Joe Ferrari. Joe was a pretty tough guy, probably the toughest guy in 19 Truck. (It was 1968 and he wore an earring. You had to be tough to get away with an earring in 1968. He looked like a pirate, a very non-conforming individual.) He eventually snatched the kid from my arms. Joe was cool under the gun. He was always making the right move, always in the right place at the right time. He set the kid up on a table so her head would dangle off, and we worked on her up there, but we knew she was gone.

Soupy Campbell was the outside vent man on that job. He ascended the fire escape, one, two, three, no hesitation, and vented the windows. He'd had the option of going in one of two windows. He'd picked the window that looked the worst. If he had picked the other window he would have come in right on the kid and maybe been able to get her out in time. I remember him saying, "Damn it. I went in the other one because it was the first place and the hardest place. I figured that would be where I'd do the most good.''

You're always questioning your own decisions in your head: Did I do the right thing? Did I do the right thing? Guys may be sloppy about their uniforms, may pay no attention to lots of regulations, but most of them—and when I say most, I mean far and away most of the ones I ever worked with—are concerned about doing the right thing in a fire. There are very few incompetents at a fire. When I worked uptown, we had a very crowded firehouse. We had three companies in there, plus the division. It was a small place and it was an uncomfortable place at times. Out of a hundred guys who were assigned to the firehouse there had to be a certain number that you really weren't as friendly with, or didn't enjoy their company as much as others, but I really couldn't knock too many of them at the scene of a fire. They were good. And the ones who weren't good stood out so badly that they were soon gone.

Chapter 8

Lieutenant Jack Fanning
Ladder 26, Manhattan

The guys who aren't afraid of fire are the guys who haven't been exposed to it enough. Thinking about what it can do, hearing about people getting burned or killed or whatever in fires is completely different from actually being in a situation where it happens.

I don't know one fire fighter who would say he's not afraid of it. But with time and experience you become strange bedfellows with fire. You respect it more, and you can do more in fire situations.

I've been in ladder trucks for most of my time on the job. Our big job is to search the fire apartment and all the other areas that are burning. When I first began doing truck work, taking one step into an apartment that was on fire was taking a big step. It's very scary. You're in there searching without a line, and you have zero visibility. All you're feeling on the exposed parts of you is heat, and you can't move around as easily as you would normally. A table or a chair can become your worst enemy. Your mask gets hooked on it. Something as simple as a small end table could take on nightmarish proportions. Maybe all you want to do is back down the hallway, but you get hung up on this table. It becomes an adventure in there. If you feel a chrome blade on a chair, you figure you're in the kitchen. You feel tile on the floor, you're in the bathroom. You swing your tool and you hear a clank, you say, "Oh, that's the bathtub; I'm in the bathroom now. All right, I'll line myself up with the bathtub

119

and there should be a small window on that wall giving a certain amount of vent up there." You step into another room and work your way along the walls, always trying to remember that this is your way out when the time comes. What happens many times is you're searching along a wall and now you want to get out, and all of a sudden you find yourself in a room you haven't gone into yet—and you're totally disoriented. You go for a window. For a guy first doing it, this could be terrifying. You're in a burning apartment. You're alone and if you want to get out at this moment you can't find your way. You're just hoping that the guys are bringing the line up and this place isn't lighting up around you. But time and experience work in your behalf. It's a good feeling to know that you could have two ways to get out—the way you came in *and* a fire escape or an aerial ladder, or something like that. That's the situation you're always trying to create. You can work a lot better once you create that situation. They teach us in school to head toward the light source when we're searching.

The first two years on the job, I caught a lot of engine work on the Lower East Side. Those jobs you always had the line to operate off. When you have that line, you have your way in, and your way out is built in. No matter how bad things get you can always sit on the floor, grab that line and follow it right out. Truck work is a lot different; you don't have the luxury of the line. You're in an apartment that's totally foreign to you. Your first priority is to find anybody who's in there, and your second priority is to do this without getting yourself killed.

When I was working in the Bronx a couple of years ago, we had this thing called the above-fire team. Things were so busy then that instead of sending two trucks to a box they would just send one truck. That truck had seven men on it and two of those seven would operate above the fire. That above-fire team saw a lot of action. Here were two guys taking the place of an entire company. It turned out to be impossible.

We always worked together as a team and tried not to get separated. Each man would be responsible for searching a few apartments.

Once I went to search an apartment where they said a woman was trapped. It turned out she was trapped, but she wasn't in the apartment directly above the fire—the one I was searching—she was in the adjoining apartment. She was hanging out the window, so they eventually got her down with an aerial ladder without me knowing it. I assumed that she was in that apartment, so I had to search it. I got cut off from the other guy after I went in there. As I got farther into this apartment, I could see the glow of two windows in the living room. If I smashed either one of these windows I knew I would bring fire into the apartment. There were no vents allowed once you saw the apartment was threatened with fire. I walked farther into a bedroom, thinking I was going out of this apartment. I got to one of the windows, and the fire was just roaring up underneath. Well, I found out later that the fire was on its way through the baseboards, and it was coming up into the apartment behind me. All I was doing at this point was trying to get out of this place. There was plenty of heat in the apartment, and I was starting to get very frightened. Many times you just have to believe that somebody's watching over us, because I finally found an opening and got out. Then that apartment lit up, and I could just as easily have been stuck inside there. I could have been just a memory.

The search is a very tough part of the job, because you're trying to do something and at the same time do it without getting killed. To do it right you have to be very aggressive. You don't even have to see a glow, but you can feel heat on every exposed part of you. The place doesn't even have to be lighting up, but simply becoming very black, with a crackling. Then you know it's time to get out fast.

When I was first assigned to 26 Truck, the guys I was working with one day—my forcible-entry team—had really given a heavy push into the burning apartment. They were right there with the extinguisher hitting the fire. There was a good three rooms going in the back of the apartment, and it was a very big apartment. The people in the hallway were saying that a baby was in there. (It turned out the baby was six years old and she was in there with her grandfather.) We stayed in there until the fire actually drove us right down the hallway of the apartment and out to the public hall. I was really impressed with how the two guys on my forcible-entry team just hung tough, knowing that somebody might be in there. They stayed until their hands and the backs of their turnout coats started to burn. I had to tell them to leave or else, because by then the apartment was just about to light up.

The apartment was an L-shape setup and to get into the bedroom where the victims were you had to go into the last room and then make a U-turn back into this bedroom, because the main doorway to that bedroom from the hallway was blocked by a dresser. By blocking that doorway, the tenants had ruined their chances of getting out of that apartment once the fire started. It was a French door with small panels of glass.

One of the guys got into the bathroom, gave it a quick search, and ducked right back out. We were lying on the floor. Where we were there was no fire, but when I hit this pane of glass, the fire shot right out of the small opening I made, and then everything started lighting up. We had to make our retreat. As it turned out, the grandfather's head was less than a foot from that opening I made. The little girl was lying right next to him on the floor.

I was destroyed for the next week. Common sense told me that room was on fire before we walked into the building, that they were dead before we got off the truck, but for weeks I kept remembering that I was close enough to put my hand in there and pull the grandfather out or pull the little one out and that she could have been alive today. Leaving that apartment was tough. I had two guys right with me—we gave it our best shot—but I had to order these guys to leave. They knew that there was somebody in there and they weren't going to leave on their own. I finally told them, "Hey, let's go!"

The fire chased us right down the hall. If we had stopped for a split second or if one of us had gotten hung up on a piece of furniture or something like that, the fire would have shot us right down. The whole apartment was flashing over at the time. All the gases get collected at the ceiling level and they get so hot that they ignite. Well, those gases lit up and raced down the hall after us. And as the flame raced down the hallway, it also rolled over us. It was burning right up inside my turnout coat.

In a situation like that a bicycle or a shopping cart in the hallway could make all the difference in the world between getting out and not getting out. As you're going through, entering, you clear the way for the engine company, but you also clear the way for yourself if you have to bail out. In the tenements, occupants have all kinds of things in the hallways. Captain Dunne of 175 Truck was killed while he was searching for a kid when his mask got hung up on a bicycle in a hallway. He couldn't untangle himself and the whole place lit up and he was cooked.

Many times a job's an endurance test—it's a matter of staying and not backing off. You can't say, "Oh, jeez, there's fire in three rooms. Let's get out of this apartment and close the door till they put the water on." When you're doing truck work, if there's fire in three rooms in an occupied building, you know there could be somebody in one of those rooms, and *somehow* you have to get in there, whether it means going through the fire or going to an adjoining apartment and coming in off a fire escape. Our job is not to sit back, our job is to get in there no matter what the cost and search to see if there is somebody in there. Most times there's not. But the many, many times you push and come up empty-handed are all paid back to you a hundredfold the night you go in and find some kid under the bed. I once found a kid under a television set. Another time we had a fire where a section of the ceiling had come down and we were searching for a kid. He was underneath the fallen ceiling, but we found him.

We look at the job from our point of view. The fireman *wants* to work. He wants to rescue people, and he wants to be involved in something that's just plain scary to everybody else. Who else wants to go into a burning house? Who wants to enter a burning apartment or something like that? Nobody else does. Just the fireman. He *wants* to come to work and be involved in that. We don't want to see tragedy, but we want to work. Our job is to try to minimize the tragedy. The harder we're working, the more tragic the situation is. But fire is a fact of life, and people are saved because of our efforts.

Once a year the Fire Department has a medal day where they give out forty some odd medals to the best rescuers of the year. I was fortunate to win two of them. In the first one, fire wasn't even involved. We were in the firehouse around supper time—I remember that because I was cooking steaks—and we got a call to a box in one of the project buildings down on Webster Avenue in the Bronx. On our way there, we got a report over the radio that there was a kid hanging inside the elevator shaft underneath the car. When we went into the building somebody told us in the lobby that he was around the fourth-floor level. Another guy and I went up there and forced the elevator door open, and there was a boy about nine years old inside the shaft. He was just hanging there. He was out of our reach, but up along one side of the shaft was a railing that is part of the guideway the elevator runs on, and there was a good-sized bolt attaching the railing to the wall. I jumped onto the railing from the landing and put my foot on that bolt. Then I swung out as far as I could. I scooped the kid in and handed him back to the fireman on the landing. By that time more firemen were on the landing and they helped me get back in.

We found out later that he and another kid had climbed down on top of the elevator from the floor above. The other kid managed to get out somehow, but this kid fell in between the wall and the elevator car. He just managed to grab on to one of the cables before he went flying home. If he had fallen, he would have been killed. I would have been, too, because the odds of living through a four-story fall are very slim. That was one of the most unusual rescues that I've had.

In most elevator incidents the car has tapped out in the middle of the shaft. It'll lose power, and we'll find a group of people just sitting inside the car. Maybe it's the middle of the summer and those people start getting hot. If there are two cars in the shaft, we'll ride one until it's side by side with the disabled car. Then we reach a hook through and trip the interlock on the disabled car. That will open the hoistway door on the landing. Many times, however, it's a single-car shaft, and we have to take the people out of the top of the elevator. For that kind of job we use a pencil ladder, which doesn't even look like a ladder until it's flopped open. We use it quite often.

Stuck elevators can get serious. We had an old man who had a heart attack while he was stuck in one in the Bronx. He was D.O.A. when we got to him. That happened on a real hot summer day, too. Sometimes you get people who are stuck in an elevator while there's a rubbish fire in the base of the shaft. Then you have some very panic-stricken people. We can see that the situation is not that serious, but convincing them is something else. You get four or five people stuck for any length of time in an elevator, and they're ready to kill each other to get out of there. They can make a situation worse than it is. But we deal with them all the time, especially in the projects. We're constantly having to remove people from those elevators because they're only maintained when they have to be. Management will have a repairman come the day *after* five people are stuck in there for two hours. They'll only react to a problem; they won't try to prevent it.

I won the other medal for a rescue on 120th Street in Manhattan. I had just relieved a fellow when the box came in. He said, "I'll take it in," because I hadn't changed out of my street clothes.

I said, "No, I'll take it."

Later on he gave me the business, because if I hadn't relieved him that day, he would have been involved in the rescue. Anyway, the fire was on the top floor of a brownstone. A bunch of people were coming out the front door when we got there, and they were all yelling that somebody was upstairs. I got to the top floor first, and I had my forcible-entry team coming up behind me. I heard people yelling. The place was tremendously charged with smoke, and there was a lot of heat. We couldn't see anything, of course, but I heard them yelling. It turned out a girl and her uncle were hanging out the rear window, screaming for help. And there's no fire escape on the rear of brownstones. The two occupants were ready to jump four stories into the shaft. The only thing that kept them in the window was the fact that the fire hadn't reached them yet. I was able to get to them, by crawling through the apartment, and one at a time I took them to the top of the stairs; from there, two of my guys took them down. Then I went up front for a search of the fire area. Three rooms were going while I was searching. I was just about to leave the area after giving it a search, because it was pretty bad in there, when I came upon a woman's foot. I think she was about eighty-seven years old. She was overcome by the smoke; she was also burned. The fire was up in the cockloft, and it had dropped down on her. The room she was in was beginning to light up. I had to pass the fire in one spot just to get into that room. Then I had to drag her back through it. We got her out, but the skylight over the stairs collapsed in the middle of this, and there was a tremendous crash. I didn't know how much of the building was going—it turned out it was just the skylight—but now there was rubble all over the stairs. The men were calling to see if everybody was okay on the top floor. I just handed her over to the other firemen, and they took her downstairs and she was all right.

But my best save happened in the Bronx. Ironically, I got a lesser award for it. I got a Class A, though, which is nice. That rescue was in an old tenement, and we were the first due truck. There was a police lock on the door of the fire apartment. That's the lock with the metal bar that goes from the back of the door down into the floor; makes the door very hard to force. There was a good fire going in the apartment while we worked on the door. The toughest part about that job, I felt, was forcing that door. We really expended ourselves on it. I wound up using the back of the ax to take the out the middle panel of the door. Then we reached inside, dropped the bar out of the way, and forced the door in the conventional manner.

When we got inside, the living room and the bedroom were on fire. I passed right through that while the guy with me was hitting it with the can. I found a woman in the rear bedroom. She was a very fat woman—she must have weighed three hundred pounds. I was so exhausted from forcing the door I could hardly pick her up. When I first picked her up and started pulling her out, I fell down and she fell on top of me. All I wanted to do was to get her and me out of there. I just squeezed her out. Then they started moving the line in to put the fire out.

If you asked me what would be the best all-around rescue, that would be the one, because there was good truck work involved with forcing the door and following through with the search. But you don't get recognition for that, you just get the satisfaction of a job well done. But you can't really get too hung up on what medals the department gives you, because I've seen guys do some fantastic things and not get anything for it. The real satisfaction isn't the recognition you get. The real satisfaction is learning a very difficult job and then using it on a particular night. For example, using everything that was taught to me over the years and getting through the door into the apartment and finding somebody—that was the real satisfaction with that job.

It's an incredible feeling, knowing that a person would have died if it hadn't been for you. At another fire a lot of people were carrying on in the hallway, saying that somebody was in the apartment. You can sometimes tell that they're not kidding and there really is somebody in there, and that's what happened one night on Fulton Avenue in the Bronx. When we got up to the site, the fire was in the kitchen. My officer and I passed the fire and got into the rear of the apartment. We were searching the rooms and it was getting worse; the fire was extending in our direction and back to the entrance of the apartment. But the people in the hall were really serious about somebody being in this apartment, and we just had a feeling that they were right. We searched the two bedrooms, and we took a shellacking in there. We didn't have masks on and we came up short of air. We were met by one of the guys who came in off the fire escape and continued to search; he found a girl in the bathtub—they say people go to a source of water in a fire. At any rate, he found her and dragged her out. We just dashed out behind him.

When he got out to the hall, he collapsed, so I went to work on the woman with mouth-to-mouth resuscitation. There was no pulse, no breathing—nothing. She was gone, but we worked on her out in the hallway for a good ten minutes. I could hear the other guys saying that she was gone. Then all of a sudden she gurgled, so we knew the mouth-to-mouth was having some kind of an effect. She came back, and it was only because we stayed with the mouth-to-mouth over that period of time instead of giving up on her and handing her over to the ambulance guys. I just stayed with simple mouth-to-mouth while one of the other guys was doing cardiac pressure. Otherwise that girl would have been dead. Knowing that was an incredible feeling. That was satisfaction at its best. I felt like I'd really arrived. I wanted to be a fireman and this is what being a fireman is about. This is what comes of it. Tragedy comes of it sometimes, but so do the highs. That was one of the biggest highs that I've had.

Many times you come to work and you feel you can get a lot done in the office. But always in the back of your mind you know that you could be one minute from a life-or-death situation, and it happens all too often like that. I'm in no way exaggerating when I say this—in one minute you can go from washing the truck or preparing a meal or sweeping the floors to pushing a line down a hallway or forcing a door or running for your own life from a bad situation. Things happen very quickly. The worst situations seem to materialize out of thin air. When the alarm comes in, you never know what's at the other end of it. I have fourteen years in the Fire Department, and I feel more and more strongly that when I walk in the door I could be a minute away from a very tragic situation.

But you can also wind up in the middle of some interesting situations, particularly in an area like Harlem. Pete Newel was driving one night when we were coming back from a box on the West Side. We stopped for a light on 116th Street and Eighth Avenue, right in front of the Royal Flush Hotel. That place is junkie city. A real tough area. All of a sudden we saw a car speeding down Eighth Avenue. It jumped the curb and drove along the sidewalk. Then we saw two squad cars behind it. Shots were being fired—the people in the sports car were shooting at the cops; the cops were shooting at them. And we were stuck at the light watching the whole thing unfold before us. All of a sudden squad cars came from all over. The TPF (Tactical Police Force) and everybody else was after this guy. I don't know what they were chasing him for but he was doing his best to get away from them. He tried to make the turn in front of us, but he slammed right into our rig. God only knows how fast he was going. The police saw that as their opportunity. The patrolman in the car right behind him went broadside to try to stop this man. They slammed him into our rig a few times. He had a passenger, but the passenger was slumped over. The driver was bleeding, but he was hell-bent on getting away. They kept banging him into the side of the rig trying to stop him, but the guy still got away. There were police cars all over the place, but he squeezed right through them and shot up the next block where they finally got him. It was like watching *Starsky and Hutch*. We called the dispatcher and said we were involved in an accident. He told us to remain on scene, but I told him we were returning to quarters, because police action was going on here. It must have been something local, because the cops had some guy spread-eagled next to one of the stores—a plainclothes policeman holding a gun right at his head. The police came to the firehouse later that night and thanked us for the use of our rig. The rig wasn't that old, either, and they'd banged the hell out of it. The cop was a real gung-ho type, and he wanted those guys with a passion. Nobody was hurt, thank God, but we had just come back from a fire and we were all hurting. We were all anxious to get back to wash up.

Another job I remember well because a fellow from one of

the cable stations was here that day doing a show on firehouse dogs. He had the cameras rolling on our dog, Lady, and they were asking us about her. He was taking pictures of us with her and of her riding the rig when we got called to a drugstore on Eighth Avenue and 117th Street to check out a possible gas leak in the basement. When we went down in the basement, I couldn't smell anything, but one of the guys called me and said, "Hey take a look at this." Between the side wall of a big old walk-in refrigerator and the wall of the basement there was maybe a foot of space, and in that space he happened to find a five-gallon can of gasoline right by the gas meters. That was trouble enough, but connected to the can was a wire—like the ones you put in a cup to boil water. The wire was attached to a timer, and all of this was plugged into the outlets. It was about 12:00 noon, and the timer was set for 1:15. The timer would turn this element on to heat the gasoline to ignition temperature and start a fire. And then we found that there were wires going elsewhere, so we figured we'd evacuate the building and call the bomb squad to dismantle this thing. One of the guys suggested that we just go over and take the plug out. However, these things are jimmied up all the time, and they're set with mercury switches so that you'll pull a plug or something like that and that will trigger the whole thing. So we stepped outside and then we evacuated the building. Whoever set this thing up certainly had no heart; the building was fully occupied. It was a five-story tenement with old women and kids living in it.

It took us a while to get everybody out into the street. Somebody said there was a drug war going on between one faction and another faction on the same block. It turned out that the wires led from this contraption to the top of the refrigerator—we hadn't even looked up there. The bomb squad found a couple of sticks of dynamite—enough to blow the whole building off the face of the earth. They figured out by the configuration of how the thing was set up that if one detonating device didn't work, something else would. So whoever set the bomb up meant business; it was a professional explosive device. We closed off the area. Then two guys from the bomb squad brought the thing up, dismantled it, and took it out to Rodman's Neck and blew it off. They found out later that two guys, who said they were Con Ed people, came in with an old valise. They said they were working on the meter.

It was unsettling to be around that thing. One of our guys, without consulting anybody, could have gone over, pulled the cord and set the bomb off. Or it could have been timed to go off two minutes after we walked in there.

I've been involved in a few situations where arsonists set things up just to get us—cut-away sections of fire escapes, tar paper over holes in the roof. A good friend of mine was put out of the job because of one of the fire escape setups. Someone had cut a section of gridwork on the fire escape and left it in place to appear that the thing was still intact and safe to walk on. My friend stepped on it, and the whole three-by-three-foot section went down with him on it. As he fell, he injured his back and was put out of the job and on disability immediately. Lucky he wasn't killed. That trap was deliberately set up for us. The same kind of people sometimes place tar paper over a hole in the roof so that the roof appears solid, but when you step on that, down you go. We ran into an awful lot of that up in the Bronx. Some of the people were out to get us for quite a long time. In the vacant buildings we often found balloons full of diesel fuel hanging in the cockloft; once a fire got going in an apartment and when we went in to put it out, the whole apartment lit up from this fuel in the cockloft. Those people really knew what they were doing. They taught us a lot. They knew fire better than we did.

That kind of thing went on in the early seventies in the Bronx, during that period of civil unrest. Those were the days of garbage cans being thrown off the roofs. People would let us go into the block. Then they would block the street off with abandoned vehicles and bombard the shit out of us. I remember a night when we were boxed into a street and bombarded with Molotov cocktails, which exploded in flames in the streets. In certain areas you really had to watch yourself. Things were always being thrown off the roof. We just tried to cover up and get out. Usually the call was just a rubbish fire out in a yard or something like that. You could leave it and get back on the rig and try to get the hell out. But you had to make sure everybody was accounted for.

A few times we chased people up to the roof, but it was all to no avail. We'd go up on the roof and find a carton containing the night's supply of Molotov cocktails all set up—gasoline in a soda bottle with a rag sticking out of the top—not the sophisticated Molotov cocktail that was developed later on, but a simpler version of it.

Most of this happened in the summertime. It would go on for a couple of nights; then it would die for a while; and then all of a sudden it would start again.

The police worked very well with us in those days. They would swarm over the roofs and chase these guys so that we could put the fire out without having to worry about being shot.

It was the thing to do back then. There are still cases, now they're more isolated. It's nothing like it was.

The junkies love to go inside vacant buildings and remove a lot of the stuff. These actions are not directed at us, but when the guys strip the buildings it does a lot of damage that we have to watch out for. They break all the treads on the steps. They remove landings, drop fixtures, and salvage pipe. They'll place a couple of mattresses on the bottom of the stairwell, remove the treads, remove the landings, and then take all the fixtures out of an apartment and dump them down the opening. This makes it hard for us to get up and down the stairs in these dark buildings. And many of the vacant-building fires spread quickly from one floor to the other through the voids left by these guys when they strip the buildings.

One thing truckies have to remember when they're working on roofs of tenements is to secure their second egress—the second way off. On a tenement you usually step over the parapet wall to the adjoining roof and you're covered. We have this luxury ninety-five percent of the time. When you're working on an isolated building, however, you don't have that alternate way off. Ten years ago I got stuck on the roof of an isolated vacant building. That was a memorable moment. The fire appeared to be in the rear on the top floor. Four of us went to the roof of a six-story building: another fellow from my company, 59 Truck; two fellows from 31 Truck; and me.

It was a routine operation; one apartment was going in the rear. We cut a nice big hole in the roof over the fire, to vent it so that the engine could move in and knock it out. Three of us were watching the saw man cut the hole, standing by with our tools to pull the flap open when it was ready. We were standing between the back of the building and the hole. Our egress was an aerial ladder at the front of the building. Inadvertently we cut this hole between us and the escape route. As it turned out the fire was in this rear apartment, and it also had complete control of the cockloft over the rear—but we couldn't read that from the roof at first. As we pulled the roof section open, the fire roared out of this opening and spread right across the roof. In the space of two or three seconds the entire roof was completely involved—between us and the aerial ladder. Because we were working on an isolated building, we didn't have an adjoining building to step off on to. We were totally and completely cut off—trapped. The flames on the roof must have been shooting thirty feet in the air at least, and that's without exaggeration. A tremendous amount of fire was vented with this one five-by-five hole. It just unleashed itself, and all of a sudden we went from a basic one-apartment fire to a multiple alarm. And here we were stuck, the four of us, and fire was pushing us to the rear of the roof.

The only thing that bailed us out was an oddity. Most tenements in the rear have a goose-neck ladder that goes over the parapet and down to the top-floor fire escape landing. This building, however, had a three-by-three-foot landing instead, with a cutout over the parapet wall and an actual stairway, which was unusual, going down to the fire escape. If we'd been dealing with a goose neck ladder we would have been in a lot worse shape, because the fire was venting out the four windows below us, too, so it wasn't just a question of just stepping onto the ladder and going down and getting away from it. We were getting it from both sides. Anyway, to make a long story short, there we were, the four of us, huddled on this little landing not knowing which way to go, and I was getting burned right at the back of my coat. I got some real good burns on my legs and on my hands. I had taken my gloves off and reached in my pocket to get a rope. I was going to attach the rope to the fire escape landing, but the fire escape was red hot. It would have burned right through the rope, so there was no point in attaching it. Then we all moved in one split moment of time, knowing we were going to stand here and burn if we didn't get out. So we all went ass over teakettle down the stairway to the floor below. We didn't do it by choice. It was either that or jump off the roof or just stand there.

Of course, we had some other guys in the backyard. A couple of them had gone for a net. That's something that we'd never do in a million years—jump into a net—but they were just thinking of options. Everybody at the job knew we were trapped, and they were just trying to think of how they could get us down alive. An aerial ladder was placed right through the flames, as far as it could go. But the ladder was completely involved in flames. So there was no getting out that way. At least they made an attempt to get us, because they are not people who stand passively, not trying to do something. My hands got burned to smithereens as I grabbed the railing and swung out over it and down to the fire escape floor below. My hands felt like they were in a furnace because the railing was red hot. My legs were also badly burned because the fire had gone right up inside my coat. Then we had to keep going down because that's where the fire was venting out the windows. One guy broke his thumb in the process.

All four of us got burned, but we were lucky to be alive. While we were up there, however, I was pacing back and forth trying to think about what our options were and what are we going to do. But I was also in a state of subdued panic, wondering what was going to happen. Then I actually pictured it in my mind: I could see myself jumping through the air six floors to the concrete courtyard.

I know for a fact that at least two of us would have been killed if that was a goose-neck ladder and not this stairway type of thing. It was a very close shave with the red devil, too close for comfort. I was on medical leave for quite a while after that. I needed the rest just to get my head screwed back on. That was a very memorable moment up there on that roof. I spoke to guys in my company. They came over later and said, "We knew you were up there. We knew exactly where you were, but there was no getting to you."

They had come up through the interior of the building to the bulkhead and the bulkhead door was open, but it was just a sea of flames; there was no getting us that way. The chauffeur tried his best to put the aerial right to us, but the best the aerial could do was sit in the flames. We were on our own, we were just on our own. But it was an impossible situation, I thought that it was the end. I really did.

I was terrified.

Chapter 9

Fireman Dan Defranco
Engine 17, Manhattan

I was a plumber over on the West Side of Manhattan. A good friend of mine—Don Wilday, who's dead now—kept telling me what a great job the Fire Department was. He pretty well embarrassed me into taking the test by saying, "You probably couldn't even pass it."

I got notified to appear at the training center on October 12, 1962. However, I still had no intention of going into the fire service. In fact, I went back to work that morning as a plumber on Pier 40 over at the west end of Houston Street. It was the Holland American Line's pier, and we were having problems on the job. I asked the foreman about extra money. He said no. I said, "I quit." Then I got on my motorcycle and went up to the FDNY training center—at that time it was on Welfare Island—and the next thing I knew I was in the Fire Department. I was just fooling around; I never thought I would stay. Well, lo and behold, I stuck with it.

I was first assigned to Engine 27 over on Franklin Street in the meat market. They had maybe twenty runs a month, so in the course of working a month, if you caught one run you would be lucky. When I got there the guys told me about all the big fires they had gone to, like the *Normandie* fire and the Holland Tunnel fire. I think I had maybe two runs before I caught my first fire. It was over a bar. This was a one-story building, but it had a big shack on top where they did some cooking. I guess they also used to sleep in there. The whole shack was on fire. After we put the fire out we began moving all this stuff out, and I found this dead man. He looked like he'd been mutilated; his hands and arms were burned off. I got scared so they sent me back to the firehouse.

I walked all the way. It was about two o'clock in the morning, and I've got all of this in my mind. It's very dark—all these piers, like something out of the movies. After six o'clock in the evening there's nobody in that area until six the next morning when all the trucks arrive. Well, I bumped into a guy, and it scared the living shit out of me. That was my first fire, and it was terrible. I was really shaken up by it. I wanted to go back to plumbing. But I stayed. I even transferred over to 17 Engine on the Lower East Side, where they were doing thirty runs a tour. I have been with 17 Engine ever since, except during the strike in 1973 when I was sent out of 17 because we had union problems there, and the chief dropped anybody who was a problem. The strike was on November 6, 1973 and the department order was on December 10. I was the first one to go to Brooklyn. I went to 242 Engine in Bay Ridge, and that killed me. It was like going back to 27 Engine—a nice company in Bay Ridge, but few fires. I left an area that I liked, and it took me eleven months to the day to come back. I had to go through politicians to do it. I won, but they made me pay for it.

The engine guy, like an unsung hero, does all the work and gets no credit whatsoever. His job is to get in there, put out the fire, and take a beating. My heart has always been with the engine—that's the machine that pumps the water and hauls the hoses. You have to see these guys—not that I'm downgrading the guy in the truck, but in the engine somehow I think you're closer. There's four guys on the engine moving in on the fire, all of them dependent on each other. Each man is expected to do his job. If an engine guy made a rescue in the course of moving in, he couldn't get credit for it, because he wasn't supposed to be out of position.

I got a little kid out of a fire once, someplace over on Attorney Street. They had a good fire going in a tenement, and we were on the line. In those days we didn't have masks. They used to say in 17 Engine that masks were for Halloween and that was the only time you wore them.

But we came into this building and actually went over a body twice. All this debris had come down in the hall. One of those portable closets had burned and fallen on a woman.

When we got into the hallway the fire was dead ahead. We went over this pile of rubble, never knowing there was a body under there. But I could hear a kid crying in the next room, and I tapped one of the guys on the shoulder and I told him, "There's a kid in there!"

He said, "Go ahead!"

I went in and there was this little baby, I guess maybe three years old, under a crib. I grabbed a coat that was lying on the floor and put it over him and dragged him out, sliding on my stomach because the smoke was so banked down. I got him out into the hall and passed him on to a man who was out there. Then I went back to the line. I knew a guy in the truck would work on the kid; I had to get back on the line, that's where I belong.

I remember the beatings I used to take. I would move on my stomach, my nose right at the crack of the floorboards, trying to push the line down the hall. I used to throw up halfway down the hall. I would be violently sick. The guys would be puking in front of me, and I'd be sliding on it. But I would just keep going. I used to say, "If I get out of here, I'm quitting. I don't need this. Who needs this? I was a plumber by trade." And then I'd go back to the firehouse and I would say, "Boy, that was some job," or "We really did good. We really kept it to two rooms as opposed to losing the whole building." Then I would just forget about it and be ready for the next one. But I guess I stayed because of the relationship the men build up between each other.

Sometimes you're scared shitless during a fire. There may be a tremendous wind, or you might push open a door and see this fire roaring down the hall, and no matter what you do you can't gain on it. Or the outside men may start to pull out the lines because the fire is coming down at you. Those are the things that scare you.

Maybe you have a couple of rooms fully involved in fire and you start making nice headway. You don't think of fear the few minutes you're doing this. It might seem like longer, but how long does it take to go down a long hall—maybe five minutes? But if you had to think about it you sure as hell wouldn't be there. I think that as you become older and more experienced something happens to you when you throw on the rubber coat and the helmet. I've sometimes found myself doing things that a normal person wouldn't do, like jumping from one roof to the other, right across the air shaft, and passing the line in, because the fire got into the other building. You put on that coat and the boots and the helmet and you think that somehow gives you a little protection. You feel nothing's going to happen to you as long as you've got those things on. Funny, as I think of it, one time I was in Staten Island when a house caught fire. I was off duty at the time, and I felt helpless. I went into the house and I was able to get an old man out of the back room and into the kitchen before the guys from the local fire company came in. But because I didn't have the rubber coat and the helmet on I felt unshielded— and I felt bad, too, in the sense that maybe I could have gone in deeper.

To be a good engine man, you've got to have the ability to hang in there. You give it your all and then if you have to go in farther you can somehow come up with a little more strength. We used to do tremendous work down here on the Lower East Side. I remember when I first came to this house, there was this old guy, Maxie Rutter, our MPO. He used to say, "Kid, you're going to see the night when you're going to say, 'I hope to Christ it's not another fire.' "

At that time I was dying to see fires and I couldn't believe that, after being there maybe less than six months, when I rolled out of the quarters on a cold night I would say, "Oh, I hope not." But sure enough, as I turned the corner I'd look up and see the sky lit up. How many sunrises I saw over the East River, working all night and being in the burned-out apartments or up on roofs and seeing the sun coming up.

You just got to have the willingness to outdo yourself. You get that confidence—confidence is the big thing. When a guy says, "Come on, we're going to back out," you have to say, "No, we can make it." That was the whole thing in the sixties and early seventies. You never gave up a line. You had to die with it, and somehow you became crazy with it. You'd be the first due engine, you'd be getting your balls beat in, and the fresh company would come up, all nice and clean. And they'd say, "They told us to come up. Give us the line." They were as eager as we were, and they were looking to pull the hose out of our hands. We'd tell them, "Screw you! Go get your own line. We brought it up and we'll stay with it."

How many times we'd come back and we would be too

tired to do anything. We'd have maybe three fires on a cold night, and we'd back the engine in, go in the kitchen, have a cup of coffee, walk up those long flights of stairs in the old firehouse, lie down, and just say, "Ah." Then the box would come in. "Let's go, first due!" The companies in our house—Engine 17, 18 Truck, and Fourth Battalion—are all real gung-ho people. Not every firehouse is the same, because they don't all have a lot of work. Without work the house could be a real zero, because there's nothing to hold you together. You lack that battleground where you are dependent on the next guy and he's dependent on you.

In those crazy days the second due engine company would never stretch hose from his engine, because he had to be available for the next fire. But they would strip the first due engine that came in. Let's say we come up to a fire and we drop off maybe four or five lengths of the hose and take off to a hydrant, which may be half a block down the street. Now another pumper—let's say 28—comes in second due. He would be almost in front of the fire. Well, instead of taking their own hose and going into the fire the second due engine walks down half a block and takes your hose from you. If you had multiple alarm, then everybody stretched hose. The companies that left last, usually the first due engine and the first due truck, would take the hose up. That used to kill me; it was just craziness.

The Fire Department is very traditional. We didn't stop washing the wheels until 1970. For about ninety years, after every run, when you came back to the firehouse you used to wash all four wheels of the truck. That custom started back in the horse-drawn days, when there was horse shit on the wheels. The men would wash it off so that it wouldn't smell the house up. The horse lived in the house, too, and it didn't bother him, but you had to wash the wheels. I can remember coming back from a fire soaking wet and the probie would get the pail. The pail was always by the house watch with soap and the broom. Then he would scrub the wheels, hose them down, get the dog shit off. That was tradition. If you went out twenty times, the probie would scrub the wheels twenty times.

Years ago, and again we're talking about tradition, when we had a multiple alarm, we used to do a hose change. We had a hose tower with one extra change of hose. But like every busy company in Harlem, Bushwick, Bed-Stuy, we'd need ten changes of hose a night because we stretched ten, eleven, twelve lengths of hose, one line, and then if somebody else came in and stretched another line. There's another seven lengths. You would take all the hoses back. If they were soaking wet and smelly you wouldn't fold them back in the bed; you would just throw them on any old way. Soon as you got back to the firehouse you were out of service. Actually we were still in service, provided we had enough hose to make one stretch. And it would be a mortal sin not to have a nozzle screwed on when you were taking up from the fire, in the event that you caught something on the way. But when we got back to the house we stripped out all the hoses—fifty-foot lengths of two-and-a-half-inch hose—and hung them up to dry.

Back then we didn't have inch-and-a-half hose like we have today. We would stretch two-and-a-half-inch hose all the way up to the fire, and we would kill ourselves trying to bend it around the corners in those narrow hallways. The only time we used an inch-and-a-half hose was when the fire was knocked down and we had pockets of fire here and there. Then we would connect that inch-and-a-half to the end of a two-and-a-half. Finally someone said, "Let's try the inch-and-a-half." But again, traditionally we always used two-and-a-half. Finally they said, "Jeez, you know the inch-and-a-half always works better because it's lighter. Fewer guys are needed to bend it and it has more maneuverability than the two-and-a-half. You don't have to put four guys on it, so we don't lose the guy who's in control." And so we changed.

Years ago we only used the straight stream nozzles; that was all we had. Those nozzles threw a lot of water, but again, we killed ourselves. Now we have this new fog nozzle, which is beautiful. If you have a good body of fire in a room, you put that nozzle on, and it gives you sixty-degree fog. If you have a good opening, which naturally you can always rely on the truck company to give you, you can take this whole room of fire and just push it right out the window. Of course this can push the fire to other floors, but in the end it's a beautiful way to put out a fire. It's a giant shower head that just wets down everything at once, as opposed to giving only a ⅛-inch column of water. With a fog nozzle you can cover a tremendous area. You whip that around in a room, it's like a hurricane. It has really made fire fighting easier.

The masks also make a difference. It's sad that we didn't have the masks sooner. So many guys I've worked with have died. And, yes, if they'd had masks, maybe they'd still be around.

During the last ten years we've come into the plastic age. When we used to go into the tenements under heavy fire condition, the whole building might be burning, because most of the contents were made of wood. But the times have changed; now everything is plastic, which has created new hazards. The telephone company fire in 1976 is probably the best example of those new dangers.

Oh, that fire was tremendous; it was actually a disaster. We just poured tons of water on it. We were there for twenty-four hours, at Thirteenth Street and Second Avenue. They evacuated I guess ten to twelve square blocks. In fact, they evacuated everyone from the Eye and Ear Infirmary, which is just north of the phone company. Not that we knew it at the time, because we were engaged in fighting the fire. I guess they call it a borough call, which is anything after the fifth alarm. They were depleted of manpower.

We'd had a union meeting the night before. The next morning we heard that the fire started at midnight. The guys from our house were all working there. So I went up there with a good friend of mine, Freddie Link. Engine 17 was at the front of the building on Second Avenue supplying a couple of ladder pipes and Stangs, so they were right in the thick of it. We got there around noontime. We were off duty; we had come in that day to get paid. But we'd brought our gear from the firehouse. We got coffee and lunch for the guys. That night all the guys on the day tour went sick, so Freddie and I worked overtime. We came back to the firehouse at—oh, I guess maybe five in the morning. We got an hour off to shower.

As I said, it was a disaster—a lot of guys got hurt. In the building we couldn't see anything. We were groping, feeling our way through and kicking over equipment. We operated on the third floor for three or four hours. We were in a doorway and a spout of water two feet high was pouring over us from the hoses. It was like being in a waterfall. The water was shooting in from all the windows. Then we were told to back the line out and operate in the basement—that was late at night. We got into the basement. Some of the areas had maybe ten feet of water in them and our job was to get the pumps going to see if we could get the water out of the building. We worked on that a long time—smashing out some gratings on the sidewalk, dropping the hose down, getting the pumps going.

We didn't wear masks there because all the fire was above us, but the smoke had been sucked down through elevator shafts and there was this haze. We were walking around feeling dizzy—very light-headed. Well, little did we know at the time that the air was full of PVC [polyvinyl chloride]. It was a different kind of smoke, and we got very sick from it. At the other fires we'd be sick for the first hour in heavy smoke; we'd be dizzy, throw up, feel better. But this fire was a little different. It was constant.

I see these new kids—I call them kids, these young fire fighters; they want to get their balls beat in. I tell them, "I wish someone had told me twenty years ago to take care of my lungs." I'm sure mine are screwed up. I was out nine months on light duty in 1979. I got burned in my throat, mouth, and lungs really bad during this one fire. It was early in the morning. Some guy had a fight with his wife in a tenement. He threw gasoline around and lit it—it was like a ball of fire. We were the first due engine. We were out in the hall of the fire building around 6:30, 7:00 A.M., and people were still in bed. I had no mask on—I was the nozzle man. The fire had come around us, and as we were stretching the hose into the building people were screaming hysterically, "There's kids in there!" The kids we found in the front rooms were almost incinerated from the fire. The kids toward the back we were able to save; the truck company got them out. We were just pushing and pushing, and the next thing I knew, I couldn't take it anymore. After we knocked the fire down I remember them carrying me out and putting me in the ambulance. They took me up to Bellevue. I was there three days. Then I went back to the medical office with the X rays from Bellevue. The doctor said to me, "You need some more time off; your lungs don't look so good."

I was sent over to the fire alarm dispatchers office in Staten Island and put to work licking envelopes or something like that—light duty, no exposure to smoke. I spent the next six or eight months on light duty in that office. Then I went to this doctor, Dr. Castellano, and he said, "Your lungs are no good. You should be getting out of this business." But that's not for me. I tell the guys, especially when I am out campaigning for a union office, "Put on that mask. Every time you put on that mask, think of it as another paycheck. And if you think of it that way, you'll want to wear it all the time." I'd love to see all the firemen, like the teachers, lying on the beach in Florida when they are ninety years old. Firemen die young.

One time, when I was running for office in the union, I was in the quarters of 9 Engine in the Chinatown section of Manhattan having coffee, talking to the guys. It was after midnight and an alarm came in: "Engines only—car fire on Allen Street," which is around the corner from the firehouse going north.

I was talking to George Duignan. It was the second time I'd been in 9 Engine during that week. Once on the day tour while I was there they had a second alarm—next to Fellini's restaurant down on Mulberry Street. Now I said to George, "Jesus Christ, I hope this ain't another second alarm."

He said, "Relax, it's a car fire around the corner."

There were only a few guys from 6 Truck up, so I walked outside. I was on the apron as 9 Engine drove out; I'm about to close the firehouse doors. The truck is going to take the house watch. I said, "Gee, they got a job; it smells like a job." I could smell smoke.

But again they said, "Car fire."

With that a car comes screeching around the corner of Eldridge and Canal right toward the firehouse. It's a station wagon full of Chinese, and they are screaming. As they're screaming I said, "They're coming. The firemen are coming!" I assumed they were talking about the same fire. With this, the bell starts to go off on the teleprinter, and the fireman walks out of the house watch office and he says, "The box is two-twelve, on East Broadway—a fire in a restaurant." Now I realize that the smell was not a car fire; it was a job. I ran across the street and got in my car. I followed 6 Truck. The truck made a right-hand turn, because all the people are screaming to go into the back of Chatham Square. The people are pointing down the street, so the truck turned into the block. As I got there I could see people in front of the East Broadway movie theater pointing down East Broadway. So I made a left to get to the front. I got there nose to nose with 6 Engine, which came up from lower Manhattan. In the meantime 9 Engine was at the car fire only two blocks away.

A commercial building was fully involved; it was something like a movie scene where a plane hits a building. The whole first and second floor and part of the third are fully involved in fire.

The tenement next to it appeared to be a good structural building with no fire in it. Later on, we realized the fire had traveled from the original building by blowing out into this building. The owner or somebody had cut giant holes from the commercial building into the tenement next door. The Chinese will often take a building and do whatever they want without anybody knowing about it. This fire incinerated the rear of the tenement with no smoke at all coming out of the front. So here the men were engaged in one building, and lo and behold, when the second due truck began making the search of the adjoining buildings they started to bring the bodies down a long, long stairway to me, and guys kept screaming.

The guys from 6 Truck—I think, Jimmy McHenry and Captain Richard Fanning—were working along with Roger Eidelberg. They took some beating. They would come down to the bottom of this long stairway, and they'd hand me a limp body, and one guy maybe would stay with me under the canopy. We'd try to get the body out of the way of all the glass coming down. Then they would bring another one down, and I'd look over and a guy would be yelling to another guy in EMS to get him an oxygen mask. I remember going over to the battalion van and telling them to send in all available EMS because we had multiple D.O.A.'s and possible D.O.A.'s. I think we had eleven possible D.O.A.'s.

The final count was eight or nine dead; but we only monitor the injured for twenty-four hours. The sad part of it is, if a person dies two days later it's not considered a fire fatality in our books. And if he or she does die later, we don't know about it. Usually if someone gets burned internally it takes two or three days to die. But that's the fire department's way of downplaying the statistics. I felt bad because, at first, I was in front of the building taking pictures. I had no fire clothes on, and you feel so helpless when you don't have turnout gear. I said, "Shit, I could have gone up the stairway. Maybe I could have awakened the people." But from what they told me the rear rooms of the tenement had plywood partitions and bunks maybe six high, like on a ship. Those poor people didn't have a chance.

During this fire I had bodies lying here and there. I ran and got a resuscitator, wondering which one I should put it on first. And it seems for some reason you always want to save the smallest—the babies. Yet this one woman, maybe she would be alive if I'd put it on her.

Across the street and up maybe eight buildings there used to be a firehouse, but it was closed. They made a Chinese supermarket out of it. It used to be old Squad 5's quarters. Who knows? Maybe if that engine company had been there, many of those people would be alive. It's always easy to second-guess it later.

In the busy days the chief would come in the kitchen and say, "You guys did some fucking job," and he really meant it because he was right in there with us. Guys like Marty Lawler and Chief Whitney would be behind us at a job, and we would hear them saying, "I thought you were a good engine company." We'd get mad, and somehow the line would be picked up and just fly through the rooms. They would give us that little zing to get us moving.

After I came back from my lungs being burned, I used to tell the guys, "We're crazy to do this. Let's wear the mask." My motto, which I used to write on the blackboard, was "The day of the beat is over." Once you come up with a slogan, however, everybody's going to mimic you. I used to find it written on my locker door, "The day of the beat is over."

Well, then we had a job someplace on Broome Street, the top floor. They carried me out of that one. We really took some beating; the whole engine and the truck were wiped out. We didn't let up. We really pushed in and we got the fire down, but I was wiped out—no mask again. Chief Whitney put the big flashlight in my eyes to see if I was dead or not. Then he said, "You told me the day of the beat was over."

Chapter 10

Captain Daniel J. Tracy
Ladder 110, Brooklyn

I'm in the job twenty-five years. In 1958 I was kind of fishing around for a direction to follow. I was attending St. John's University. I had been in the service. I had worked at several jobs, and I wasn't happy in any of them. Opportunities at the time weren't that good, and I didn't see any future in what I was doing. Because I had several friends who were encouraging me to take this job, and because I admired fire fighters, I decided to give it a try.

I was a little nervous at the beginning, because I was assigned to a busy company. I didn't know that places like that existed. I always thought that a firehouse was a neighborhood spot, very quiet, and they went out every once in a while. And here I was in the heart of the ghetto. The men were doing a relatively high number of runs, about 1,600 a year at that time. I think the only company that was doing more was 26 Truck up in Harlem, and they were doing around 2,000. The going in and out, which doesn't even compare to what you have today, took me aback, and I wondered if I had made the right decision coming in to the job. I thought about leaving it.

I had a good friend named Eddie Wetzel. He retired as a battalion chief recently and became a deacon in the Catholic church. He said then, "Give it a chance. Stay around. See how you like it. Don't give up too easily. Give it a good shot."

And that's what I did. And, of course, I fell in love with

the job, as most of us do. I settled into the firehouse routine and got used to the idea that it is a demanding job. I found that not only was it demanding, but it is a very rewarding job. And, as I say, I've been in love with it ever since, and it's been a great love affair.

At my first fire—the first one that wasn't a mattress or a couch, I mean, or something hidden away in a rear room where you only saw smoke—I realized what a dangerous job we have. It was in a paint store. It was really a hardware store, but it had a lot of paint in it. It was on Livonia Avenue in Brooklyn, in an L-shaped structure. A wood frame building with the store on the ground floor and three stories of apartments above. We were the first due truck, the unit assigned to respond when the initial alarm is reported. Engine 283 had gotten to the fire ahead of us. Just as we pulled up, all the front and side show windows blew out, and a ball of flame rolled out into the street and enveloped the entire front of the building. That was the first time I had ever seen fire erupt out of a building, and I was absolutely astounded.

Prior to that it would be a mattress or some other piece of furniture that had been carelessly ignited, and we had to do the hallway routine. That was very punishing. But I just didn't understand what fire was until that night at the paint store. It was like daylight in the middle of the night. It was a real eye opener. Fortunately, there were no civilians injured at the fire. Everybody had gotten out of the apartments above the store, but it was a big indicator of what was to come over the years. I've seen plenty more like that where people were injured and, unfortunately, killed, but I was very impressed by that one particular fire, on that particular night. It's always stood out in my mind.

Being a professional, you like to think that you're not afraid. You're aware of what can happen, you're aware of the dangers, you're aware of the injuries that can occur. You try not to be fearful, but you're working in total darkness, and all of us are fearful of darkness. The lack of air and unfamiliar surroundings—it's all very fear-inspiring. But we're trained, we're experienced, and though the fear hangs over us, it doesn't guide our actions.

Have I ever been frightened? I guess I have by explosions. One time when I was a lieutenant, we had an obvious arson fire in a frame building on New Jersey Avenue, just down the street from the firehouse. When we went into the hallway, there was a sudden eruption of flames. We couldn't understand what had caused it. Later we found that someone, probably the guy who set the fire, had gone into various areas of the building and placed little storage baggies with maybe a pint of gasoline in each one. As the fire approached these bags, the gas would ignite and explode. We were able to put the fire out pretty promptly. Then we discovered more of these bags hanging in closets and in various rooms. We knew then what had happened in the hallway that had frightened us—a bag of gasoline had exploded. I guess if you are frightened, you try to dispel it with your professionalism, your experience, and your training.

What part of this job have I found most rewarding? Well, that keeps changing for me. Over all, I think we do a tremendous job. I think the city of New York gets its money's worth out of the Fire Department. I've felt that way since day one when I walked in the door. Early on, I felt that the most rewarding part of the job was the saving of lives. Then, later, there is the feeling that you've done a terrific job just keeping this fire from going from one apartment to another. That's a great satisfaction. You've got the jump on this thing, and you've got to keep control of it. You realize you've prevented a lot of damage from being done. I think that realization carried me through the first ten years as a fire fighter and many years as a lieutenant. But then, you just kind of evolve.

As a lieutenant I got a great deal of satisfaction from dealing with the men in the Fire Department who have the leadership required to make a good fire fighting team. A couple of them, right off the top of my head, are the lieutenants I worked with: Curt Landgrebe who's now battalion chief in the Eighth Battalion; Larry Lee was a lieutenant I worked for for many years. He's over in the Thirty-fifth Battalion now. The present chief of the department, John O'Rourke, was my lieutenant for several years. My first captain on the job was Joe Gates; he was an outstanding fire officer. Of course, as you develop into a leader yourself, you try to emulate these people, or at least imitate them to a degree.

When I became a captain, I found the satisfaction that comes from passing my experience on to junior fire fighters, trying to train them to be effective and to operate in a safe manner and to maintain very high standards. We have to be demanding on this job. It's an emergency operation. You have to have immediate responses to orders, and you have to have particularly dedicated men.

The fire officers whom I've admired through the years all have a common philosophy. If you had to pin that philosophy down, I guess it would be that, number one, you get the job done. In other words, you put out the fire, protect property, perform well at emergencies. And, number two, you look out for the welfare of the other members of your department—and these thing all dovetail. For example, if you're looking out for the welfare of the members, you're training them to perform their duties in a safe way. And when you do that, you are achieving goal one, by making them more effective at putting out the fires.

To be a good fire officer you have to be very tough-minded. Sometimes you have to be rough in order to achieve the goal of extinguishing the fire and protecting lives. When somebody's not performing the way you feel he should, you have to call it to his attention. You expect him to perform up to the standards of the department—though it is a rare thing when they don't.

You also have to be aware that we perform a difficult job, and when those goals are very well accomplished by the firemen, you have to reward them. Unfortunately, we're civil service, and so we don't have a big system of rewards. There isn't much we can do for the men who have performed well. We can't give them a day off or tell them to take a little vacation. But I've always felt that peer approval and the approval of my officers was my reward. When somebody says, "You are a damn good fire fighter," that's always the highest thing anyone can say about a man on the job. It hasn't changed any in twenty-five years.

I think this job has—through the years that I've been in it anyway—the continuing problem of providing satisfactory amounts of good equipment. When a tool is lost or damaged at a fire, we have a great deal of difficulty replacing. We have to go through a lot of red tape. If I had to criticize the New York City Fire Department, it would have to be along those lines. It's a result of the penny-pinching that goes on. You get a tin cup attitude—"We don't have the money."

If I had to criticize the fire department in any other area, it would be the very short period of training that they give new fire fighters. When I came into the job, the training period lasted for three months. It has been reduced through the years to six weeks of training—it's almost ridiculous. The new members come to the firehouse prepared for certain things, but really not for fire duty. It's the fiscal realities, the higher-ups will tell you—there's not enough money available to train them for longer periods. They want them out of the probie school and into the firehouse as quickly as possible. And for as long as they're on the payroll, they want them performing at the firehouse. I suspect that they want to reduce the amount of overtime they're paying. This is where the problems seem to exist.

Thinking about the most significant events in my career as a fire fighter brings to mind my two close associates who were killed at fires. One was Bobby Meil who was killed in July of 1961 at a fire in the Grateful Laundry. We were in 120 Truck at the time, in Brownsville. I wasn't working that particular tour but my close friend Bobby Meil was. He was a second grade fire fighter—in other words, he had another year to go and he would have been a first grader with three years in. He had just come back from vacation, and it was his first night tour. Around midnight there was a fire at this laundry on Junius Street. They were operating on the roof to get ventilation. The fire had really been roaring on the inside and it produced enough heat to twist a very large I-beam. I think it was a three-foot I-beam, and of course when an I-beam is heated and twisted, it can force out a wall. This wall collapsed and a section of the roof opened up like a trapdoor right under him, and Bobby fell into the fire. Three other members who were on the roof with him were able to make it to another wall and jump off the building. The fire fighters made a tremendous effort to move through the interior and try to get to him. They used a couple of lines, but they just couldn't get to him in time.

When Bobby hit the floor, he went toward the rear—I don't know how he survived that long, but he went toward the rear of the building, even farther away from where the members were trying to get to him. He was burned to death. That had to be a very significant turning point in my life, because I was still a young fireman at the time and it was the first close-at-hand death I had ever experienced. Several members had been killed in those early years and I knew about them, but nobody that I had worked closely with.

Then, in 1971, exactly ten years later, John T. Dunne, the captain of 175 Truck, got killed in a fire. John had been up in 26 Truck where he was the captain of a second section. He went down to the Chief of Department's office and worked there for a while, before being asked to take over this new company that was being formed, 175 Truck. He had contacted me because he knew I was looking for a company in Brooklyn. He asked me if I'd like to work down there and I said, "Great." The firehouse was convenient to travel to, and there was a little bit of action there. It looked like an exciting proposition—a new company.

John was working this particular night in March 1971. I had worked the day tour, and he had relieved me that night. I got a call about five o'clock the next morning that he had been killed at a fire. What had happened was they had responded to a fire in a frame building over in Bushwick. There was a report of children trapped on an upper floor, and as the second due truck, they initiated a search of that floor, but they were forced out of the apartment. John Dunne took a fall in the apartment and got his mask tangled up with a bicycle. It was a strange kind of accident, but he burned to death.

These two deaths were really significant incidents in my career in the Fire Department. They brought home to me a reality that you have to keep filed in the back of your mind— that your life can be over in a very short period of time. You have to maintain your vigilance, and you have to stay on top of the operation. And you try to pass this along to the younger people. It's a dangerous job and this is how you have to do it. We emphasize that; we pound it into them.

I don't think those deaths changed my outlook on the Fire Department, because the department *is* my life. Just as I said, they reinforced my understanding that this is a particularly dangerous job. You can get killed in it. Bob Meil was a tremendous fellow, a very nice, pleasant guy; he never even cursed. You kind of toss the language around in this job, and you remember the ones who don't curse. He was one of them. Of all the fellows on the roof that night, if you had asked me which one I thought would get off, I would have had to say Bob, because he was very athletic. He was a powerful young guy. He's the last one I would have thought would get killed. John Dunne, with all his savvy and his know-how, with all his experience—it came as a tremendous shock to me that he was killed in a fire. He just impressed me. I knew him as a very talented, experienced fire officer. When he got killed, it really shook me. But it didn't change my attitude. My attitude is still that we have a dangerous job and the only way to deal with the danger is to know what you're doing.

It's hard to say which was the most dangerous experience I've had. One incident that comes back to me happened when I was in 175 Truck. We were the first due truck, and we went, once again, into a frame building. We went in under the high stoop, and we were on the first floor. The flat had very heavy fire conditions in it. We got into the hall, and there was a pair of sliding doors. We wanted to make a search, but we decided to leave those doors secure. We used a side service entrance to get into the fire apartment, and we began our search. I was with two fire fighters, Reginald Crenshaw and John Foley. As we started to make our search we realized that the fire was taking off on us. I told them that we had to get out. So we started for the door that we had come in by, but the fire must have just gotten into the ceiling, and now when we looked out into the hall, we saw flames. We decided to go out a rear window. I ordered John Foley and Reginald Crenshaw to get out, and they jumped through this window. However, it got so bad that I couldn't follow them. I just had to do something. I got down on the floor, and I remembered that when we came in we saw a cellar entrance right near the front door. So I pushed over to that door and sure enough, the cellar door was ajar. I rolled down the stairs into the cellar. Now I'm under the fire and the other two fellows are out at the rear. I knew they would be wondering what happened to me. I went over to where there's a little cellar window looking out into the back yard. I saw John Foley and I said, "John, John." He heard me calling him. But later on, he said that after he got out into the back yard with Reggie, he turned around and saw a ball of flame shoot out the window. He figured that was the end of me. Then, when he heard my voice, he thought it was an angel calling. We always laughed at that incident. John Foley thought an angel was calling him from the cellar.

That was a harrowing experience. Why that cellar door registered in my mind as I passed it, I have no idea. I tried to think back on it, I hardly even took notice of it, but it must have registered. That again is the experience that you pick up along the way in twelve, fourteen, fifteen years of fire fighting. You have a sixth sense of what you saw coming in, which is usually the way out. You should make mental notes all the time. I'm always noting where the doors are, which way I turned, and how I can get out of this place if things go sour.

I've always been assigned to truck companies. When I first came into the Fire Department, I was assigned to 120 Truck, and I worked there for just under ten years. I worked in 175 Truck as a lieutenant for six years. I've been a captain down here at 110 Truck for just under eight years. A truck company allows you to be an individual. We often talk about that. In an engine company, you are part of a team. You are required to stay with your group and get the water on the fire; your job is to extinguish the fire. As a truck man, you kind of go over and around the fire, not right to the seat of it. You're operating as an individual that way. You do have your forcible-entry team, which tries to locate the seat of the fire. It consists of the officer and two firemen. But you also have your roof man and your outside vent man. They become the above-fire team, and that's where a tremendous amount of excitement is. In a truck company you have to rely on your fire fighting experience. You have to make decisions based on conditions as you judge them. It gives you a great deal of satisfaction to operate as a truck man. You have to have the framework of the job knowledge. That's what you hang everything else on. You have your sequence of what has to be done at a particular assignment. For example, as a roof man, you go to the roof and ventilate, check the perimeter, then descend to floors above the fire and make searches.

I've never worked in an engine company, but I'm not trying to put that job down. Engine work is very demanding, very difficult, and because it's so difficult, it has to be very rewarding, but it's different from truck work. Throughout the years, I've always thought that it is really advantageous for the truck company to be in the same quarters with the engine company they do most of their work with. You're personally involved with the guys in the company, and as you perform your operation, in the back of your mind you have the idea that these are your friends in there, and the faster you do your job, the better off they're going to be. They're getting the shit beat out of them. And if you don't ventilate quickly, you'll hear about it from them. They'll say, "Where the hell were you when we were getting our brains kicked out?" That helps you perform your job a little better. Looking out for our "midgets."

I always thought that sharing quarters was a good idea, but sometimes you work with an engine company from another firehouse. If you're doing all or most of your work with another company, they can be both an inspiration and an inducement to perform well. When I was a fireman, we had that kind of a relationship with the 231 Engine. They were tough little guys, and they were very demanding. They didn't take any guff from us because we were starstruck in the truck company. They were just as tough as we were—a lot tougher probably.

Looking back on fires, they kind of all blend together to tell you the truth. So much overlapping. But some fires, just because of the difficulty, do stick out in your mind. I recall one fire on Howard Avenue, just off East New York Avenue, in a new-law tenement. Every apartment on the top floor was fully involved. It was such a difficult fire to extinguish. The bulk of the fire was inaccessible to outside power streams, so we had to use inside hand lines. It was difficult to force the doors and open up so the engine company could extinguish the fire. A lot of members were hurt. It was my first experience with the pressure building up in the cockloft to the point where there would be a smoke explosion. The products of combustion mix to a certain point; then they ignite and explode, bringing the ceiling down. I've seen it several times since then, but that was the first time I was aware of what was happening. The ceiling blew down on Engine Company 283, which was operating in the apartment. Everyone in the company was injured in that fire. They were burned, helmets blown off, and they lost control of the line. They had to beat a retreat from the apartment.

Another fire that sticks out in my memory was in the American Dinette, a first-floor store on Rockaway Avenue just off Livonia. The building was an old-law tenement, but there were no people living upstairs. The American Dinette

Company occupied all the floors throughout the building, and they had a display area for dinette sets on the main floor. We were able to go into the store standing up. There was smoke all over the place and an obvious fire condition, but we couldn't locate it. We had proceeded to the rear of the first floor of the store when suddenly another one of these ceiling explosions occurred. The entire ceiling was gone; all the flames rolled out of the ceiling. We hit the floor. A lot of us made for the front door and got out, but we had to go right back in and start operating. Now we've got a fire. Now at least we know what we're dealing with. That makes a difference. We had a line in there, but with all the confusion and mad dashing to get out when this ball of flame erupted, we had to regroup and move back in for our operations.

I remember one fellow from Squad 4. He had a mask on. When that ceiling blew he ran for the front of the building and out through the broken plate-glass window, and although he wasn't injured, he took off his mask, put it down on the ground, and kept walking. This was a culmination of a series of fires that he had been through in which he had these near misses. He went out of the job shortly thereafter on medical leave.

What was it like to be there? Well, there's a lot of yelling and shouting, but it's not confusion. You're trying to communicate and the only way to communicate is to shout, though one of the bad marks you can get against yourself at a fire is to be considered what they call "a shouter." You have to train yourself to keep a grip on yourself and remember that you're a professional. Everybody else is running around, all the civilians are running out, and they're all excited; everybody's panicking. But you're the professional; you have to keep a cool head, get your organization moving, and do what you have to do at a fire. A great deal of shouting goes on when things happen, such as a collapse of some kind. But, as I said, it's not confusion; it's really an attempt to communicate over the din.

It's very hard to describe the interior of an occupancy that's fully involved in fire. Hose lines are operating. If you have one or two lines going, the rush of the water out of the nozzles makes a tremendous noise, so it's very difficult to hear what anyone is saying. We do a lot of our communication by tapping one another and by pounding on each other's backs. Sometimes you have the power saw operating above you, and those saws make a tremendous noise. You can't communicate on the radio, either. You can't understand what is being said on the Handie-Talkie because of the din.

I recall having this problem at a fire I went to one time in a new-law tenement. Unfortunately, a few people were killed in it—two girls and their mother. We had gone up to the fire floor and forced entry into the apartment that was on fire. The lieutenant said he was going upstairs to see if he could check the apartment above. We were going in to secure the door so it wouldn't blow out into the hall.

I was with a fellow named Bob Love. He is now the captain of 2 Truck. He's one of the toughest men you'll ever meet, including at fires. He had the can, and I had the forcible-entry tools. We were going down the hall and he was using the can. I tapped him on the back twice and he moved forward. He operated a little more when I tapped him on the back again. He couldn't talk, and I couldn't say anything because it was so hot and smoky. We did that three times: I tapped him on the back and he moved up a little farther. Finally, we had to beat a retreat. The can was expended. We made as much of a search as we could, and then we went back outside to take a little bit of a blow.

I said, "Bob, why the hell didn't you come out when I tapped you on the back?"

And he said, "I thought you were telling me to move forward."

So there's sometimes a lack of communication at fires.

That particular job was very exciting. There was a boy-friend involved in that fire. He fell asleep on the couch. He must have been smoking, because he lit up a pillow. He got up and he extinguished it. But now, because he'd thrown water all over it, he couldn't sleep on it anymore. So he went into a bedroom where a couple of young boys were sleeping, piled the two little guys into one bed, and he slept in the other. We got this information out of him later. And because he didn't extinguish it properly, the fire on the couch reignited, took off, and consumed the apartment. The boyfriend was able to go out through a window into the courtyard. The fire escape in this apartment was in the kitchen and it was also on the courtyard. He was in the bedroom, about eight feet from the fire escape, I'd say—in other words, across this enclosed courtyard. Somehow or other, he got over to the fire escape. How the hell he did it, I don't know, but somehow he was able to get those two little guys by the hand and swing them over to another fire escape, and they escaped. But the woman and the two girls were trapped in the fire apartment at the rear with no fire escape whatsoever, and they were killed.

The stupidity of that man! I mean, he was very heroic for saving the kids' lives, but the stupidity of setting that fire really stayed with me.

Another fire that stands out in my mind happened after we had just initiated an interchange program in the Fire Department, maybe 1965 or 1966. Interchanging means going to another company in an outlying area. You operate where they normally operate, and they come up to your quarters and operate. It was an effort to spread out the workload in order to rest the members who were involved in a lot of fires. In order to qualify for interchange, you had to accrue a certain number of points. I forget exactly how it used to be, but in order to qualify for interchange you had to be just about worn out—practically on your knees. So the program was pretty welcome at the time.

In those days we had a covered apparatus because of the harassment at the time. People were throwing bottles and stones at us from the roofs, so we had to have a cover over our rig. That's why they cover all the trucks today. Well, anyway, the outlying company didn't have a covered rig, so when we interchanged, they used our rig and we used theirs. And while we were interchanged we got a multiple alarm over in Bushwick. They special-called us, not as the relocated company, but as 120 Truck, since the chief at the fire knew we were one of the few companies that had a power saw at the time. But he didn't know that we had exchanged rigs and that we were now driving an open apparatus. It was zero degrees on that particular night. I was the tiller man and we responded to Bushwick and Johnson.

It was a very unusual fire because it occurred in a row of four tenements with a common entrance that fronted on Bushwick Avenue; but the entrance was on Johnson. The common entrance to all four of these buildings was on the first floor. In there was a guy who manufactured pizza pie boxes and he had them all stored there. The fire started in this occupancy. It blew out the front windows, rolled up the front of the building, and totally involved all the floors. Most of the people were able to get out by way of the rear fire escape to the roof and get away from the buildings that way. Word was that the two truck companies that responded to the first alarm moved something like fifty people down their aerial ladders—146 and, I believe, 108 Truck.

Well, anyway, this thing was really going by the time they called us. We got to the fire, but we didn't have the saw, so they gave us an assignment to search. They had labeled the buildings A, B, C, and D. We had the job of searching the C building. We went up to the third floor. That's as far as we could go in the stairway. Then we initiated a search. We had split up—one part of the company went to the rear, another part of the company went to the front. Suddenly part of the floor above us collapsed. Now the guys who had gone to the front thought that the guys in the back were hurt and vice versa. But we met on this pile of rubble. They were looking for some people who were missing. The lieutenant went down to the chief in charge of the fire and told him that the floor had collapsed and that we had found a body in the rubble. From that, we surmised that there were some people on the top floor. They called one of the two tower ladders—Ladder 1. They got in front of the building and put the safety chief in the bucket. Up he went to the top floor and made a search. He discovered some more bodies, and then he knew this was a major tragedy. In that top-floor flat thirteen people were found, burned to death in the fire. It was probably the most disastrous fire I've ever been to in my life. It was a memorable fire for several reasons—because of the temperature, since it was zero degrees, absolutely freezing outside; because of the number of people who were killed; and because of the extent of the fire throughout all the building. It was a total disaster. Removing thirteen dead people from a fire is one of the most depressing things I've ever been involved in.

I have two Class III and two Class II awards. The first one I received was a Class III for a fire on Amboy Street in the Brownsville section of Brooklyn—a very high incidence area at the time. This was during the 1960s.

This particular fire was in an old-law tenement, on the first floor, and an interesting thing happened there—the kind of thing that reinforces how much you have to be aware of on this job. The first due company was Engine 283, and they had stretched their line. We used inch-and-a-half hose at the time. That's not a powerful hose, but in the hands of a determined company, it can be a very effective one. Engine 283 was a determined company, and they had the jump on the fire. They were in the first floor and they were moving along pretty good when a length of hose burst down in the street. The burst length meant that they had lost their water, but they were well into the flat that was involved in the fire. Because of the swiftness with which that company operates, they pass a lot of fire. They put out what they have to in order to keep moving and get the bulk of the fire knocked down. Then they usually backtrack. So they were moving along pretty well and they had gotten pretty deep into the apartment when they lost their water. Of course, once they lost it, they had to back out. In the meantime, 231 Engine was second due and had stretched their line up the stairs, relying on 283 to hold the fire. They had gone up the stairs trying to force entry with the truck when 283 lost their water. So the whole company was caught in the hall above the fire. They all jumped into the courtyard from the hall window—all of them, two stories into the courtyard. Thank God they weren't up higher.

At this particular fire there were two people—a very old man with just one leg who was confined to a wheelchair and a woman who kept house for him, a sort of caretaker. I was able to get in by dropping a ladder on the fire escape and entering the apartment from the floor above the fire. Things had gone sour at this point, and we couldn't get out the front door. I got the man over to the fire escape and handed him over the fire escape down into the courtyard. The difficulty of that, of course, was maneuvering this old-timer with one leg.

I received the second medal for removing five children from an apartment above a fire on Howard Avenue. I got them out on the fire escape, and my friend, John Connolly, came down from the roof and helped me round up the kids. When we were taking them down the fire escape, one of the kids said, "Billy is missing."

I went back in and found Billy unconscious. That was a very fortunate experience. The apartment below was fully involved and there was a line in position operating, but there was a great volume of fire. It was very smoky, and the kids were in real trouble. The only one who had her wits about her was the one nearest a window. She was trying to get out. She thought she was at the fire escape but she wasn't. The others were in the room with her so I was able to round them up rather easily. They were small kids. Of course, when she said, "Billy's missing," I went back in to find Billy and he was in the living room which was two rooms away from the fire escape route we were taking down.

I got a couple of Class II medals, also. One of them was at a fire in a corner building on Dumont Avenue. When we pulled up to the building, it was one of those classic examples of everything letting go at once. There was a store on the first floor, and the front windows let go just as a man, his wife, and their daughter were coming down the fire escape from the top floor. The man was on the first landing trying to get the drop ladder down and the other two were up above him. While he was trying to drop the ladder, the fire let go out the two windows in the store and engulfed him in flames. They had to use the can on him—his clothes were on fire—but they were able to get him off the fire escape. He was seriously burned, though. In the meantime, the woman and the girl had gone back up to the top floor.

Now, if you can picture this, the fire is blowing out the store windows, engulfing the fire escape so that way out is gone. They put up some ladders to the top floor—I don't recall if it was a four-story building—and we initiated an attack through the interior. There was another entrance on the side of the building, but the problem was that the store had a back door which is, I believe, illegal. It entered into the public hall and that, too, was on fire. They put the can on that and tried to hold it. I went up the interior stairs to the top floor and found this woman and her daughter on the floor. I was able to carry the girl. The woman was semi-conscious, but she had her legs under her and she was able to come down the stairs with me. By the time we hit the second floor, the rest of the interior team could give me a hand, and we got them down and out of danger. They weren't burned, but by now they were unconscious and had to be revived in the hospital.

I got the other Class II for a fire on St. Mark's Avenue just off Eastern Parkway in Brooklyn. I was the outside vent man at the time—the rear man they called it. There was a report of a trapped kid. This was a two-family house with an apartment on the first floor and an apartment on the second floor. There was a basement below and I think that was also occupied by a family. That made the building a multiple dwelling—it wasn't, however, a legal multiple dwelling. Anyway, the fire started down in this basement area, which was fully involved when we got there. What complicated matters was that the gas meters were in the front of the basement and they ignited right away. Now, these fires that involve gas are pretty serious. They screw things up for the forces operating in the front of the building trying to get a line in. The men weren't sure if they could extinguish this fire. They were trying to figure out what would be the best approach.

Meanwhile I had proceeded to the rear of the place through an adjacent building with another fellow in the company. He boosted me up to a window one floor above the ground, and I got in. I found the trapped kid on the bed. The fire was already burning through the floor of the apartment. He was actually just about a whisper away from death—the lamp over his head was already on fire. I grabbed him and ran to the rear. I didn't exactly know where the window was, though I had smashed it out before I came into the apartment. I hit the sill with my knee and went ass over teakettle straight out the window still holding the kid. Donald Healey was down below in the yard. He caught us as we fell and broke our fall. Thank God it was just one floor. Donald Healey, by the way, is retired now; he went out on three-quarter salary two years ago.

These were my exciting moments. I had a couple of minor awards for lesser actions, but these were probably my personal highlights.

I often think of those kids, you know, and I wonder what they're doing now. I feel like I gave them a new lease on life. I don't know, there must be a word for it—like God is watching out for us—you know, like you have guardian angels. All these thoughts start coming into my mind. What put me in that particular place that particular day and why was I at that fire? It's very mysterious. I'm almost certain it was fate in some circumstances. At times you just feel that things are preordained by God to happen a particular way. It just had to be. Too many things happening by coincidence make it impossible not to think there's some guiding force somewhere. Like I said before, it's very mysterious.

Of course, being a professional fire fighter, if you should think for one minute that a rescue was your own most outstanding singular achievement—yours alone—you'd be really full of shit. I mean, it's just ridiculous to think that way. Rescues are the direct result of teamwork; they're not just one person's singular achievement. If somebody doesn't do his job at a fire, there aren't going to be any rescues made. That was really brought out to me at one fire. Curt Landgrebe was at a fire on Sheffield Avenue one time, and he performed one of the most outstanding rescues I have ever seen or heard of. After it was all over, he told me that he knew exactly when I performed my own assignment at that fire, and he said that if I hadn't performed my assignment the way I did, he never would have been able to rescue that child.

Landgrebe made that rescue during a fire on the top floor of an old-law tenement. When we pulled up to the site, two apartments were involved, and 290 Engine and 103 Truck were committed to the first flat. Curt landed with the forcible-entry team and went through the interior to the floor above the fire and entered the second apartment, which was also heavily involved in fire; probably it had auto-extended. Anyway, he went up and penetrated the fire because there was a report that a kid was trapped on that floor.

My assignment at this particular fire was outside vent man, so I proceeded to the rear and initiated a vent. When you vent, you change the direction of the flow of heat and the flow of fire. Curt said that when he got to where the kid was supposed to be, he couldn't move an inch farther because of the tremendous heat. He was going to get burned to death himself. He said that just when he was about to give up, he heard the glass going—that was when I made the vent—and felt the whole nature of the fire change around him. And he said just at that moment the whole situation changed and he was able to move a couple more feet. Then he found the kid and got him out. The kid was really burned, but he recovered. I used to see him in the street quite often. He is badly disfigured, but here's a kid walking the streets even though he's disfigured. He's still alive and he seems to have adjusted well. Curt performed an outstanding act of heroism on this job—but heroism is a common occurrence among fire fighters. I thought he was just too willing and too quick to give the credit to somebody else, and that really impressed me. He's a great guy, Curt is, and he always impressed me.

A lot of funny things happen too. I can remember one thing

where we were roaring; I still laugh today when I think about it. It was on Watkins Street. It happened with 120 Truck where we had some cast of characters. One of them was Willie Forsberg who was quite a character. He was a great practical joker and was always pulling jokes on people. He had a predilection for firecrackers. He liked to throw firecrackers around when you least expected them. Little did we know that he himself was scared shitless of firecrackers. Well, we were getting ready for a semiannual inspection. Now they have annual inspections, but at the time, we used to have them semiannually. We had a thirty-five-foot portable straight ladder that weighed a ton. It was made of wood, of course, and the tip of it had been burned in a fire. Don't ask me why, but at the time if your ladder got burned at a fire, a lot of questions were asked, so we used to try to hide these things. The captain was going around looking for a better place to hide this thing. The cellar's no good; the chief is sure to check on it. So he figured that if he put it on the roof, probably the chief wouldn't go up there and it would be safe. Well, anyway, we had a courtyard behind the firehouse, adjacent to the kitchen. We took the portable ladder out there into the courtyard. We decided we were going to use the rope evolution to raise this portable ladder. We were going through that evolution and had hooked the ladder up on a rope. The guys were pulling it up. Now we're all standing out there in the courtyard, and Willie Forsberg is standing there with us. A couple of guys on the roof are pulling the ladder up, and a fellow named Eddie Casson had a two-shot repeater firecracker. You light it up and throw it, and it goes *pop*, and it shoots another firecracker into the air. The second one is much bigger. He throws this out the window and it goes *pop*, and we all said, "'You son of a bitch. That's a dirty trick.''

All of a sudden there was a boom. We all thought the ladder had fallen, and we dove through the window into the cellar. Of course, Forsberg was the leader of the group diving into the cellar. It was probably his firecracker.

Another incident involved Jackie Boyle. He is now the captain of 5 Engine, but at the time he didn't even have a wooden locker. Back then, if you had a wooden locker in that firehouse, it was a sign of prestige and showed that you'd been around for a while and had some seniority. But he didn't have one and so he decided to take a pole out of the pole hole and where it had been, he put in a floor. Of course, the pole hole had doors on it so he put a lock on the door and a couple of hooks and hangers there. Now he had himself a wall locker. Larry McCarthy, whom we worked with, decided that he'd pull a joke on him. So he gets the lock off Jackie's locker and goes out on the roof. He sets up a box propped up by a stick with a string on it, and he puts some popcorn or Cracker Jacks under the box to attract a pigeon. He traps the pigeon and takes it and puts it into Jackie's locker and of course the bird shit all over everything.

But, like I say, it's so goddamn exciting—the fires, I mean—that you run the risk of giving the impression that you're in this business for the excitement of it. Most of us *are* in it for that. There's a certain macho element in the Fire Department.

We reflect all the time that this is an exciting business. But I think if we really knew what was waiting for us at some of these boxes, we wouldn't be in the job. As I said, it's so exciting that the adrenaline just goes. The challenge of it grabs you—fire is a formidable enemy. To tackle it and overcome it really is probably one of the most exciting things you can do. It's just an unbelievable experience.

When my daughter was very tiny, for some reason or other, she used to like to stand at the top of a flight of stairs and put her toes over the edge, just for that feeling of almost falling, but not quite. Whatever it is in human nature that makes a little child do that is still in us when we're grown men, and that's what I think goes on at fires—you're teetering on the brink.

Chapter 11

Lieutenant John Vigiano
Rescue 2, Brooklyn

I did not like the life of the insurance adjuster. The going to and from the office on subways, the pettiness of working with people who were constantly talking about their salaries—how much this one makes and how much that one makes. I wanted to do something that had a meaning. I took the firemen's test and the policemen's test. My father had been a fireman, in fact he retired after thirty-five years. But since my parents were separated when I was young, I really didn't know much about the Fire Department. However, on the fireman's test I got pretty good marks and I was called by them first.

When I first came on the job I was shocked to find out that on a fire truck, when you went to a fire, you rode with four men and an officer. For some reason I thought when you went to a fire you went with twenty men on a truck. But the best part was to work with these people. At that time we didn't have the manuals or the formal schooling we have now. What you learned, you learned from your co-workers. And I was fortunate—I worked in a unit where there was a lot of *esprit de corps*. There was a lot of work, so consequently we had a chance to do those things that had been demonstrated or explained to us. We developed from that.

Once I'd joined, my outlook on the Fire Department changed. It was nothing like the stereotypes that you read about—you know, the guy with the red suspenders, the Dalmatian dog, and checkers. I don't think I've never seen a checker game in a firehouse. I've only seen one Dalmatian. He was in a parade. And red suspenders seem to be something somebody would wear for a joke. It's a unit of hardworking men. A lot of humor, and at times a great deal of tragedy. But for the most part it's more fun than anything else.

When I went to my first fire, I think I'd only been in the company for two days. It was the start of my night tour. We had to relieve a company that was operating at the fire. It was on Belmont Avenue in the East New York section of Brooklyn. We got there and the fire was in a tanning factory; they take rabbit skins and make furs or whatever they do with them. The building was what they call mill construction. I now know that trying to put a hole in the ceiling of one of those buildings is impossible, because it's just thick beams—there is no ceiling per se. But with the smoke you can't see that, and me being the new kid on the block, I didn't know mill construction from cardboard construction. I didn't even know there was such a thing. I remember trying desperately to put a hole in the ceiling, and all I kept hitting was beams. Because I was a probie, I had a hook and the can. It ended up we had to knock down a wall. When the smoke partially cleared on the other side of this wall I saw a fireman smoking a cigar, and he's telling me, "It's all right, kid; we got it." I was overwhelmed. I asked, "How can you be smoking in all this crap?" It really wasn't much of a fire because we were relieving a unit that was already there.

The first fire that I could sink my teeth into and say that I did something I'm paid for—though by my standards now it wasn't much of a fire—was on New Lots Avenue in Brooklyn in an apartment over a store. We got in there first. The engine company was having trouble getting a hydrant, so I was told to go down the hall with a can, get in the door of the fire apartment, and put out whatever was burning. It was a mattress, I believe. It's amazing how much fire you can put out with an extinguisher. But you really don't think about what you're doing. All they want is the can. You have a guy with you, and he's telling you, "This way, that way," and you know that everybody is watching. They are not really looking at you, but you wonder if you're going to measure up—are you going to do your job? You do it, and when it's all lifted and everything is almost normal, the guy with the irons comes over, and says, "Hey, that's the way to do it." And

Captain John Quinn said to me, "Nice job." You find out that even after twenty-two years those words probably mean more coming from one fireman to another fireman than anything else. At the time I knew the captain was happy with my performance. I was happy—Christ, here I went to a fire.

Today I would call that a routine nickel-and-dime fire, the basic type of fire that firemen fight—the one room that's put out with a can. I don't even know if they charged the line, or for that matter if they even stretched the line. They probably did. I don't know, all I remember was I had a chance to use the can and it went well.

The first multiple alarm that I went to was also the first loss of life I saw. Again, it was on Belmont Avenue—Belmont and Powell, 184 box. It was in the winter; it was cold. I remember seeing Christmas trees in some of the windows. It was the first time I got roasted by the other men. It was a second alarm in a four-story tenement. We had fire on two, maybe three, floors, and at that time that was a lot of fire, especially for me.

I don't know where we ended up; I know we were above the fire someplace, on the third or the fourth floor, because we were a second due truck company. We had to breach a wall in one of the apartments to get in, and there were two occupants in there. One was a kid. They were burned. It was tough. I had never seen death directly. Growing up in the street, I'd sort of seen some of it, but it was usually from a knife fight or a gun fight—and they were rare. My view of death had always been over somebody's shoulder or between somebody's arms. I heard about it and ran down the block, but ninety percent of the time it was over before I got there.

At a fire where somebody is actually dead, the first thing you ask yourself is "Could we have saved this person? What could I have done?" And as you think about it, you realize there is nothing you could have done. You're just part of that whole mechanism that puts out these fires. As a junior man you have to put this person—this body—into a body bag. It struck me then, and it has stayed with me for the whole time, how solemn that moment was. The kidding around stopped. No jokes. There is no gallows humor at this time.

We wrapped the child in a sheet or something off a bed and placed it in a bag and tied the bag up. Then we had to do the same thing for the adult. And again I felt I was being watched.

You know. Am I going to bug out? Am I going to get sick? But I knew it wasn't the time to fool around. I did what I had to do, and then the bodies were carried out and were put in an ambulance.

The next day there were some jokes, mostly about me. "Jesus did you see the kid? Looked like he was going to throw up," and stuff like that. But the only thing that really struck me during the fire was how solemn this was. Everybody felt that the deaths were their responsibility. It's a strange feeling, and it passes, but it is there for a moment. That was my first multiple alarm—1684 box. I don't remember the day; I just know it was around Christmas, and it was cold.

There's many facets of this job that I find rewarding. Saving a life, naturally, is one of the top ones. But saving a life is a chancy thing; you may or may not get that opportunity. I've worked with some great firemen who never saved anybody. These men don't have any limits, and I'd give anything to be like them. They're excellent firemen. They did their job day in and day out. They just never had an opportunity to be there when somebody had to be pulled out of a building. But when you put out that fire or you make the search, or when you take that door and you get in there at the head of the line and you've done it right, that satisfaction is nirvana. You look around and everybody's smiling, everybody's happy.

I enjoy being a fire fighter. I thoroughly enjoyed having the can or the irons. I thought they were the most challenging jobs. With the irons you have to force that door. Everybody's waiting; nobody moves until the door opens. It's you against *it*. You challenge *it*. If you're the can man and the door is open, you've got to get in there to use that can to hold that fire in check, because you know somebody is going to be making a search. And in those days it was really a race with the engine company. And Christ, if you could ditch water on the fire before the engine did, that was something to break their chops with. Most of the time, though, if it was any kind of a decent fire, forget it. They were going to get in there ahead of you because there is just no way you're going to get in.

Then I got assigned to an engine company, when I first got promoted, and that was another feeling of accomplishment.

Taking a line down a hallway. Make a room and knock down the fire in it, then make two rooms. You're talking to a nozzle man. "Come on a little more, do this do that."

As much as I liked being a fire fighter, the satisfaction was multiplied tenfold after I became an officer. Now I could direct, I could suggest; the guys would do what I wanted them to do. Working in Rescue 2 is *ba-a-a-ad!* I put my books away. I have no intention of studying, because I don't want to be promoted; I don't want to leave this company. If somebody would guarantee that I could come back here as a captain if I got promoted, then I'd say, "Well, I'll take a chance." But I really don't want to risk being sent somewhere else. If I *had* to leave here, I would want to work in an engine company. When I first came on the job, the engine was the place to be. I used to laugh, because the men in the engine companies are the little guys we used to make fun of all the time. I have nothing but respect for them today.

A rescue company does everything and anything. Rescue 2 today is a throwback to when I came in the job. I went through the roaring sixties into the seventies. I had the opportunity, or the luck, to live through and work in probably the busiest, toughest time in the history of the New York City Fire Department. From the riots to the second sections and interchange, the relocations, forty runs a night. Ten thousand runs a year! Numbers like that are staggering, but those days are over. When you did that day in and day out, you learned your trade and you learned it well. During that time you built something. The men were cocky, but they were good and they knew they were good. They would go to any fire and they would treat it the way it had to be treated.

In a company like Rescue 2, everybody is right where he wants to be. You have to volunteer for this unit. We go to every major fire in Brooklyn—sometimes we go to Manhattan, Queens, and Staten Island as well—and we go to any and all emergencies. If I say to my guys right now, "I want to go out and work on a Hurst tool," they won't say a word. In fact, most times they'll ask me, "When are we going out to a drill?" And our drill isn't according to the clock—say, from 9:30 to 10:30, or from 1:30 to 2:30. It's from when we start to when we finish. We've had drills that lasted five hours. It seemed to be the thing to do that day. When these men go to fires, they never ask for relief, they never ask for any R&R.

The guys will work with burns on them the size of a small dinner plate; the skin will be peeled right off, but they will get it bandaged up and they'll work that way for the next two or three weeks. If the burn gets infected, they'll just keep putting Silvadene on it. It's a carryover from the sixties and the seventies. These are the same people I worked with back then. The best ones. When we go out to a job, the job will be done, if it can be done. Whether it's my group, Captain Downey's group, Artie Connelly's group, or Jimmy Rogers' group; it makes no difference. You can take the officer right out, and the guys will still do the job. It's a tremendous company. And I have to believe all the rescue companies are capable of that kind of work.

There's a couple of Emergency Service cops who hate us. Emergency Service has had their times with us. We've had our times with them. I think it's competition. I mean, if you're riding in your car or if you're walking in the street and you see a cop, what's the first thing that crosses your mind? You say to yourself, What did I do? I think sometimes we perceive cops as the enemy. Yet when you see a fireman you know he is a nice guy. The cops think that the only good publicity they get is when they perform emergency service work. They take a guy off a bridge, they pull some kid out of the river, they help somebody out of an accident. And that's what we do, too—except the bridge rescues. I'm sure if we were told we had to do bridges, we'd become experts in that, too. So the cops find us a challenge. And I'm not talking about a street cop, I'm taking about Emergency Service. Big difference. We're their competition. And they don't want to lose the publicity they get from making rescues. I don't think I've ever had a problem with a street cop. They're out there, they're fighting the elements, and when we have a fire they direct traffic or give us a hand if we need it. But with Emergency Service cops, we have locked horns more than once.

One time an Emergency Service cop was killed while he was trying to get a guy to release a hostage. They do a lot of the same type of work as the Rescue. So when they had his funeral, one of my guys and I said, "Let's go." Most guys thought we were crazy, since we're always, it seems, standing on opposite sides of the fence from the Emergency Service. But I said, "We owe him that much respect." I later found out that he was the brother of a fireman who used to work for me. But at the funeral we were right in the middle of a crowd of E.S. cops. They just looked at us and we just looked at them. Nobody said hello, nobody said thank you; not a word was exchanged. But that night when we were working, two E.S. cops stopped by to thank us. That made me feel good.

I've had some good jobs with emergency cops. One was a year and a half ago below McDonald Avenue. We got a call—a woman under a subway train. We had been practicing removing people from under a train for a couple of years. The Transit Authority Emergency Service units are specialists in it. They trained all the Fire Department rescue companies, and they were training Emergency Service cops, also. We got there and sure enough there was a lady under the train. It was summer and it was in the early evening, so it was still pretty light out. There was a cop in the trough between the tracks and he couldn't budge her. Transit PD had set up their air bags, and we came along with ours. Between the three units we lifted the car up and we got her freed. And actually the difficulty wasn't so much that she was pinned, because the train wheel had severed her arm off, but her face was bonded to the side of the wheel. That was one of the reasons we couldn't budge her. We actually had to pull her face right off the wheel. When the brakes are applied a tremendous amount of heat is built up in the wheels and the rails. Since she was under the train, the wheel stuck to her face. The amazing thing about this was that the woman was alive. She was hit by a train and dragged forty, fifty feet; she lost an arm and had half of her face burned away; and she was still alive. It's remarkable how much the human body can take.

At first I thought she was dead, but then Al Steinhart, who was underneath the car, said, "No, she's still alive." Al went under the car head first. Craig Shelly went in from behind the wheel truck; he was trying to push the leg. I was on the outboard side with two of the other guys. We raised the car up about three inches. The whole job took only maybe eight or nine minutes. And there was no animosity between any of the three services—the Emergency Medical Service was also there. We got along great with them. I think most of the problems between cops and firemen are individual problems.

It's personality—that one cop or that one EMS guy or that one fireman.

We've also gone to numerous subway fires, and you feel for the people who are stuck on a rush hour train on a Friday afternoon trying to get home from work. To be taken from one car to another, when it's 100 degrees and it's black, with the smell of smoke, the unknown—Christ, what an awesome feeling that is. Especially for the old ones. We take the passengers down through the cars and occasionally across catwalks from one train to another train. Other times we take them right down into the trough and walk them up onto the platform. It depends on where the car broke down or where the fire is. Those are just long-lasting jobs. Usually the fire isn't confined just to the undercarriage, so we have to cut out the floor of the subway car. A lot of smoke, very hot, humid, and debilitating.

In the instance of a subway fire the engine companies definitely have to wait until they know where the fire is and what platform to go down. Do they go down the emergency stair? Jesus, if they stretch to the wrong platform it could be another thousand feet to the fire. Their problems are monumental. In most cases the ladder companies find the location for them. Occasionally we have to find it and tell them where it is. A lot of manpower is wasted, but there's nothing you can do about it. Once you get underground, the radios are only good for about fifty or sixty feet, so unless you set up a relay you lose communication. You wonder how you did this job in the sixties when you didn't have any radios. I wouldn't want to do this job again without a radio. The radio is one of my best tools.

In the rescue company we go to some places that are incredible. Just last year we had a job in the Hudson Street power plant. It's a big building—Christ, it must be six stories high. It's full of power units; it's a maze. The fire was in a transformer, and it just kept lighting up. They had already extinguished a portion of it when we got there. At least six or seven extinguishers were already depleted. We were kept standing fast in the street for twenty minutes after we arrived, so somebody from Con Edison was fooling around in there; somebody was trying to put it out without calling us in. When we got inside, we asked them to give us all their CO_2 and foam extinguishers, but ironically, we ended up putting the fire out with a water extinguisher. No matter how much CO_2 or how much foam we put on it, the metal was so hot it just kept relighting the oil. We had to cool the metal. Nothing cools better than water. So we used a water extinguisher. And your training bulletins? In a fire like this one, you throw them right out the window. The safety chiefs would jump out the window if they heard of using water on a transformer in the middle of all this awesome electrical power—more volts than I can remember, 100,000 volts, 200,000 volts. Incredible. I mean these Con Edison people throw volts around like you're talking about the national debt. And they walk around in that power plant with all the confidence in the world. They just tell you, "Make sure you don't go out of this area." We had to work in an area about ten by twelve feet. And we stayed in that area. It's funny how we perceive things, and how those guys perceive them. We'd ask them, "Any holes in the ceiling?" And they would say, "Naw, naw, it's all solid." So we'd say, "But how did the conduit get to this floor from the next floor?" And they'd reply, "Oh, it's all encased." But when the smoke cleared, we could see daylight overhead. We know then that when they were putting that conduit in they chipped away a little more than they should have, so there's a hole there. "Oh, yeah," they'd say. "Well, that's always been there." They don't perceive fire the way we do, either, that it travels through cracks and up stairs. That particular night we were there for about an hour and a half.

Con Edison, like most of these major companies, has its own small fire brigades. They try to control everything themselves before they let outside people come in—meaning the Fire Department. I think their motives are selfish, however. They know if we go in we're going to shut them down. And when they get shut down they lose money. It's the same with the Transit Authority. They don't want us to shut down their train. It's money, it's people, it's time. They don't really want the Fire Department there, they'd rather handle it themselves. When the Navy Yard had a fire on a ship, the *Constellation*, they waited a long time before they called in the Fire Department. They wasted time while they tried to handle it themselves. They had a tremendous loss of life because of it. Most of these big companies don't want to call the Fire Department, they know we don't put up with nonsense. We say, "You've got power? Turn it off. We're going to work in that area." And even that's not a guarantee that they'll turn it off. We've been on trains and subway lines after being assured that the power was off, when all of a sudden we'd see a light blinking and hear a train coming at us. Somebody screwed up. When they say the power's off, maybe ninety percent of the time you can believe it's off. But you treat it like it's live. We have what's called a third-rail tester. It's a primitive tool, but it's very effective. It has a little battery box you use to test the tester. Then you test the rail. Then you test the tester again to make sure it's still working. If you touch this tool to the third rail and the light goes on, you have power; if the light stays off you have no power. That little piece of primitive equipment has kept us out of a lot of trouble lately, because you really cannot trust the Transit Authority. You can't trust anybody—I've been burned too many times. You don't assume anything. You go on what you know for sure. Go with your facts.

There was a fireman from Rescue 1—he was later transferred to Engine 303 in Jamaica—who was struck by a diesel train in the Jamaica yards. All the power was off, they said, so the firemen were in there doing their job, and a diesel train came through. It didn't kill him, but I always remember that guy who got hit by a train. How could they leave the power on while we're in there? Now when we go to any of these incidents I treat it as if all the tracks are live and all the trains are running.

Same thing happens at fires once in a while. We're told to go in and make a search. We've got some great companies in there doing the job already, and now we have to go through there. Then somebody from another company says, "Hey, I did that. What's the matter, don't you trust me? Don't you take my word for it?" And what do I tell them? I'm in a Catch-22 situation. If I take his word for it and then find out that the job isn't done, my credibility is ruined. I have to be diplomatic and say, "Oh, we're looking for something specific," or, "I lost something." And we end up making a second search—only in some cases it's really the first search.

The most significant event in my career as a fire fighter was the feeling that I had that day in City Hall when I got my first medal. They had the band from Power Memorial High School, and we didn't just stand in front of City Hall, we marched into City Hall Park. I remember hearing the band

and seeing my friends, the guys I worked with. Then when we got into City Hall Park they called us up and the mayor gave us our medals, and we heard everybody cheering. I started back to the ranks and saw thirty guys from my company there. I had my family there, too. My father was there, and he was still in the job at the time. A feeling of real achievement.

I'd only felt like that four times before. Once, and it might sound a little corny, was the day I graduated boot camp at Paris Island. I'd spent three months down there really going through a lot of shit, so when the D.I. came over and said, "You're a marine," I had that same feeling of accomplishment—and pride. I really had chills down my back when the band was playing.

Another time I felt that way was when my first son was born. Maybe the feeling is synonymous with firsts. But I was working that night and I got a phone call that I had a son—Christ, there was nothing I couldn't do that night—and I probably would have tried to do it all, but they told me to go home. The lieutenant said, "Do us all a favor. Go visit your son in the hospital." And I did.

The third time was when I received my bachelor's degree, after kicking that around for twelve years, at Carnegie Hall. That felt good, too—maybe because of the fact that I was playing Carnegie Hall. I had my family there for that, too. My boys were old enough to understand what I'd had to go through to get that sheepskin. God knows, they had to suffer. They would say, "I got a ball game tomorrow," and I'd answer, "I've got a term paper that I've got to knock out." I'd only stay for a quarter of the game.

My fourth time was when I won the Fund for the City of New York Award; it is something that the Ford Foundation puts up—a five thousand dollar grant, tax free, which was really something. I was only the second fireman to win that award, so for me it was awesome—to be picked out of the whole Fire Department when there are so many dynamite guys out there. It was great for my family, it was great for this fire company, and it was great for me—and the five grand didn't hurt either. My wife's biggest dream—she wanted to go to Hawaii. So we took $3,500 of the grant money and put it in one of those money market accounts. The rest I spent on the family—bought them a VCR, bought myself a better stereo system, bought a new TV for the house. And six months later somebody broke into my house and stole it all. But that money was a family gift, everybody shared in it. It was nice. And I look back and I've got a plaque on my wall and some fine memories.

The first time you get an award you say, "Wow, I did this!" But with maturity you realize you're just representing the guys who didn't get it. They call your name out on medal day and you walk up there and they hand you a ribbon with a piece of gold on it. It's nice. Your family thinks "Hey, my father is a hero." "My husband is a hero." There's nothing more exhilarating for a fireman than to be recognized. Now, instead of recognizing only twenty-five of us, like they did in 1968 when I got my first medal, they're giving fifty of them. That means fifty guys are going to have that feeling that I had. And I think it's great. They give you a reward. But the medal is just a little bit more. So you take it as a token that you're representing all the guys who did the job but didn't get the recognition. And if you keep that frame of mind, you won't go crazy; you won't think you're somebody you're not. I have guys in my company who should have ten medals, but they never got any, never got the recognition. You have to reward some of these people. Especially engine companies. They take a pounding day in and day out. They get shit for it.

I worked with a guy in 103 Truck who has twenty-four years on the job right now, and he doesn't even have a Class B decoration. But I know he carried me out of a burning building, down three flights of stairs, when he found me unconscious in a hallway. On that particular night we were responding to a box and there must have been a screw-up somewhere along the line. The dispatcher had reports on fires in two locations and was sending the assigned company to the other location. He sent us to a four-story NFB—non-fireproof building. A regular brick new-law tenement, but it wasn't a big new-law tenement. It was longer than it was wide, much longer. At that time we were riding with seven men. Bob Blume was the lieutenant; he's now a chief in the First Division. When we got there, fire was showing on the first floor front. The building was fully occupied: we had people showing out of about five windows. And we were all by ourselves. The chauffeur threw the aerial ladder up to the roof. It was an isolated building, so we wanted to make sure the roof man got up there. Fire was coming out the rear, so it cut off the rear fire escape. I was the outside vent man. We threw a thirty-five-foot portable ladder to the top floor. I went up the portable and found a couple of people and got them out.

That building was split, there were apartments in the front and apartments in the rear. Blume had Billy Golden with him. Billy had the irons. Bob Daley had the can, and he was relatively new to the area. He got cut off by the fire. He was off on one end of the hall with flames coming out of the door. We couldn't use the fire escapes. Flames went right up both fire escapes, front and rear for several floors. He couldn't go up. He couldn't go down. He couldn't go anyplace. He had some expression on his face.

When the engine company finally stretched the hose, they discovered that a bottle had been stuffed in the hydrant. It clogged up the line, and they lost water. So things were going from bad to worse, and we knew no other fire companies would be coming in for a few minutes; they were going to be delayed. To make a long story short, we pulled people out of just about every floor. I think I made three trips in and brought people out. Then I started across the interior hall to get the rear apartments on the top floor now, and I met the roof man; he had come down. Fortunately he had vented the roof. That was one of the good moves. No way we would have made it across that hall unless he got the roof. So we went to the rear, and he had already gotten some people out on the fire escape. He was taking them to the roof. He just couldn't bring them down because of the fire below. So I said, "All right, I'm going to go back and tell the chauffeur where I am." The next thing I know I passed out. Frank Posa came up looking for me. By now the engine had knocked down the fire on the first floor and second floor, and Frank carried me out of the building through the interior. He never even got a pat on the back.

There's a perfect example of a guy with twenty-two years in one of the better companies on the job and nothing, no recognition. And yet you've got guys who have six months on the job and they're singled out and they win medals. So you can't judge a man by medals or awards. You have to judge the man by what he is. But unfortunately medals become a barometer in this job, in the military, and in the police department. "Gee, he's got all these letters after his name so he must be good." The equation happens, and I guess that it's a human, or an American, fallacy. How we measure people. I'd like to see every guy I work with get a medal. I know if I'm working and they do the job, I won't lie, I won't distort the facts; I'll make sure I have it accurate, and if they are entitled to something they're going to get it. It works fairly well in this company. We have a reputation, we have credibility.

When I was a fireman, before Captain Gallagher took over, there was a different S.O.P. [standard operating procedure], which was probably one of the many reasons why I went back to a ladder company for a time. The main thing I didn't like was that when you went to a fire the chief would say, "Stand fast, Rescue." That killed me. I wanted to work.

When I got promoted, Captain Freddie Gallagher asked me if I'd come back to Rescue 2. He had a totally different outlook on us attacking a fire. Freddie's concepts were great. He was a super tactician. He's a football coach and you can see why he's so successful. He read John O'Regan's "*Ladders 3*, the FDNY manual that spells out the essence of ladder company operations." In it everybody has an assignment—at a fire. Based on what he read, Freddie asked how a rescue company would be most effective in a fire. Well, first thing you have to do is get to the fire. How do you get to the fire if they don't call you? Make yourself available. And God only knows how, but eventually every time a 1075 comes in, a rescue company is on the road. The joke around here is that we would like to go to all 1084s—that's the signal given when a first unit arrives at and acknowledges its presence at the scene of a fire. So if we went on 1084s we'd go to every box in the city. Some people out there think we do. We've been accused of a lot of things.

Many times when we get to the fire the initial charge has already been made, the tactics have been laid out, the fire is progressing, mistakes are made, rescues are made. If the first due engine or the first due ladder company screws up, someone has got to try and correct it. We might make the correction, the second due ladder company might do it, or even the second alarm companies might end up correcting the problem.

In most areas of operation the department has come a long way over the years. Everyone's fairly well trained. And initiatives are made according to tactics. The line goes where it's supposed to, companies operate where they're supposed to. But we will all ensure that the roof is opened.

Here's how our company is organized for a fire. Two men make up the "floor-above team." Both have masks; one carries a hook and a radio; the other guy carries a set of irons. The can man stays with the officer. Our chauffeur ensures that the line is going in and not coming out, or if they just need hose he'll feed that hose. Before we send anybody above the fire we put a guy on the line.

Putting this extra man on the line has caused a lot of hard feelings at times with other companies. Their attitude is "You don't trust us? Why are you putting a man on our line?" And we can't explain it all the time. Which is tough. We say to them, "If you need help moving that line that's what our man is there for. He has a mask, he's got the capabilities, and if you need somebody to feed you line, he'll feed it, but the line has got to move." And what the engine companies and the ladder companies don't know is that the chief will tell us in the street, "Move the line." The line has got to move. You can't put a fire out from the hallway. You have to move the line to the seat of the fire. And sometimes all it takes is an extra pair of arms to pull the hose, or an extra shoulder to push a guy. It works.

In the high incidence areas the companies are soaked with reputation. They're dragging you down the hall, they're going, they want to go. But you get a company that doesn't go to that many fires and they may be a little unsure of themselves. If you send a guy in there who's been to a lot of fires, he knows what it's like. He'll start talking to them, "Come on, you can do it a little more, move it in." That's all they need. Firemen will go anyplace they're told to go, or directed to go, or asked to go. They're all the same, the problem lies with officers. If an officer doesn't move the men, the men are not going to move. If the officer balks at the door, the company is going to balk at the door. Though it's not a hundred percent. Occasionally, an officer will say, "Let's go," and the firemen say no, but fortunately that's rare. In most cases the line moves. All they're looking for is encouragement, a little help. That's all it takes.

If, for whatever reason, we lose water or a ceiling comes down, injures a few guys, and they back the line out, I want to know about it. I have two people crawling around upstairs with no protection. Our man on the line also has a radio and can communicate with me.

At a fire, everything is a judgment call. There's no cookbook recipe. We like to quote the football players: "We've got a game plan when we go in, but we can call the automatics as soon as we get their." It seems to work.

I've developed my own way of attacking emergencies. Going into an emergency I try to find out as much as I can over the radio. When I get to the scene I only take two people out of the rig with me. One is proficient in emergency medical techniques (EMT), and the other is proficient in the use of tools. I'm not proficient in tools anymore. Christ, I haven't used tools in eight years. I have an idea of how to use them, but unless you use them every day you lose that balance. When we go into the scene I report to the chief. While I'm talking to him and getting his verbal size-up, I have my two guys immediately sizing up the job—one from the inside and one from the outside. The EMT man will get into the car, if it's a car accident. If it's a kid stuck in an elevator, he'll get in the elevator with the victim. A lot of times all you have to do is cut a guy's shoelaces, take his foot out of the shoe and he's free, but my man has got to ensure the extent of the pin. The other guy is sizing up what tools we're going to need to get the victim unpinned. And he'll say to me, "Lieu, I think we need the Hurst tool," or "I think the air bags will do it." And I'll either confirm it and call back to the rig for the required tools, or I may say, "No, I was here last year. A different type of tool will do the job." It's a prerogative you have as the officer.

Meanwhile the chauffeur and the other two men back at the apparatus are taking the basic tools off the truck. For car accidents the Hurst tool comes off; at elevator accidents the air bag starts to come off. If I order a change, we have got the manpower to bring whatever is needed. However, in most cases the stuff is already in motion. If the chauffeur doesn't hear from me, he'll call me on the radio. When the tools are brought to the scene, I'm touchy. I want my people to use them not somebody else. I don't even want the truck or the engine company to be there; I want them out of the way. And I'll ask their officer or the chief, "Can you get these men to move the spectators back—give us a working area?" When you do this type of work day in and day out, eventually you're going to lock horns, somebody is going to get pissed at you. But basically we have a good rapport with just about everybody, though some better than others.

It is not that the other companies won't do the job, but the average company does not have the ability to pick their people, especially today. Fortunately, at the rescue we have hand-picked guys; they're all experienced. Without a high number of fire incidents, it can take someone today three years to gain the good solid foundation that an engine or a ladder man needs. Today a guy could be in a company for three years and never get the nozzle. According to some companies' policy, the nozzle only goes to the senior man, or the nozzle only goes to blond-haired guys—whatever the system is. Most of them I think are on a rotation basis. But, say, every time a guy works on a certain rotation there's no fire. He can go months without actually putting out fire. Whereas people in this unit are coming from high incidence areas and they have the experience.

The Waldbaum's fire was a very traumatic point in my career. I was scheduled to work that day, but I needed to take a personal leave day. The fire was in the morning, I guess around eleven o'clock. I was taking care of business and heard over the radio that there was a collapse in Brooklyn, but there was no mention of any firemen trapped. About an hour later the guy on the radio said some firemen were trapped. I called the firehouse and some one from the other company told me everybody was out. It bothered me that I hadn't been there. It was my crew that was working, and it was possible that one of my guys was seriously hurt. Later I found out that one of them had been on the roof. He fell through into the cockloft, found a hole, and fell through the hole onto the floor of the store. Only by the grace of God is he alive today. Happily he's a lieutenant covering around here. I see him on occasion and it's nice to see him alive. But for months after that it bothered me that I had taken the time off. It took a while for me to straighten my head out and accept that I had no control over it.

I've been a couple of places where I thought it was fairly dangerous. The most recent was two years ago on Albany Avenue. It was a tremendous fire. After it was over, I think there were five unit citations—four or five individual meritorious acts. And I think four or five medals came out of the same fire. We got in there just about the time the chief was getting a fairly good picture of the fire. It was a rapidly extending fire in a four-story non-fireproof multiple dwelling. Fire had full possession of the interior hall, the first-floor apartment, the second-floor apartment, the third floor, and I think it was getting into the top floor. It was quite obvious that somebody had poured some gasoline in there. When we got there we couldn't even see the bucket of the tower ladder that was into the top floor. We dragged four people out. We heard later that 111 Truck and 123 Truck did an outstanding job.

We were assigned to get to the top floor, so I chose to go up the rear fire escape, since the interior stairs were jammed up with the first two engine companies, who were trying to make it up the stairs. Once we got the report that the squad had pulled a kid out of the top floor rear I sent a fire team around the rear to get the top floor. Then I ran to keep up with them. When we got around there, one of our guys from the above-fire team was coming out of the top floor with a child. He had found a young boy. He came down the fire escape, and we told him to keep going, take the child out. Then the other guy and I started up the rear fire escape. There was an officer on the fire escape, and he told us watch out because the windows were going to go. But we replied, "We'll give it a shot." We ran up the fire escape and literally dove in the window. We were on the exposure-four side. We made it to the interior hall. It's an incredible feeling to know that you have fire below you, above you, and on one side. The only thing on the other side of us was the exterior wall. We were searching and searching, but we couldn't find anybody. We could barely see; there was a lot of smoke, mostly heat. The flames were all in the walls. We could see the fire in the ceiling above us, we could see it in the wall next to us, and we could feel it coming up underneath us. So we knew that the floor below us was not that safe. There was no hose line in there yet, especially in the rear. We wanted to find if there was any more kids in there. That was uppermost on our minds. It was Gary Howard and me. I guess when you get nervous you talk fast. We kept saying, "Find anybody yet?" "A little more, a little more, maybe we can make it to the next room." We actually talked ourselves through those three or four rooms. We got to the interior hall, but we couldn't get past it. It had collapsed in the front. So I said to him, "All right, let's get out!" We got back out on the fire escape, went down to the third floor, and just as we got there the fourth floor let go and the flames came right out the window we were just in. After something like that happens, you look at yourself and say, "Were we lucky!" Then you wonder, was it a calculated risk, or was it stupidity? You don't know. But with that, Engine Company 227 came up with a line. They knocked the fire down on the third floor, and we went back up and inside the second time around. That time we found a young boy in the third room. How we missed him the first time I still don't know. But it was too late. He was dead. That was a hairy spot.

Another time, we were coming back from a job and on the radio we heard units responding to such-and-such location. My chauffeur, Jack Kleehaas, knows the area like nobody I've ever worked with, and he said, "It's just a couple of blocks. Do you want to take it in?"

I said, "Yeah, by all means."

We turned the corner, and we saw a heavy volume of smoke and flame pushing out of what appeared to be the third floor of a new-law tenement. We gave the 1075, told the chief it was an occupied building, and took off. We got into the interior vestibule and there was an elderly man, who said his son and wife were upstairs.

We started up the stairs. The door to the fire apartment was just cracked. We dropped a can man off on that floor, and I went to the fourth floor. It's amazing how much confidence you have in your own people. You know the fire is coming out that door and yet your guy is there and you feel secure. I got upstairs; the door was open. I got into the apartment and started down the hall. I made it to the rear. Later on, we figured that hall was forty-eight feet long. Forty-eight feet of crawling, when you can't see anything, is like going a mile.

This place was charged. There was no ventilation whatsoever, other than the fire coming out of the front windows on the floor below. I got into the rear room and it really wasn't that hot; it was warm, but not hot. I made a complete 360-degree turn, but I could not find a way out of the room. I said, "It's impossible, new law tenements don't have one-room apartments.'' I continued to grope around and eventually found my way out of that room.

So I came back down the hall, and I'm still assuming there's a woman and a child somewhere in the apartment. I heard a very slight whimper. I couldn't find anyone. I said, "Jesus Christ, they've got to be somewhere in here." Someone had taken a wall and made a new doorway in it; then they sealed off the original door. I got into the second room strictly by chance. And again I could hear someone. I started crawling toward the voice and I found a young man in what is usually the front bedroom. I was shocked to find this guy—who happened to be a twenty-one or twenty-two-year-old air force kid home on leave. He passed right out. So I put my mask on him, which probably was a mistake, because my head was pounding by this time. With the turns I had gotten disoriented. I didn't know where I was. Unfortunately for me the fire had vented in the air shaft, and it was coming up the shaft windows. Now I had fire in front of me and I had fire behind me. I could see it. I could see the window, and then I got my bearings. I dragged the young man into the kitchen. By then the rest of the guys had come up. I told one of them to take him out. I had to go back and get his mother. I went back into this oddball-shaped apartment. I wound up in the back room and I couldn't find her. By now flames had come up and burned away the glass in the room I was in. The curtains started going, and fire started to go across the ceiling. The chief of the 57 Battalion, Jim Duffy, was in the street, and he saw the whole thing. The engine had just come in and was stretching the line. I gave him the report on the radio that we'd found the kid and were looking for the mother. He said, "Get out, get out *now*. You got fire on the top floor!"

I said, "We're still looking for the mother."

He said, "Get out! I'm ordering you out! The woman is accounted for. There is nobody else in that apartment. Get out!" As I went back past that window, the flames came into the room. In just a matter of two minutes the fire had possession of those two rooms.

The engine had done a nice job on the floor below and then stretched upstairs to where we were. When we all got out in the streets it was one of the few times that the chief came over and literally gave us a hug. He was very happy. We got a unit citation. I was put in for an individual award, which was like icing on the cake. But it was a hairy spot. Any time you're alone and things are not the way they should be—and you know you have to get somebody—it's difficult.

The first time I made a rescue was in the 1960s, around Christmas time, and I had to slide along a clothesline. Larry Lee, the lieutenant in the adjacent company, who is now a chief in the 35 Battalion, used to get a kick out of testing us all the time. We were probies, and he was a sharp guy. He told us to always carry a small length of rope, because you never know when you're going to need one. So I went out and got a clothesline, and he'd ask me questions on what I should do with it. He was with the "enemy"—120 Truck—and I was in 103 Truck, but I learned an awful lot from that man. He was a teacher. He used to use the rope mostly for venting the top floor or the floor below that from the roof. He had always said, "It will be your way out someday." That ratty old rope was with me for about five years. By today's standards it never would have been in service. But here we were, Christmas time. There's a couple of jobs in the neighborhood, and they've got relocated companies—interchange companies—so there's really nobody in the firehouse who should be there, nobody who really knows the neighborhood.

We get this call over on Berriman Street. In the front it is a two-story building, but in the rear it's three stories. No fire escapes, just balconies. I was assigned the roof position, so I went via the adjoining building up to the roof. I opened up the scuttle to vent the roof, and tremendous heat came out of there. I gave the report that the roof was open. Then I looked over the rear and there's a lieutenant and a fireman stacking picnic tables on top of one another to try to reach one of the balconies. I yelled, "What's up?"

They said, "There's a woman on the top floor. We can't get to her."

So I said to myself, "How do I get down to the top floor?" I then took out my clothesline, tied it onto something on the roof, and I slid down this clothesline onto the balcony, a matter of fifteen or twenty feet, but that clothesline worked, and it worked well.

On the balcony was a regular storm door. I took the door off and, boy, was it hot! I made a dash into the room, and—I guess because of inexperience—I ran into this bed and it knocked me over. I fell right down. I didn't know where the hell I was now. I had lost my helmet and I'd lost my bearings. And I had to compose myself. I said, "Hey, you're in the Fire Department. Get a grip, now. Find out where you are." I looked behind me and I could see the fire coming out from the first floor under that balcony, so I said, "I know where I am now." I started crawling around, and in between the two rooms I found the woman. She was really sobbing. But when I grabbed her, she just let go and passed out. I guess she figured, "Well, he's gonna' save me." So she stopped hanging on.

She was deadweight and I had to drag her. I dragged her until I got to that bed and I just didn't have enough strength to carry her over it. She was a heavy woman and I was tired; we'd had a couple of jobs earlier that night, and I was taking a pounding. I had to leave her. I had to go and get air. I went back to the door and I found a chair on the balcony. I took the chair and I smashed out the window with it. It was the best thing I ever did. I should have done it before I came in the first time to let out some of that heat and smoke. Then I went back in and found her. I dragged her over this bed, and at that time I felt it was the most physically demanding act I had ever done in my life. Here was a woman who weighed over two hundred pounds, and it took every ounce of my strength to get her up and across the bed, down onto the floor and out to this balcony. It seemed like the whole room was a bed and I couldn't find my way around it. If I had gone back later on, I might have found out it was just a regular twin bed, I don't know, but at that time it appeared to be the biggest obstacle I had ever come across. And she was part of it, her weight. I felt I called on everything I had that night. I got her out to the balcony. Then *I* passed out.

When I came to, I was in the street and somebody had a resuscitator on me. I looked over, and there was a body next to me that appeared to be the woman. I didn't know where my helmet was, my tools, nothing. I went to Kings County Hospital and was admitted for a couple of days because of a high carbon monoxide level. The woman fortunately lived, but it turned out she had TB. They gave me all kinds of tests, but it never communicated. That was hairy, but I was young.

Probably the scariest episode for my family was on Holy Thursday, somewhere around the early seventies. I had ridden to work with a probie from the company; we had a car pool. That night we had a series of small fires and then we picked up a job on Dumont and Williams. I was the chauffeur. When we got there everybody was committed. Then some kid came around, grabbed me, and said, "Hey, fireman, there's a lady in the window up there." He was pointing to the alleyway. So I ran around to the alley next to this new-law tenement. I look up and sure enough I see a woman in a window. She's on the third floor, and the fire's got the first and second floor totally consumed. I knew I couldn't get up the fire escape. A thirty-five-foot ladder was the tool to use, but they're tough to climb alone.

I grabbed one of our buffs—a young man who is now a lieutenant covering in Rescue 3. In those days he always hung out at the firehouse. Some kids are just pains in the ass, but he was nice. He minded his business; he just liked to take pictures. I said, "Come on, Jack, give me a hand." Between the two of us we raised the thirty-five-foot portable ladder. I told him, "Butt the ladder!" He butted and I climbed up, but I couldn't get in the window where the woman was, so I climbed from the ladder to the third-floor balcony. We couldn't extend the ladder for some reason; I don't know why. I just remember I stood on the top of the ladder, grabbed the railing of the balcony, and hopped over, and the railing was hot as a bastard from the fire on the second floor. It was like standing on a barbecue grill. I just dove in the window.

Now I'm running around trying to find this person. She was in a foyer. I said, "Come on, I'm taking you out." She was hysterical, a young girl, sixteen, seventeen years old. I get her out, but realize she has no shoes on. I said to myself, "Oh, shit, I can't let her stand barefoot on that hot patio." So I told her to stand on my feet. I got her on top of me and we reached over and got on the ladder. As we were coming down the ladder she told me, "My brother is still in there."

I said, "Don't tell me that. Your brother is still in there?"

And she says, "He's still in the apartment." He was trying to get out through the interior. She didn't use those words, but that's what she was telling me in her broken English and her hysteria. I got her just about to the ground, handed her to this kid, and said, "Here, take her."

I went back up and through the same act again, but it was easier the second time because I knew what I was doing. Now

I have to find this kid. I don't know if he's a little boy or an older boy. But sure enough he had got to the interior hall and opened the door, and that's where he was lying. I had to drag him back down the hall and out the window. This kid was just about semi-conscious and there was no way I could carry him, there was just no way. He was too big and I was too exhausted. I kept smacking him, telling him, "Come on, you're awake, get up." Because of his youth—he was sixteen years old—he was in a lot better shape than I was. He came to right away, and we got on the railing, repeated the act, and came back down the ladder. It was a nice job. A buddy of mine from the squad was trying to get up to the apartment from the floor below by way of the interior stairs. He made it to the landing, but he never made it to the apartment. He got wiped out; they took him right to the hospital.

We ended up going from there into a second alarm in Brownsville. And that night we had two probies working with us. So we were running around in this building making searches, and I had these kids with me. You're responsible for them and you always look out for them. And I remember we were telling the guys to pull the ceiling here, pull the ceiling there. The officer had two other guys in the other end of the building and the next thing I knew I was almost out cold.

Where I was I don't know. But I could feel bodies around me, I could feel bodies dragging me. You piece it together later on. We had been pulling the ceilings, and they said I just passed out. I guess to a probie it's a traumatic experience to see a guy just fall over. They ran to the window and they were screaming that I was dead. With that the guys came up and carried me out to the street. I have pictures from a fine photographer of all this, that's the only reason I can put it together. The next thing I remember, I'm in the hospital, looking toward my feet and I see a priest, and I'm saying to myself, "Boy, somebody must be fucked up to have a priest." Then I realized the priest was talking to me. He was asking, "Do you want me to call your wife?"

"My wife? What do you want to call my wife for?"

He said, "You've been unconscious for quite a while."

I said, "Nah, don't call my wife. That's the last person you'd call."

Then they put me in a ward, and all night long they took

blood and all that kind of crap. Around ten or eleven o'clock the next morning my car pool went to my house, and my wife came out and asked, "Where's my husband?"

He said, "Didn't they tell you?"

And she asked, "Didn't they tell me what?"

He said, "Well, you better call the firehouse."

This probie just got into his car and left. So my wife got on the phone and was told that the 103 had been relocated. She couldn't find anybody to tell her where her husband was. She got frantic and started calling my buddies, and now they started calling the firehouse. Then she called her relatives and they were calling people. They found me in the County around two o'clock in the afternoon. It was a case where the officer going off duty had left a message saying, "Make sure you call Vigiano's mother or his wife at such and such a time. Don't call her now; call her later. He's okay and this is where he is." But the paper on which this message had been written got mislaid and the company was relocated. The next company came in. Whatever the situation was, nobody followed up. My wife was beside herself—we had two young kids at the time. So that afternoon I had the union guys visiting me, people from the job, guys from the firehouse. Finally a relative pops in, "Nobody knew you were here."

I couldn't believe it. "Nobody called my wife?"

He said, "No."

Well, I said, "I want out of this joint." That was on Good Friday.

The doctor said, "No, you can't get out; you're staying here. Your blood gases are still in the critical stage. In fact, the blood we were taking from your vein looks like blood from an artery, that's how bright it is."

So I sat in this ward. I never even got a private room. I just watched people die. Kings County wards are not a pleasant place to be. I ended up talking to a doctor and a nurse most of the night. On Easter Sunday my relatives came and drove me home. Probably the worst time for my family was that time. Probably the worst time for me, too, and I never even realized it. In the sixties and the early seventies, when I was a fireman, nobody wore masks, and I believe that is one of the major differences between then and today. Today we all wear masks in this company, and guys don't readily get knocked out so often.

One night we all wore white coats, and when we responded to a box, everybody was looking at us. One guy called us the Wild Bunch. We walked up to this new chief we knew, and with as straight a face as I could manage, I said, "Chief, Rescue 2 has these new test coats, and we were told to take over as many lines as we can to see if the coats will hold up." He turned around and told the engine, "Give Rescue the line." You should have heard the engine men! There was all kinds of words going back and forth. The chief announced, "I'm ordering you! They get the line!" The next day we had to apologize to the engine men. They were a little pissed over it.

When I was a fireman in 103, we had a captain who was a fun person to be around. He had a very dry sense of humor and was a super student, a very intelligent man. And nothing seemed to rattle him. In that company there was always somebody putting peanut butter in the receiver of the phone, then telling you that you had a phone call. Or they would pull the fuses and we wouldn't have any lights. A guy would be really engrossed in watching TV and then they would pull a fuse. Oh, you'd hear the screaming and the bitching.

One particular night it was boring so the guys figured they'd get the captain. They pulled all the fuses on the top floor. He was trying to get into his office up there. After bitching and moaning, he finally told the house watch to check all the fuses. Finally the captain gets into his office, but none of the lights work. He goes over to his desk and strikes a light with his cigarette lighter. On top of his desk is a fireman lying naked, à la Burt Reynolds in the *Cosmopolitan* centerfold. Then the captain holds the cigarette lighter up and he sees a guy sitting on the file cabinet naked, a guy lying in his bed naked, two guys sitting on the floor naked. He just let the light die out and walked out of the room as if it never happened.

At one time I worked with a buddy of mine, Bill Trotta. He and I were nicknamed the Katzenjammer Kids. We were so bad together they wouldn't let us work together. We were constantly pulling pranks. This one particular night we had rigged up some firecrackers in with the burners so if somebody would turn on the stove, seconds later the firecrackers would go off. We had this one lieutenant in 290 Engine who was very straight. He was the type of man who if he walked into a room naked you'd probably salute him, because he just had that aura about him as an officer. Every night at ten o'clock he brewed a pot of tea. He went to the teakettle, filled it up, and put it on the stove; it was like a ritual. We had set up our firecracker trick earlier, but I forgot I still had one in this burner, and here comes the lieutenant. He fills up his pot. We were watching TV or shooting pool—God only knows what we were doing. I looked at my buddy and he looked at me and I said, "Oh, no!" The lieutenant puts the teapot over the stove, turns the jet on, turns his back to the stove, and the thing lets go. Well, it wasn't just a firecracker; it was actually a cherry bomb. The pot went about eight inches off the stove. When that thing blew up I ran, and I just kept running. He turned around and he was beside himself. He takes the pot and runs into the truck office and he's standing there yelling at Lieutenant Matty Farrell, and Farrell is looking up. Then the lieutenant asked, "Do you see what they did? Do you see what they did?" He's shaking the pot and the water is going all over. Farrell, who is very quick, says, "No, what did they do?" The lieutenant says, "Look what they did to my teapot!" And then I guess he realized how ridiculous it was. And he said, "You're just as bad as they are," and threw the pot down and slammed into his office. Farrell started laughing, and he came into the bunk room. He asked, "Where are you?"

I was hiding behind a locker, and he goes, "Just get a new teapot by tomorrow morning." He had that knack of never losing his cool. He was great. What a boss.

Oh, yeah, the firehouse kitchen burned down one day. The captain had made us whitewash the walls. The whitewash dripped on the woodwork—it looked like some kind of a cantina—so we threw sawdust on the floor. Then somebody appropriately wrote on the walls, "There's no law west of the Pecos and no civilization north of Livonia Avenue."

And I said, "Gee, it really looks like a cantina." I borrowed a serape and a sombrero, and I bought a live chicken. I brought him to the firehouse. They had him on a leash. He wasn't actually a chicken; he was a bantam rooster. That banty was great. A pain in the ass. He stayed with us all night, through the next day between tours, and the next night. But I forgot that they wake up very early. And I had hid him. I had covered the bottom of a locker with cardboard so you couldn't see his legs when I put him in there. He'd wake up at five o'clock in the morning and start crowing; the firemen wanted to kill him. But it took them two days to find the little son of a bitch, and when they did they put him in my locker. You can imagine what a chicken does to your locker after one day. Oh, man, I had chicken shit all over the place. Finally, one guy took him and put him on a farm upstate.

That reminds me, we had a fellow in the engine company—I won't mention his name—and he was a real wise guy. No good at a fire, no good as a fireman. Some fellows were very aggravated with him. He wasn't aggressive; he had to have four men with him, and he was always out on the street. He was what we call a kink chaser: "I'll stay in the street and straighten the hose out." He had no physical strength, either; he was built like a pear.

We had a couple of wild guys working one night, and we go to a fire. The engine goes out first. Then he slides down the pole. He said, "Oh, well, I missed the engine. I'll ride with you guys." He gets in the back of the truck. We're following the engine to the fire, and he's making light of it. So one of the fellows says, "You hump! Your guys are out there. You missed the engine and it doesn't mean anything to you. You have no pride in yourself!"

He says, "Oh, well, I'll get the next one; there was no fire anyway." It was a false alarm and we were turned back by the dispatcher over the radio.

So we started to take his clothes off, and we said, "You don't even deserve to ride with us." So we push him outside the truck. He was holding on to the back of the rescue truck balls-ass naked. We pass the engine, and the front of the engine doesn't even know he's missing. Well, they see him and they do a double take—here he is on Queens Boulevard with a helmet on and nothing else, trying to get back inside the truck.

Chapter 12

Lieutenant James Curran
Rescue 1, Manhattan

When I was in probie school I kept turnout gear in my car. Sometime during late February or March 1962 there was a fifth alarm in a taxpayer on Ditmars and Thirty-first Street in Queens. I drove up to the fire, put my gear on, and reported to the chief.

Smoke was emanating from numerous stores, and burglar alarms were ringing. Firemen had forced entry into the stores. After I reported in, I wondered, "Now, what am I going to do? What do I really know about this?" I knew that I was anxious to be part of the team. The chief had assigned me to a truck company, Ladder 116, and I was with two firemen, Donald Milney, who is still a fireman with 116, and another fellow by the name of Tom Hayes; he's dead now. They steered me around, so to speak, "Do this, do that, come over here, let's do this now." I was sort of a robot.

It was frightening. When we went inside, I was in awe at seeing fire over our heads in the ceiling area. Every time we poked a hole into the ceiling, fire emanated, and as we pulled the tin down it was just total fire. They had a couple of hand lines going, but the fire was rolling from store to store. Finally they pulled everyone out before it collapsed. Then we went into exposure three. There was a multiple dwelling in the rear. We had a hand line, and we stayed up on the third floor and put water down into the fire building. The fire gutted about five or six stores, including a large supermarket. Sections of the roof collapsed. This was before we got the tower ladders (erroneously called cherry pickers by the press) that we have today, which are quite effective in controlling taxpayer fires. The fire started around 7:00 P.M., and I was there until maybe midnight. The chief took my name and wrote a letter to the division of training commending me. Coincidentally, when I graduated from the Division of Training I was assigned to Ladder 116 in Long Island City.

But Ladder 116 wasn't active enough for me. I had seen a television show that was aired on Channel 5, *The DuPont Show of the Week*, entitled "Rescue One." Walter Matthau narrated it, and it won numerous awards. After that I wanted to be part of a rescue company. I went over to Rescue 4 and was interviewed by the captain. He told me he wouldn't be calling me until I was at least first grade, which meant three years on the job. However, five months later he called and said that if I still wanted it to put in a request for transfer. He'd have me detailed there while the transfer was pending. I spent twelve years in that company, totally satisfied.

In 1973 the Fire Department went on strike. However, I didn't go. I was the only one in my firehouse who didn't. It was the most difficult thing I ever had to do and probably ever will have to do—to go against sixty people that you work with. I had been, prior to that, considered one who just went along with the crowd. I never took a stand on Vietnam, or a stand on anything. Also, my wife had gone through Queens College, which was a tremendous threat to me at that time. Here I was working, and my wife went through college and graduated with honors. I wouldn't be the pillar of strength in the family anymore. So I had a little bit of therapy and came to the realization that I am responsible for everything I do. There was no such thing as he/she/it, God, or the devil made me do it. And I thought about it, and I felt I just didn't want to go out on strike. At that time we had a union leader and a Chief of Department who were very strong-willed, and their strong will and antagonism toward each other caused the strike. We were told to remove all our clothing from the firehouse prior to the strike. I felt maybe I'd call in sick. Just have everybody call in sick and then keep some people on overtime, and that might suffice. But I thought about it some more. I lived nearby in Woodside, and I felt I had a responsibility to go to work. I was born and raised in Woodside. My father lived two blocks away. My mother died in my arms when my company responded to the call when she had a heart attack. I felt I couldn't hold my head up high in my father's eyes and in my wife's eyes, or go against something that was just so natural for me. The idea of going on strike for money was ridiculous and ludicrous to me. Hey, I'm a fireman, the first and last line of defense. And we're going to go on strike for money? It's ridiculous. So I showed up at the firehouse that morning and there were the pickets, going around. I walked on the line for about ten or fifteen minutes and it just hit me: I cannot do this. I think that the other guys knew. They saw me in extreme depression and anxiety. I remember the firemen verbally cheering each other up, "How you doing? How you feeling? When is this going to end? Oh, boy, what are we going to have for lunch?" Meaningless statements, just to sort of justify what's going on.

My car was parked in an illegal spot, and one of the firemen suggested that I move it. I got in it and went around the corner. I had prepared a letter resigning from the union. I walked back around the corner, with my helmet and my gear, and I handed the letter to the union delegate. A couple of firemen came up and asked if the strike was over. And I said, "For me it is."

I walked into the firehouse. I was fearful for my life. I thought that anything might happen. They might storm in after me. Threats were being lodged. I went up to the office and told the captain, "I'm here to work. I'm not having anything to do with the strike." I said, "I'll drive the rig, I'll do whatever you want," though I was not considered a qualified chauffeur. One of the lieutenants, who was a very strong union person, said I was emotionally upset and I shouldn't drive and started ordering me to do menial tasks like clean the kitchen. I had caused a lot of turmoil. Now the officers had to make a decision. What were they going to do now that they had a fireman who wanted to work? They were removed from the strike as long as they didn't have any subordinates who wanted to work. They went back and forth about who would work. They said, "Let's call the union. Let's see what they say." Then it flashed through my mind, what the heck is going on in this world? Am I totally out of touch with reality? Is there no one who just says, "I'm gonna do what I want to do and not what I'm told"? There is the attitude of "We have to stick together and with the union."

But how do you live with yourself if someone dies as a result?

Well, as it turned out, the whole strike was a lie. The union said an overwhelming majority had voted to strike. But I think it was actually 4,200 to 3,800 votes *not* to strike. The ranks were lied to, duped, and they gave up an awful lot of themselves for the sham. To this day some of them still hold a grudge against the union. It was funny, though—the fellows who voted for the strike got what they wanted. Afterward there wasn't too much animosity from them. But the fellows who voted not to strike and went on strike, they were really hurt and angry.

A lot of things were done to me behind my back after the strike. It could never be the same being in that firehouse. It became a nightmare. But in time, it made me a much stronger individual. Much stronger. I know now that I can't blame anybody for what I do. I can't even blame my mother or father for the way I am. I just hope there's never another strike. As they say, you never know who your friends are until you're in trouble. In those days I didn't need more than two or three fingers on one hand to count who my friends were. It was extremely uncomfortable being there. I remember going to a party, and at the party one fireman from a particular company came up to me, and he mentioned that another individual was a no-good son of a bitch. I asked, "Why?"

He said, "He didn't go on strike."

I said, "I didn't either."

And he said, "Yeah, but I didn't know you then."

So it hit me: he wasn't mad at the man for what he did, though he vented all his anger on that individual; he was angry with himself, mad that he'd been duped, cheated. I came to the conclusion that I had to change venue. The fire commissioner had sent letters out saying that he would do anything he could to help those of us who worked during the strike. So it was just a matter of making calls and a few days later I was in Rescue 1.

I got promoted in 1976, and was sent out for a time to Jamaica as a covering lieutenant. I enjoyed it, but by August 1977 I was able to return to Rescue 1, and have been there ever since.

I have found tremendous satisfaction being in the rescue.

We fight fires in various types of buildings—from those with deep subcellars to high-rises. We go to subway accidents, ship fires, and various collapses. We also have a scuba team that has been trained to fight fires under the piers. Because of the many different situations this company goes to, our men must be able to think in order to be good.

When I was in Rescue 4 we did a lot of extrication work. We had one in Flushing, in 1968. A Vietnam veteran had come home, borrowed his folks' car, and gone out partying. He hit a tree doing sixty or seventy miles an hour and wrapped the car around it. We were called out to extricate him. When we got there he was screaming. The chief was there. He said, "See what you can do, get him out." The screaming set off panic in the situation. He was the driver, yet it looked as if he was a passenger in the rear. The left front wheel was almost behind the front seat. The floor of the car had just accordioned up. One of the driver's legs was just about severed; the other leg was almost as bad. It took us about fifteen or twenty minutes to extricate him. We wound up using the Porto Power to jack his foot right out from the metal. There was almost nothing left of it. They had a doctor there. He gave him one shot of morphine, but couldn't give him another. Well, it took us a while to get him out, but it was difficult working with that screaming. What we did do—and I've done it many times since then when we couldn't keep the victim quiet—was stick a roll of gauze in his mouth and tell him to bite on it; that quieted him down. We could work more professionally. And once he was quiet, the people at the scene quieted down, too. And the chief quieted down.

We had another extrication in a machine shop. A fellow had gotten his arm caught almost up to his elbow in some sort of a roller. When we got there this Spanish-speaking fellow and his friends were almost crying for us to get him out. We looked at it and we asked, "Can you reverse that machine?"

They said, "Yes."

We said, "All right, put it in reverse."

They did, but then they hit the button—his arm went in farther. Now the screaming intensified from him, his relatives, and his friends. Anyway, we just tuned out what they were saying. We put Halligans on either side of the rollers that were on his arm, then we put some blocks of wood under the Halligans and caught a piece of the metal. Two fellows pushed down on the Halligans and that was enough to roll his arm right out. As his arm rolled out, his eyeballs rolled up and he passed out. This I guess was due to the blood rushing to that area. Fortunately he had no broken bones.

We had another incident where a fifty-three-year-old man fell off a motorcycle and broke both of his wrists. We splinted his wrists and talked to him all the way to the hospital. When we got back to the firehouse we found out that he had died. Whether it was heart failure or some internal injury I don't know. That was sort of a strange experience, since we initially felt we did a nice job.

When I was in Rescue 4, we once had twelve D.O.A's within three tours. We had an extrication problem where there were five teenagers in a car—three in the front seat, two in the back—underneath a tractor trailer. The three in the front were decapitated. The two in the back were relatively okay. Banged up, but such a vast difference. The car went under the tractor trailer and the impact just swept off the windshield, peeled back the hood, and their heads. One of the kids who died was a brother of a fellow in the back. As we were taking care of the kid in the back, he was asking, "How's my brother doing? My brother, my brother."

To get him through, we told him, "He's fine, they took him to the hospital, he'll be all right, don't worry. We have to take care of you now. He's okay."

We went from that incident to a fire in Woodside where we lost a man. Then we went to a fire over in Jackson Heights where we lost a mother and four children.

If you do lose someone it's really devastating. I've known firemen who have grabbed people, and as they were pulling them out, the room lit up. They had to get out and they couldn't get back in until the fire was knocked down. By then the people were dead. Of course the firemen didn't know whether they were dead already. It can frustrate you, particularly where someone gets away from your grasp and falls or jumps to their death.

This particular fire in Woodside, with the mother and four children, was very emotional, because we found the mother right by the window with her infant wrapped in her arms, both burned extremely bad. Another kid was under a bed, another was in a closet, and the third was in the hallway. The father and older son survived. The fire had started in the cellar. The father came running out of the cellar, leaving the door open, and the fire came up, chased him and his older son outside, swept up to the second floor, and trapped the wife and the three other kids up there.

That fire was in a brick semi-attached house. When we first got there, we went up to the adjacent house and breached a hole through a wall into the burning house. But so much fire came through the hole that we had to shove a mattress against it just to keep the fire from coming at us, until we brought a hand line up. We operated the hose through the hole, but they were all dead. The fire was emanating out of windows on the first and second floors when we arrived, so there was no hope for anybody inside.

We went over to Ridgewood the next night to another fire where a couple more teenagers died.

It hits you two, three days, a week later. You realize how you've got to grasp on to every second of life. You see so much death in a short period of time. Sometimes you wonder if the whole world is turning upside down. You have to get hardened to tragedy and learn to live with it and put it aside when it's over. You can't let it eat at you, or the rest of your life will be ruined by it. I don't say most people can do it, but I think firemen can do it easier, because they see it in their profession. If you're a fireman in a rescue company, you sort of adapt to tragedy, but you don't get into each other's heads that much. Unless you're really tight with a couple of people—and you reach out to each other—you keep things on pretty much of a surface level.

The firehouse routine is quite jovial. Especially in the group. When it's one-on-one or sometimes one-on-two you can get into something heavy, but with the TV going, house watch, kitchen, the fact that at any second you could be called out to a fire, we tend to keep things light and lively. If you were to ask another fireman, "How do you really feel about death?" he would push the question aside. Actually, in front of our peers we always want to appear strong. Machismo gets into a great bit of our interaction with ourselves and other people. We're probably as insecure, maybe more so, than other people, but we're in a profession where we can work it out. We're expected to be the big brave people who save the city, though this responsibility can be devastating to some firemen.

If a civilian gets burned, he is treated and sent home. He's never going to see another fire—at least that's what he thinks. It's wiped out of his mind. If a fireman gets burned severely, he is treated, too, but he's got to go back to work if he wants to continue with his profession. And when he thinks about the pain and the fear he went through when he was trapped and the disfigurement, if there are scars or skin grafts, he might decide it's not worth it to go back. No way. He'll forget about the good times. He'll think only of that last fire. If he goes to the next one will he be able to perform? Will he be able to hold his head high in the opinion of his peers? Probably not, but he wouldn't want to admit this to other people.

I've spoken to firemen who have been burned, since I've been president of the New York Fire Fighter's Burn Center Foundation, and these people are the true heroes, because they've given more than a lot of others. They've given their skin, almost made the supreme sacrifice. It's very difficult for them. They can't look at their families and play the role of the big hero fireman, because they're scared shitless. It's tough for them to talk about this. They can talk to another fireman, but he might not be able to relate to it unless he's had a little bit of similar experience. They could go into therapy, but a lot of firemen reject this. They probably feel it's belittling, or they feel they can handle the problem alone. Then there are the jokes that have gone on in the kitchen about being crazy, loony if you go into therapy—this one's crazy or that one's crazy. These men who've been burned would rather die than be thought of as crazy. They'd rather suffer the pain of mental anguish than seek help.

It comes from the machismo associated with firemen. Some civilians say we're crazy for going into the building—"You should let it burn," they say. Sometimes you probably say that maybe we are crazy, especially when it's a vacant building. We do, at times, make aggressive attacks even when it seems illogical and impractical. And this is something that I guess we wrestle with until we achieve a certain maturity and experience, and realize that the real bottom line is coming back alive. To be able to say no to your peers and not be afraid of their intimidation rather than just go along with the pack—that's something I think firemen struggle with a lot. Most of them want to keep a strong image. There may be others who just don't care, but they may not be considered good firemen. As in every other job, we have all different types of people. My experience, though, particularly in working with rescue men, tells me that most firemen have very strong egos, extensive experience, and great motivation. And the firehouse is a nice environment to work in, where everybody has a common goal to do as good a job as they can to accomplish a task. So you all sort of glide along together; it's not one person pulling everybody else. As a matter of fact, you have to keep moving because your peers are right by you; that keeps you going. In the long run most of the time this sort of teamwork brings a successful conclusion to a task, and it can be done gracefully because you have six people who are optimistically task-oriented.

I made a rescue about three years ago on Forty-ninth Street. Jack McAllister made a rescue at the same fire. We went into a five-story U-shaped building with three entrances, one from the middle part of the U and one at either end of the U, and there was fire in the courtyard. A woman had already jumped. Fire was emanating out one window. There were people on the fourth floor. A Spanish-speaking fellow was screaming out of one of the windows, and he had a kid in his arms. I went into the middle entrance and went up the stairs with another lieutenant. As we were going up the stairs we began to realize we were in the wrong part of the building. My forcible-entry team had been stopped by some civilians seeing us run into the middle part, and they said, "No, go over here!" So McAllister went up and into the apartment they directed him to. He crawled under the fire, got one of the fellows out. I went to the fourth floor of the adjacent building with Lieutenant Freddie Daniels of Engine 54. The two of us kicked the door in, went to the end of the apartment, and looked out the window. Five feet away there was the guy screaming with his kid in his arms and the fire blowing out the window next to him. So I straddled the windowsill, tied a rope around my waist, tied it to a pipe, and told Freddie to hold my leg. Just as I stepped out of the window with my one leg, the man dropped the child—a three or four-year-old girl. She fell four stories down, but a fireman broke her fall. She lived. The woman who jumped also lived. Another girl got out another way.

Now the fellow who was perched on the windowsill had his

hands on the sill and the fire started to come out over his head. So he was looking for a spot where he was going to jump. I reached over with my left hand and I had my right hand on the inside wall of his window. I said, "Come on, man, grab my hand." With that he reached for my hand, but as he made contact, he fell. We made the perfect left-handed handshake. He swung back and what I had in my mind was "Oh, boy, this guy is not going to pull me out of the window." Fortunately he only weighed about 140 pounds. When he made the left-hand grab, as he started to swing down, he grabbed my wrist with his right hand and swung back and forth about three times. I realized now that I had him, and he had a grasp on me. I said, "Let me go, Freddie, get him! Get him!" And as we pulled him up, the whole next window, where he'd been standing, erupted in fire, like a blowtorch. We pulled him in. He ran downstairs.

Freddie and I went next door to the fire apartment. The engine had moved in with the line. I followed them in and in that same room, on the bed, was this guy's wife. She had burned to death. She had probably been unconscious from the smoke, because I never saw her appear in the window.

Later on I said, "There's the guy I got out."

McAllister said, "No, that's the guy I rescued."

I said, "What do you mean? That's the guy I rescued." I didn't know he got the guy's brother out—two brothers with goatees—they looked like twins.

The worst fire for me was a fire I had while I was in Rescue 4. It was on Myrtle Avenue—possibly Brooklyn, possibly Queens, a borderline box. It was in a three-story building, twenty-five by sixty feet deep. (The size of the building will determine to a certain extent the amount of fire you can have, whether it's on one or two or more floors. If you can imagine a twenty-by-sixty multiple dwelling, six-story, non-fireproof, you have a picture of it. So knowing a building's size sort of tells you the area of fire, whether it's life hazard or not.) There was a haberdashery on the first floor, two apartments on the second, and two apartments on the third floor.

When we got there it was an all-hands fire. The other companies were extinguishing fire on the first floor. We were told to get to the second floor. There was an entrance to the residence from the side street. As we went up the stairs there was an engine company advancing just in front of us. Visibil-

ity was very limited, because there was so much smoke.
There was carpeting on the stairs, so I took my gloves off and
started feeling my way along the edge of the carpeting. As we
went up the stairs I noticed the molding was very hot. I called
back to get a second line ready because we had fire underneath us in the stairs.

As we got up almost adjacent to the nozzle man from the
engine company, the hallway ignited overhead. The gases up
at the ceiling flashed with a noise and then went out. The two
fellows up near the nozzle turned around and literally dove
over our heads. There was about six, seven other fellows
ahead of us on the stairs. They turned around and dove right
over our heads, and we sort of handed them down. Then I
went up next to the nozzle man and told him to open it up and
just keep the water moving over our heads in a circular
fashion. He was on the landing and I was on the top step. We
might have been doing that for five or six seconds when the
top step just let go. I dropped! The mask bottle on my back
caught on something, and at the same time I was spreading
my arms, so I stopped myself from going right through into
the fire. I pushed myself up and out. I then dove down the
stairs. I went out to the curb, knelt down with one knee on
the sidewalk and the other in the street, and doused myself
with water from the gutter. I had first-degree burns from just
the heat. The fire didn't even burn through my clothes.

The chief said to me, "The third floor hasn't been searched
yet. Rescue, can you get it?"

Another fireman and I went up the fire escape to the third
floor. He ran out of air, so I said, "Okay, you take the rear
apartment, I'm going to get the front apartment." I went from
the rear out into the hallway to the front. As I was searching
the front there was a pretty good visibility—all the windows
were broken. Then I heard yelling behind me in the hallway.
And I felt heat—six rooms below me had lit up. I went back
to the hallway door and saw that the hallway was pitch
black—filled with smoke and a lot of heat. I closed the door,
but I couldn't lock it, because I had kicked it in. As it turned
out, just closing it wasn't enough, though. As I turned around,
every window I passed had fire leaping up from the floor
below. I rushed from window to window yelling, "Help!
Help! Help!" I ran up to the two windows on the Myrtle

Avenue side. Every time I passed a window all I saw was the fire from below.

All of a sudden the pressure of the heat pushed open the door to the hallway and the smoke and heat belched in. With that I ran out of air. I took my mask off and threw it on the bed. My only chance was to jump out a window. Fortunately, people across the street on Myrtle Avenue saw me, but the firemen in the street couldn't see me because of the smoke and flames. The people told an off-duty fireman from Ladder 124, who buffed the fire, that there was a fireman trapped, so on my second time back to that front window I saw that there was the bucket. I went right out the window into the bucket. He took me down to the street, and I gave him a big kiss and a hug.

A few minutes later the fire on the second floor was extinguished and we were told to make a secondary search. We went up, went through the apartment. I went into the bathroom, the bathtub was filled with water. I stood inside the doorway, reached in with my hook, and swept the tub to make sure there was nobody in it. A few minutes later the officer came up to me and asked, "Jimmy, are you sure you made a good thorough secondary search in the bathroom?"

I told him yes. The reason we were being extra cautious was that prior to this fire—maybe two, three months earlier—a rescue company was told to make a secondary search, and while they were doing it, a report of another fire came in, so they went to the other fire. They had told the chief their search was negative. After they left, a kid was found behind the refrigerator D.O.A. So the department called the rescue men downtown and, in so many words, said, "You're a rescue company. When you make a secondary search, you're supposed to be extra thorough." A secondary search is made after the fire is under control, when you can see what you're doing.

Unfortunately, this time I made a mistake when I stepped into that bathroom. I knelt on one leg and swept my hook back and forth in the tub. I looked at the lieutenant who was standing outside the door and said, "See? There's nobody here." With that the whole bathroom dropped. The only thing left was the sink on the wall. The tub went right to the basement. I landed on the first floor. I felt a pain in my elbow. I started touching myself to see if I was okay. With that, two firemen came in on the first floor, reached under my arms, picked me up, and ran out to the street with me. I went to the hospital and was checked out.

I later learned that the lieutenant just about had a heart attack. He figured that was the end of me.

I went back to the firehouse later, had a sandwich, and went home. That night I started to get scared, and the next day I got really scared. I felt my number was up. At one fire, three near misses—the stairs, the apartment, and the bathroom. I started to question whether I should stay in the job. I was out on medical leave for about a week. When I went back to duty I was very, very leery. It took a good month and a half before I started to get my confidence up. For a while there, I was afraid to go in on a fire.

We had a cellar fire sometime after that, and I was really afraid to go more than right inside the doorway. But I went in there. I went back to the trenches and worked it out. Had I been in a hospital with a severe injury for a month or two and then on light duty for another couple of months, I really would have been devastated. You relive your last experience, and the more you relive it, the more the fear will overtake you, the more you may not want to go back.

Some people retire so that they won't have to live with the fear. They're not firemen anymore, so they don't have to worry about going to a fire. Then a year or so later they overcome their fear, and they wish they were firemen again because they believe they can now work with any injury they might have.

I think this happens to a lot of firemen who are on medical leave for extended periods of time. There was a fellow from Rescue 2 who went through the roof at the Waldbaum's fire. I saw him about a year after that happened. He still had the fear with him, but he said he could work it out and he did. But the fear was there; he could admit it and talk about it. And he was still visibly shaken a year later. That is very common and very, very natural. I can relate to it because of my experience. However, his was more devastating because the people around him were killed. And if it hadn't been for lucky timing—the fact that he kept moving once he hit the deck on that cockloft and crawled off to fall sixteen or eighteen feet to the floor—he would have died, too. As it was, he got banged up, but he survived. He's a lieutenant now. He was able to work out his problem and go back in.

The true hero is someone who overcomes fear. We all have fear. If you don't have fear, then what you're doing is not courageous. You're either stupid or ignorant of what lies ahead of you, or you haven't had enough close calls. You put it all together and you realize that each step you take is a tactical risk. But based upon your experience you will not overstep your limits. It's like a battlefield—if you've been there before you can get a little bit closer to the action this time and hopefully stay away from that stray bullet that might get you. You don't stand up in an open field of machine-gun fire, but you can still advance.

At one fire, in a hotel on Seventh Avenue off Forty-second Street, we stretched a house line, a standpipe line, in the hallway on the ninth floor. That kind of hose sometimes sits in a building for years and years and may not ever be changed. It dry-rots and when you stretch it out and charge it with water the pressure from the standpipe can burst it very easily. At this fire, the hose burst and I was past it. It was uncomfortable because the fire was blowing out the window next to me, and when I opened the hallway door, I found that the hallway was too hot to go through. So I closed the door and went back to the window. I thought about breaching a hole in the wall to the next room, but it was thick plaster, so I laid my personal rope on the windowsill and tied it around the pipe riser. That hotel had ten-foot ceilings, so there was no way the aerial ladder could reach me way up on the ninth floor.

If the need arose I was gonna slide down the rope to the floor below, kick in the window, and make my escape. But for now I waited. Two or three minutes went by. Meanwhile they got a new length of hose in, got water on the fire, and when I crawled back to the hallway door and opened it, one of my men came in and said, "I thought you were a goner. I couldn't get to you." I took in my rope, folded it up, and put it in my pocket.

Just having a rope is a deterrent to panic. It's similar to a cop having a gun. He might have to use it, but if he didn't have it he couldn't take certain actions. If I hadn't had that rope, I probably would have gotten very scared and started hacking my way through the wall or dashing out into the hallway and trying to run through the fire to get out. Or I might have gone into the hallway and tried to escape the other way, and it might have been a dead-end corridor.

I believe we make our own luck, to a great extent. We take advantage of situations as they present themselves. In a situation where a fireman walks out and abandons the building just as it collapses, it could be luck or it could be a decision based upon his experience—knowing how long the fire's been burning, the type of building involved, and the fire load. He knows he has to get out before it collapses. It's an ongoing learning experience. Even if you're on the Fire Department thirty-five years there's always a fire you haven't seen. No two fires are alike. You have your strategy for certain types of fires, but there's always a few small variables thrown into it.

A type of incident that doesn't come along too often is the high-rise fire. One that sticks out in my mind, going back several years, was the Westvaco Building fire, at 299 Park Avenue, over on Forty-eighth Street. That was a big fire. We knew it was a good fire on the way over there from the progress reports. When we got into the lobby we went to Chief Grimes. He had reports of fire on the nineteenth, twentieth, twenty-second, and thirty-second floors. And as we got into the elevator they said there was heavy smoke on thirty-two. "Well," we said, "let's go as high as we can go," which you should never, never, never do in an elevator because you can get trapped up above the fire or the elevator could open up on the fire floor. Go two floors below the lowest reported area of fire or smoke and take the interior stairs up. But we had reports of people trapped up there and we got fooled, because there was no smoke in the lobby, no smoke in the elevator. We went above the fire.

We got off on twenty-two, and there was a good amount of smoke. There was an access stairway between twenty-two and twenty-one. (An access stairway is a wide-open stairway between two floors. The Fire Department doesn't want them because they're a hazard. But the developers bargain for them, and maybe the department will permit them if there are sprinkler heads all around the stairs.) As we went down the access stairs, we found a cleaning lady on twenty-one groping around in the smoke. I gave her to my chauffeur and said, "Get her down below the fire." We now knew the fire was on twenty. So we crawled down the fire-tower staircase to the twentieth floor. An officer from a truck company was already there. He had stretched a standpipe house line and was operating on the fire. The engine company was in the process of hooking up to the floor below and stretching the two-and-a-half-inch line. We were on the south end of the center hall, and the fire was in the northeast quadrant moving north down the corridor. So we split up into two teams. I had one team go toward the west end of the building, the other team start searching the south. They overlapped when they hit the bathrooms, because that's where people have a tendency to hide if they can't get out.

At this particular job the fire was on the twentieth floor, but the smoke had banked down to sixteen. The fifteenth floor was clear. The smoke rose, but it was summertime, and because of the air conditioning, that smoke was cooled and stratified, and so it banked down below the fire floor.

The fire was of such intensity that the aluminum frames around the windows melted and the glass fell out into the street. The whole northeast quadrant was burning. What kept the fire from progressing through the entire floor was the subdivision—there were partitions around every 7,500 square feet. The partitions went from the floor up to the underside of the next floor.

There were three hand lines in operation. On one, the engine company ran out of air and abandoned it. Because of smoke banking down, incoming companies didn't know where the fire floor was. The communications were not as good as they should have been. People were getting knocked out, our people were running out of air trying to hold a position, and relief didn't come. That happens when you have a fire of such magnitude, with a tremendous amount of smoke.

The building had a fire tower, which is a separate enclosed staircase. To get to this fire tower you had to go through two doors: you'd go through one door into a vestibule, then through a second door into another staircase. In the vestibule there was a guard rail that surrounded a shaft. One of the two doors had been left open or burned through, and the guard rail, which should have been about four and a half feet high, had melted right down to the floor from the intensity of the fire. The companies coming up the fire-tower staircase couldn't get up above the nineteenth-floor landing to operate the line, because the place was so hot. The other line that went in on the floor was west of that fire partition, and those men couldn't get through the fire partition because it was so hot, so they just kept cooling everything there and applying water as best they could.

I left one fireman from Rescue 1 on the house line and one on the two-and-a-half-inch line; there was no one else there. I took two more guys, and we crawled west and then north. We found glass that was hot. I figured it was window glass, but it turned out to be the glass in the vestibule lobby. We broke that and a lot of heat came our way. I said, "This fire is wrapping around the corner of the building." I went back to find my guys still on the line, pegging water at the fire. I said, "Hold it as long as you can. When you can't, come down. I'm going to go down and get us help. I'm out of air." I crawled into the fire-tower staircase and went down one floor, and the smoke was thick and black. I went down another floor—smoke thick and black there, too. I went down three more floors—smoke thick and black. Then I started to lose consciousness. So I just started backpedaling down the stairs. Thinking to myself, "We must have two or three floors of fire." Finally I crawled out of the smoke and located another fireman. I said, "Get up to the twentieth floor. I've got two guys up there and they're out of air!" He went up and crawled in on the floor.

Someone had brought resuscitators up and we were passing them around to each other to give ourselves oxygen. "Come on, hurry up, give it to me," I said. I was so weak. Any fireman I saw with a mask on I told to get up to twenty, because two men were on that floor. Finally, my two men came down, one of them helping the other. We were lying around on the floor taking oxygen, just totally exhausted.

A short time after that came a Mayday message: a fireman from Engine 23 was missing. I was so exhausted I had no strength left. If they'd told me it was my sister or my daughter I don't think I could have gone after them. I was so weak, so overcome, so exhausted; that was a weird feeling. There was a fireman missing and there I was a rescue lieutenant, and I had no strength to go get him. It took, I don't know, fifteen, twenty minutes, it seemed, before I was able to get enough air to muster my strength just to get up. Then we went back up there.

What had happened was Engine 23 had moved in from this fire tower. Things got so hot they had to go back out. One guy's helmet got knocked off. They found his helmet but not the man; they didn't know he had gone down to another location. So he actually wasn't missing, after all. We searched the fire floor anyway. By this time the fire had been knocked down, almost extinguished, but the area still retained a tremendous amount of heat, and it would for hours and hours afterward. The concrete spoiled, the steel twisted, and the floor dropped, opening up a crack. The fire got into a rug and a couple of cabinets on the twenty-first floor.

I think 130 firemen went to the hospital at that fire, most from exhaustion and smoke inhalation. A few people might have had minor burns. But what was the most frustrating for me was that I had never before been physically beaten to the point that I couldn't respond to an urgent Mayday message, where I had no strength to do anything but gasp for my next breath. I feared that I might have lost two of my own men and I did not even have the strength to go after them. It was very, very frustrating, in spite of the fact that we got a unit citation for that fire.

There were a lot of pictures in *WNYF* magazine of those windows blowing out. Quarter-inch plate glass coming down twenty stories—it'll kill you. There were pictures of the apparatus, showing where a piece of glass had come down and gone right through the roof. We had all sorts of scrapes on the truck, even though we were on the south side of the building and the fire was on the northeast.

In high-rise fires we try not to break windows because of the danger to people down below. If we do break them, we break them in the corner and pull the glass inward. If the fire gets to where it pops the windows, then we advance in that direction, but if it's a smoldering fire in the inner core— maybe a room where there's no window—it's tough for us to find. We've got heat all around, and we have to use our hands to sense the direction, sort of like radar. Where the heat is more intense, that's the way we go.

The best policy, for firemen and for people who work there, is to know where all the staircases are in these high-rise buildings. If you go to one and there's smoke, then go to another and so forth until you find a safe way down.

I was right in the middle of writing a roll call one morning, about a quarter after nine, when the dispatcher called us, "Rescue One, you're special-called to Brooklyn." As we were responding down the West Side I switched radio frequencies to the Brooklyn channel and heard them say, "There was a collapse—numerous firemen missing."

I said, "Oh, my God." We put the pedal to the floor. I guess it took us twenty minutes to get there. The fire was in Waldbaum's supermarket.

As we approached the scene, we came in on the avenue, on what we call the exposure two side. Chief Stankarone had that position. A fellow by the name of Pete Bondy from Rescue 2 crawled out of a truck loading area, and we questioned him as to where he thought the missing firemen were. Then I saw another fireman from Rescue 2 come out. The remaining fellows from Rescue 2 had been taken to the hospital. One of them fell through the roof, but was alive. The timing was right when we got there to make a push. The roof trusses had collapsed, but the amount of fire could be controlled with hand lines. You could cut a path, so to speak.

We took a line from the engine company and told them to get a second line to back us up. And it was a very professional maneuver. I'm pretty much in charge of our company, in that I advance with the nozzle and send men ahead, one to the right, one to the left. If the fire or smoke condition gets too bad, they come back to the nozzle. We operate by pushing the fire away and then pushing in deeper.

At this time we did not have more than a slight margin of hope of finding anyone alive unless some of them had made it to the corners of the building. The roof area had collapsed completely. So it was very unlikely that anyone was going to be alive. But we still wanted to get to them as soon as we could. Twelve fellows had gone into the fire. Six of them had been pulled out immediately, but the other six were still missing.

We were eventually able to penetrate into the middle of the building. Pete Bondy found a helmet and passed it back. I looked at it. The front piece was gone, and I couldn't tell whether it was from an engine or a truck company. I passed it to one of the battalion chiefs. He said, "They found another helmet." So he passed it back to me. I held it up again and as I looked past it, about thirty feet away I could see one of the firemen. He was upside down, draped over the aisle divider. I hollered to Bobby Burns, a fireman in Rescue 1, "Look up!" He looked up and about two feet away from him were two dead fire fighters. They were roasted—burned beyond recognition. One of them had the microphone of the Handie-Talkie, with the remote microphone wire on his chest. The other one was draped over the first man, both of them face up. They had probably tried to climb up the trusses, or what was left of the trusses, to get up to the roof.

The other four were within a radius of maybe seven or eight feet of the first two, one right on top of the other. They were all within reach of each other in this one aisle, mixed in with rolls of roofing paper. The partner saw that what they were using had just about disintegrated from the intensity of the fire.

Most of the time in a situation like that, I can operate very professionally; I can remove myself from the emotionalism. I learned that years ago in Rescue 4. The firemen told me to almost think of people as inanimate objects, so I could perform my job. And that training or experience helps me handle something that can be emotionally devastating. You see, I don't think about it until after it's over with and then it hits me. I knew one of the firemen who was killed, a lieutenant; we had gotten promoted at the same time. But I didn't know it was him until later on. Not knowing might have made the task a little easier. When we found the bodies they were still smoldering. We had to wash them down to cool them off; they were too hot to handle. We covered them up and passed them out one by one.

There was one fellow from our company who was in sort of a daze, looking at his fallen brothers. It was starting to get to him. So I reached over, grabbed him by the arm, shook him, and said, okay, do this, do that, to keep him busy so he couldn't think about it. Because if we stood around and just stared, we all probably would have cried or gone into a state of shock. But it didn't happen. That fellow had only been in this company a short time, maybe a year. The other men were very experienced.

As soon as we finished the operation, I went to a pay phone and called my wife to tell her I was okay. Then we went back to the firehouse and there was a discussion. Everyone was sort of somber about it, reflecting on what had happened, knowing it could have been them. Some time later, when I got the final report on that fire, I reviewed it with them, since it does happen every so often that a group of firemen can find themselves in the wrong place at the wrong time.

• • •

There was a fire on Forty-second Street in a dirty-book store. The store was only about nine or ten feet wide, but it went back sixty feet. When we turned the corner, we saw flames shooting out into the street, and the whole of Forty-second Street was obscured by black smoke. There were four stores in this one building, and the firemen were pushing into the middle store. Seven or eight men from Engine 65 and Ladder 4 knocked down the fire and went all the way to the rear of the store. In the rear of that store was a doorway leading to a common corridor that ran across the back of this building. Each store had an exit into this corridor, which led to a rear doorway. It would have been the second means of escape, but someone had blocked it up.

I came out of the front of one of the stores with another fireman, Dennis Dale, and we were in the street talking to the chief. We told him there was no fire in that particular store, but the fire had gotten into the common ceiling—in other words, the same ceiling that extended over all four stores. As they were operating the line, knocking down the fire, the weight of the water caused the ceiling to crash down. It buried the hose line and a couple of men from 65 Engine. They crawled into the rear with fire overhead. Their radio message was "We're cut off! We're trapped!"

The deputy chief on the scene, Elmer Chapman, said, "See what you can do. We'll get you more help." Chief Grimes went in first, as we started putting on our masks; the smoke was down to the floor. He came back out coughing and gagging. He didn't have a mask on, so I took the bottom of my mask off and I said to him, "Where are they? Did they fall into the cellar?" He just took the two of us and said, "Get them! Get them!" and pushed us into the store. We went along the wall taking the bottom of our masks off periodically and calling out to the trapped men. We couldn't follow the hose line because it was buried under debris. But we could hear them operating the line in there. The captain of the engine company had bent the hose line back on itself and was able to control it to knock down the fire. But that was driving the heat toward us. Judging from the amount of heat coming our way, I thought they had fallen into the cellar and we were going to find a hole. We went along the wall to the rear of the building, and we could hear their alarms going.

With the older masks, when you were down to four hundred pounds of air pressure they would sound an alarm—*bing, bing, bing*. As we got to them a couple of the fellows had taken their masks off and were yelling, "Get us out of here! Get us out of here!"

The rest of the members of Rescue 1 were pounding away with the backs of the axes to breach the wall in the rear to get them out that way. They heard the men inside calling out for help. We didn't have Handie-Talkies with us, so we couldn't tell the chief we had located them.

Once we got to the trapped fellows in the back, they dropped the line and half of them got out of there. But a couple of them were coughing and had no air at all. So we stood in the doorway telling them, "Come on, keep going! Keep going!" The next thing you know six, seven, or eight of them got out. But we figured we were going to find more fellows in that corridor. We went to the end and it was extremely hot, but everyone was out. We could still hear the rescue banging away, so I took my mask off and hollered, "They're out! They're out!" Then we scooted out.

A fireman from Ladder 4, Bill Hyland, wrote a poem about us. I have treasured it. It ends with "We owe you many a brew you men of Rescue." No one ever wrote a poem about me before. It was nice.

In the wee hours of the morning of January 29, 1982, we were dispatched to the construction site of the Trump Tower on Fifth Avenue. When we got off the rig it was a spectacular sight—the entire twenty-seventh floor was completely involved in fire.

The concrete for the twenty-eighth floor had recently been poured into wooden forms. These forms are soaked with an oil so that the concrete will not adhere to them when it dries. Canvas tarpaulins had been placed around the twenty-seventh floor and kerosene heaters lit to help warm the space. The wind must have blown one of these tarpaulins, which also get soaked with the form oil, into one of the heaters and up it went. It was like having a lumberyard on fire, only it was twenty-seven stories above the ground.

More importantly, however, a crane operator by the name of Tom Bracken was trapped above the fire in the cab of his machine. He was sitting above a 300-gallon diesel fuel tank, and the flames were lapping at the underside of the cab. Tom was the first one to see the fire. He'd notified the building's security people on his radio. Then he raised the crane's hook from the street; being the son of a retired fire fighter he knew that the hook might hamper the incoming apparatus. After he got the hook up, he tried to reach the crane's access ladder, but was driven back to the cab by the superheated smoke.

Chief Landgrebe told us to try to rescue the crane operator, but because of the thermal updrafts, the use of a helicopter was ruled out. In the meantime, the chief told Lieutenant Tommy Pilner of Ladder 4 to take his men and the guys from Engines 21 and 65 across the street and up to the roof of the twenty-six-story Steuben Glass building. They were to set up heavy-caliber streams and try to knock down some of this raging fire.

Tom Bracken's situation was worsening. Cans of ether, which are used to start the crane's engine, exploded because of the intense heat. Tom started to swing the boom of the crane toward the Steuben building, intending to drop the hook onto the roof of that building, climb out across the boom, and slide down the cable to the roof of the Steuben building. But the fire burned out his electrical controls before the boom was in place.

By this time we had taken an exterior construction elevator up to the twenty-sixth floor. We were met with showering fire. We could hear pieces of concrete exploding on the twenty-seventh floor because of the intense heat, which also prevented us from climbing the stairs. We tried to find another way up. John McAllister and Tommy Baker were using wooden planks as battering rams to clear away the plywood covers on the holes in the concrete ceiling. It was our intention to put up a ladder in an area where the heat wasn't so intense. Before we could do that two huge sections of the twenty-eighth floor collapsed with a tremendous roar. The building shook vigorously and a blast of heat came down upon us. We got down to the twenty-fifth floor because we feared an additional collapse, since the concrete on the twenty-eighth floor hadn't fully set.

We still had to try to get up above the fire to Tom Bracken. Fortunately I located the shaft in which the steel framework for the crane rested. Above us the steel was cherry red, and the heat radiated through my gloves when I tried to climb the access ladder.

Engine 23 arrived with a charged hand line and began cooling down the steel. Again I tried to go up the ladder, but I was driven down by the radiant heat from the floor above. Then Joe Pierotti climbed the ladder and secured himself with a leg lock. He operated the nozzle to knock down the surrounding fire while Harry Wehr from 23 and I held him.

Lieutenant Byrns from Ladder 16 and I put our masks on and wrapped our arms and hands with rags. We were able to climb up to the crane's cab. We waited with Bracken until the guys from 23 had darkened down more of the fire.

One of the things that helped save Tom was that the underside of the cab was actually a counter weight of reinforced concrete. Otherwise the tank of diesel fuel would have exploded.

The next day Tom Bracken was back at work. He told me if he did not go back then, he might never have.

On the evening of January 23rd, 1985, Rescue 1 was returning to quarters from a fire on the Lower Eastside of Manhattan. When we reached 10th Avenue and 20th Street the dispatcher radioed us to respond to box 798—our home box. Every firehouse in the city of New York has its own home box—it is the one that is closest to that particular house. I turned on the siren, the chauffeur, Tom Baker, put the accelerator close to the floor, and the men in the back of the rig started putting their turnout gear back on.

I first thought we were responding to one of the tenements on 43rd Street and 10th Avenue.

Over the radio we heard the officer from Engine 54, one of the first arriving units, say, "It looks like we have a job." In other words, a working fire.

As we turned the corner at 43rd Street we saw the engine stretching a line while the men from the truck were forcing the front door of the fire building—not a tenement, but a large commercial building next to our firehouse.

When we reported in, the chief assigned us to assist Ladder 4 in searching for the location of the fire. I split up my company. I took three men with me to the cellar, and sent two others to search the first floor.

There was heavy smoke emanating from the cellar. When

we got to the cellar door I had fireman Tom Prin remain there and pay out a search line to us. As we moved into the cellar we were hit with intense heat. I told Baker to go back outside, around to the rear, and vent. Fireman Barry Mead and I then crawled about forty feet toward the rear of the cellar. The heat was very punishing, and we could hear what sounded like oil frying in a pan, but there was no visible fire. I called the engine to open the line, but it didn't alleviate the heat. It became unbearable in there. We crawled back along the search line to the doorway.

Firefighters Cochran and Feilmauser were joined on the first floor by Captain O'Flaherty and firefighter Killoran, both of whom had been off-duty in Rescue 1's quarters. The captain reported to Chief DeRosa that the steel plates covering the wooden floors of this building were so hot that they couldn't kneel on them, let alone crawl across them. Firefighter Baker meanwhile radioed that heavy fire was blowing out of the rear.

Chief DeRosa ordered all of us out of the fire building. As soon as we hit the street the fill-cap for the building's heating oil tank blew into the air, and we had a geyser of vaporizing oil. Obviously the oil storage tank was involved with fire. Thirty seconds later, fire was blowing out of the cellar. Then the first floor and, in less than a minute, the second and third floors lit up. Within a few minutes heavy smoke was pumping out of the fifth-floor windows on the exposure four side of the building, where our firehouse was located. At the rate that this fire was spreading, we realized we were not going to control it.

While the chief was transmitting calls for greater alarms, I knew our firehouse was in jeopardy. Since we had to wait for the tower ladders to arrive, I ordered my men to go into our house, get their keys from their lockers, and move their cars away from the front of quarters. At the same time, firefighter Dan Defranco was able to remove some irreplaceable memorabilia from our house.

Then with the men of Engine 65, we stretched a handline to the roof of the firehouse and began pouring water into the fire building. But visibility on the roof quickly became extremely limited, and we were ordered off the roof and out of the firehouse. While we were abandoning the house we saw brown smoke pumping through the wainscoting. I told firefighter Baker to go into the basement and shut off the gas; the last thing we needed was an explosion. When we got outside, I asked one of the tower ladders to play their high caliber stream on the wall of the fire building that abutted our quarters. It was a last desperate attempt at saving our building.

I have been to thousands of fires, but I had never seen as much fire emanating from one building. By now it was blowing out of every window on all eight floors, and even through the roof. As we watched from across the street we heard an ominous low rumble before the roof and top floor collapsed, causing a 30×50 foot section of wall to fall onto the roof of our firehouse.

At first I thought our building held, but when I looked in the front door I saw that the roof and the two upper floors had pancaked down onto the apparatus floor. The first twenty feet of the building remained intact, but everything behind that was gone.

It was a defeat, and I felt a great loss. When a fireman loses his firehouse it's like losing his home. As fireman Al Fuentes put it, "We loved that house." It was as if an old friend had passed away. I went through sort of a mourning for the place, but in time I realized that ultimately it's not the place, but it's the men who make up the company, and that's the most important thing. Fortunately no lives were lost at this 10-alarm fire, and Rescue 1 goes on. As a matter of fact, at one-thirty that morning, while the fire was under control, we were special-called to extricate a man who had gotten his arm caught up to the elbow in a large printing press on West 17th Street.

The loss of our firehouse, however, has been tempered by the generous reception of the firefighters of Engine 34 and Ladder 21 on West 38th Street, where we have been temporarily relocated.

That night, however, Commissioner Joseph Spinato promised Captain Brian O'Flaherty that our house would be rebuilt, and as Tom Baker said, "The Phoenix will rise from its ashes."

Chapter 13

Deputy Chief Vincent Dunn
Third Division Commander,
Manhattan

When I got appointed to the Fire Department on February 1, 1957, I didn't know anything about the fire service. I had never been in a firehouse. I never knew any firemen. My father had signed me up for the Fire Department test while I was in the navy. At first I didn't want to be a fireman, but after I'd been on the job about six months I knew that I was born for the fire service.

Like most teenagers, I had difficulty believing that everything wasn't some sort of sham. There wasn't anything to look up to. I figured when I came on the Fire Department that these guys were going to figure some way to get out of fighting fires.

On Saint Paddy's Day night—six weeks after I started—we had a fire in Harlem. We stretched a line up to this tenement and started charging the line. The firemen opened the door, and I saw this black smoke come out. I figured something was going to happen and they wouldn't go in. Then they started jumping over each other to get at this hand line, and they moved it. They went into this dark hallway. The black smoke was coming out. Then they went right through this apartment extinguishing the fire. You never could see the flames, but you could hear the dishes crashing and the hose stream striking the walls and the ceiling. There was a terrible racket in there as they pushed out of the hallway and extinguished about three or four rooms of fire.

I was out in the hallway because I was the probie. When I went in after them I didn't realize that you have to crouch down. I got hit by the heat and the smoke that was on the top part of the doorway, and I was forced out. I couldn't believe that they had gone into that apartment. I think I was twenty-one at the time. That was my first fire, and that was the first thing I met in life that was for real: I saw men do exactly what they said they were going to do.

When I went back to the firehouse that night I couldn't get over the roar of that fire. The noise was more dramatic than the flames, which you couldn't see.

One of the things I believe is that fire fighting is misnamed. We really should be called smoke fighters, because there is very little fire. Smoke is the predominant product of combustion. When you see fire you really have got it made. A fire in a building is ninety-nine percent smoke and one percent fire. Smoke is the enemy; it kills more people than flames do.

When you first go to a fire you really don't know what to do. You just become engulfed in the situation and are often very ineffective. Trying to do something at a fire takes tremendous concentration. I'm talking about fire fighting at the moment of truth. You have to blot every other thing out of your mind just to take off your gloves, take off your helmet, put the face piece of the mask on, connect it up, put the helmet and gloves back on, and pick up the nozzle. It sounds like a simple thing, but at a fire people are yelling, the fire is roaring, everybody is running around, and the doors are being forced. You can't believe how hard this is until you realize that in the next second, when they open that door, you could be blown down the stairway.

I got a call the other day from a volunteer fire fighter. He had been at this fire and the officer had told him to get a particular fitting. The guy asked him exactly what fitting he wanted. The officer started screaming. The guy said to me, "The more he screamed, the less I could do." Imagine trying to button your shirt as a kid when your mother or father or somebody you were afraid of is screaming at you, "Button that and hurry up." The task just becomes tremendously difficult. The bigger the fire behind that door the more difficult it is to think about anything.

In fire fighting the only way you can do it well is to go to many fires, learn to block out every single thing and just think of the task at hand. You only do basic tasks; that's why everybody has a specific assignment. When you open that nozzle as an engine man or make that rescue as a truckie, that is the moment of truth. You might do this only once in your career, and you don't want to blow it. That's why firemen are always training.

I think what you've done as a fireman influences your view of firemen when you become an officer. If you goofed off as a fireman then as an officer you think all firemen are goof-offs. If you worked very hard and were conscientious, then as an officer you believe all fire fighters are conscientious. I tend to hold the latter view.

I find being a deputy chief is the best rank. Some guys are born to be fire fighters. Others are born to be lieutenants or captains or battalion chiefs. But I was born to be a deputy chief. When I got to this rank something happened to me; I felt like a big weight was taken off my shoulders.

A deputy chief is really a fire-ground organizer. A deputy runs big fires—second and third alarms—whereas a battalion chief is in charge of a first alarm fire. If I go to a first alarm, I am going to do one of two things: if the battalion chief is successful in controlling the fire, I'll supervise the winding down; if he is not successful, I'll go for a second alarm and institute a larger fire ground. Of course, if I am not successful and we go into a fourth or fifth alarm, then the borough commander or the Chief of Department may oversee the operation.

Many people believe that battalion chiefs and deputy chiefs are the same, but we aren't. The battalion chief is very aggressive. He goes right into the building and supervises the first three hose lines from the first three arriving engine companies. He is successful ninety-nine percent of the time.

The deputy usually gets there after the initial shot has been taken. He usually sets up his command post in the street. He has a little better ability to size the situation up, because he is not as emotionally involved as that first due battalion chief. When the deputy changes tactics, nine times out of ten he goes to an exterior attack. The deputy is more of a defensive fighter. As a deputy I learned how to pull fire fighters out of buildings. I never did that as a battalion chief. The battalion chief's strategy is to attack the fire as quickly and as forcefully as possible. The deputy also has to be very concerned with possible collapse, because when he gets there on a second or third alarm the fire is really destroying the structure.

A deputy chief is also a communicator. That's the name of the game; if you can't communicate at a fire you really can't be a deputy and you're only kidding yourself if you think otherwise.

The other night we had a fire in the Bronx on Webster Avenue and 189th Street in a one-story, 150-by-100-foot commercial building, which housed a Spanish restaurant and an auto parts store. The fire started in the restaurant and spread to the auto parts store. The initial alarm came in about three o'clock in the morning. The interior attack was not successful because there was too much gasoline in there.

I got there on the all-hands. They had two hand lines stretched and were in the process of stretching a third when the fire came roaring through the roof. I decided to go for a second alarm. We pulled the fire fighters out of the building and set up an exterior attack. I had an open lot on exposure two—that's the left side of the building—so there was little danger of the fire spreading in that direction. But on the exposure 4, or right, side of the building, I had a hardware store. To protect that exposure I sent men in there with a hand line and told them to pull the ceiling to make sure the fire was not coming through the wall. We set up one tower ladder in the front of the building and another in the vacant lot and supplied both of them with water to deluge the fire. But we had a problem. There was a large Catholic cathedral in the back, the exposure 3 side. We thought that if the fire came through the roof in the rear it would get into the stained-glass windows. I sent the second alarm truck, an engine, and a battalion chief back there. The engine stretched a line into the ten-foot space between the church and the back of the fire building, while the guys from the truck company and the chief inspected the cathedral for signs of extending fire. But as the fire progressed I continued to be worried about the church, so I filled out the third alarm and sent another engine and truck in there.

I was also concerned about the exposure 4 side, because there were at least ten other stores on that side. If the fire got into them we would have another disaster. Another tower ladder was special-called and positioned between the fire building and the adjoining stores. We just poured water on the fire building from the hand lines and heavy-caliber streams.

When I first arrive at a fire, my aide confers with the battalion chief's aides so that we know which companies are present and where they are operating. Knowing this helps me to maintain control and to make sure that nobody gets lost. On the second alarm the Field Communications Unit comes in. They set up a metallic board, called a situation board, which has little magnets with company numbers on them. Then an overhead plain view of the fire building is placed on the board and the appropriate magnets are arranged to indicate the location of each company. When the third alarm comes in, I get a communications coordinator. He is a chief whose job is to keep in contact with all the companies present at this fire and to update the situation board. As the fire continues we have to give periodic progress reports to the dispatcher over the radio. These reports are recorded, as are all radio communications, so that a log can be kept of the operation. There have been occasions where the transcripts have been used in various court proceedings.

At this fire in the Bronx, a problem developed with the wall on the exposure two side. The chief who was protecting the church said he saw that wall move several times. So we got everybody away from there. I had earlier gotten everybody out of the building. Fortunately, the wall never collapsed and we were able to extinguish the fire before it extended into the exposures. It was your typical Fordham area fire where we have many one-story commercial buildings with stores in them.

Back in 1958 we had the Wooster Street collapse down in SoHo. It was in a loft building that was used for commercial storage. Now it is a parking lot. Few people who walk by that parking lot realize that two firemen and four Fire Patrol men were killed there. In the early stages of that fire the floors just pancaked down one on top of another, while the walls stayed up.

I worked the night that collapse occurred. They wanted volunteers to go there. We went in the morning. It was a cold, icy day. When we got there they sent us into the cellar of the building on the exposure two side. We operated a jackhammer and breached through the wall to get at the trapped men. But once we got through the wall more rubble fell. We tried, but we really weren't too effective.

Later, when I was a lieutenant in 33 Engine in 1966, we were sent on a second alarm to a fire on Broadway and Twenty-second Street in Manhattan. We arrived about ten o'clock at night and reported into Chief Harry Goebel, who promptly sent us around to Deputy Chief Thomas Reiley on Twenty-third Street. I told Reiley who we were and asked him what he wanted us to do. He said, "Hold up a second."

With that, a guy from the Fire Patrol came out of a building directly behind the fire building on Twenty-second Street, and said, "Chief, we got fire around the baseboards in back."

We were on one side of Chief Reiley and the guys from 18 Engine were on the other. Reiley said, "All right, 18 Engine you stretch the line into that building, and 33, you stretch into the Broadway building."

So we went to the corner and stretched our line into the corner building that fronted on Broadway. Reiley, his driver, and the men from 18 Engine went into the Wonder drugstore, which was in the building that the Fire Patrol man had come out of.

We took our line into the Broadway building and were met by Sixth Battalion Chief Freddie White. He told us to go to this bathroom down the hall and force the door. We could then operate the line out of the window. We just opened up the line when word came to evacuate the building. Now it became a big outside operation.

Then we got word that they had a collapse inside the drugstore and twelve guys, in every rank from probie to assistant chief, were dumped into a burning basement. They were all killed. What the men in the drugstore hadn't known was that the basement of the fire building extended partway under the drugstore and that basement was fully involved with fire.

The call again went out for volunteers, and by morning there were hundreds of people there. The cellar of the drugstore was filled with water. So they got guys who were over six feet tall and had them wade through this underground lake and try to locate bodies. But all of the firemen had gone into the fire.

They started to bring the bodies out one at a time. It was

very somber, and of course every time they brought one of them out it was worse. Every once in a while you'd see a woman show up, and she would either be a widow or a girlfriend. The press would be following her around. The commissioner showed up and he had his dark glasses on. It just got to be a big event after a while.

If you are to continue on this job you have to put certain things out of your mind. It wasn't until six years ago—when I ran into a guy I worked with at that fire who said to me that they could just as easily have sent us in there rather than the guys from 18 Engine—then I really started to think about it. But that is how you survive, by putting tragedy behind you.

I don't think you can completely overcome fear. But what I do think is that at that moment of truth you are concentrating so deeply on your task that you don't have time to realize how much danger you're in. It's only after you go home at night and you're out of the situation that the fear hits you. But you come back into the firehouse the next night.

Sometimes you can lose yourself when you're at a fire. You just get so caught up in it. We had this fire in the back of a taxpayer and it was coming right through the roof. A fire fighter from the truck company put up a portable ladder on the adjoining building and brought the saw up to help another guy from the second due truck cut the roof. The fire building went back seventy-five feet, but the adjoining structure was only thirty feet deep. The fireman just walked right off the back of the adjoining building. He broke his ankle, but was fortunate in that he wasn't cut with the saw, which he was carrying when he fell. Later on, we asked him how he managed to walk off the building. He told us that he just got fixated in watching the fire and wasn't looking where he was going.

Fire is alive, there's no question about it. We call it "the red devil," or "the beast." It breathes, it moves, it's your adversary. As a fire fighter your objective is to kill it.

If there is one thing I like more than putting out fires it's writing about the fire service. I have been writing mostly about building collapses, because I have a morbid fear of losing men in a collapse.

Every year approximately 140 firemen are killed and 100,000 are injured in the United States. The National Fire Protection Association, which keeps these statistics, claims that ten per cent of those firemen die as a result of building collapse and a larger percentage die as a result of being hit with falling objects. But I think that the actual percentage of death and injuries due to structural collapse is larger. For example, a friend of mine, Frank Tuttlemondo, died in a frame building collapse. He was a chief in the Forty-fourth Battalion, and he was pinned under all this rubble with other firemen when the building collapsed. The *New York Times* and other newspapers' reported that he had a heart attack while he was buried. I believe that the NFPA statistician also attributed his death to a heart attack, but I would have classified it as a building-collapse fatality. About a month before his death, I had called him up to get some information from him, because I was writing an article on frame buildings. I was driving home with my wife when they announced his name on the radio. I said, "Oh, Christ. I know he thought of me when he was pinned underneath all that rubble, because of our talk." He went in to get those guys out. But it was just the wrong moment.

Seven years ago Captain Stelmack was putting his mask on in front of a fire building when a fifty-five-pound coping stone hit him on the head and killed him. I believe that was due to a weakness in the mortar of the building. Again I would have said his death was the result of a structural collapse.

Then three firemen from 143 Truck were killed on Liberty Avenue in Queens. They went into the back of a restaurant to search, and the ceiling collapsed. They were trapped back there. The windows and the doors were all sealed up. The other men were not able to get through the wall before the fire got to them. I'm sure that their death was attributed to burns and smoke rather than structural collapse.

We all have a crusade. Mine is to bring about an increased awareness of structural collapse and its impact on the fire service. I spend a lot of time thinking about how and why buildings fall. I visit these sites. I take photographs and I keep amassing information.

I'm often asked what are the warning signs for a potential collapse. There are some, but with all the investigation that I've done, I realize that a building can fall down without any warning and nobody could have predicted it. I tell every fireman and every officer that if all of the occupants are known to be out of the building, then they have no business being in a place where they endanger their own lives.

A perfect example of this was an arson fire I had one night in a vacant building on Washington Avenue in the Bronx. We put up a tower ladder and it did a wonderful job. We didn't have anybody operating in the building. We were lucky there was no chance of the fire extending to the exposures. When the fire was darkened down, I had to send men in there to make sure it was totally out. But they could now operate in a much more cautious way and nobody was hurt.

I think about all those firemen who have been badly hurt, and about what happens on this job, and I don't mean those little John Wayne injuries, but when a guy gets badly scarred or crippled. Those guys just disappear. Nobody ever hears from them, because when they are around, fire fighters get uncomfortable. They can see what could happen to them.

One time there was a good fire going in a vacant building on 116th Street in Manhattan that had once been a drug rehabilitation place. The captain from 91 Engine and two firemen were moving the line in when the floor collapsed. The fire was in the cellar, but they didn't know it. One of the firemen hung onto the edge of the floor, but the flames came up and he was so horribly burned that he'll never use his hands again. The captain had fallen into the cellar. They eventually put a portable ladder down to him. He had to come up through the flames, and he had to take his mask off first because he was out of air. As he came up he was badly burned around the face and the neck. The nozzle man was spared because the collapse occurred behind him. He had to jump back over the hole and get help to get the other men out.

Some time passed. Then one day I was here in the division and a guy came through the door delivering calendars for the union. He had his collar up and his face was gray. I sort of recognized him. When I got close to him I could see that he was badly scarred. I said, "Jesus, what happened to you?"

He said, "I'm so and so. I was the captain in 91 Engine."

Now I knew who he was. He just walked out of here and I never saw him again. Here was a captain who fell into a fire, got injured, was given a disability pension and then told to go away.

If you look at the statistics you see that most fire fighters die in two age groups. The first is the twenty- to twenty-six-year-olds. The second is the forty-five- to fifty-one-year-olds. The younger men get killed more often by fire products—collapsing walls and things of that nature. I think back to when I was becoming a first grade fireman. I was almost ready to commit suicide to become known as a good fire fighter. But once you have extinguished fires and had those moments of truth and you begin to realize that you can do the job very well, then you can relax. But those young firemen who are trying to impress everybody with their ability are very vulnerable. The older fire fighters tend to die of heart attacks. This is a job where you go from sitting in a truck to running at full tilt in less than a minute and without any sort of warm-up. It is something that no athlete would ever do.

When a fire fighter thinks there is someone trapped in a burning building he seems to shift into overdrive. For example, back in 1958 we got an alarm on Seventh Avenue. When we were about four blocks away, we could see flames coming out of a window. The dispatcher said, "There's a report of a baby trapped in there."

I was with the engine company, and we stretched the line up and extinguished the fire in two or three rooms. But there was chaos in the hallway. At that time we didn't have specific assignments and everybody was trying to find the baby. But we couldn't find it. The mother was down in the bar drinking. We sifted through the ashes, but no luck. The mother then came up and said her baby was in the other room where there was no fire. So we looked in that room—in the bed, under the bed, in the closets, out the window, but there was no baby there. So we went out to the street. It was a cold winter's night and we had been there about thirty minutes. The lieutenant told me to go in there and search one more time. I had the flashlight and I looked under the bed—nothing. Then I happened to look behind the radiator, and there was this little baby with big diapers on. It was wedged in there. The radiator was hissing, but the room was cold. The baby must have crawled toward the hot radiator for warmth and somehow got wedged behind it. Fortunately the baby was still alive. We handed it over to his mother. Once in a while I wonder about what ever happened to that kid.

I also think about my own life and how much I owe to the fire service. One of the people who greatly influenced me on this job was my former aide, Walter Fornes. He is a family-oriented man. He is hardworking and is very confident, but he is a character. He looks a little like Popeye and he has a very colorful way of speaking. But he is a very kind person. In the sixteen years I worked with him I never saw him get mad. I saw him get hit with bricks thrown from roofs, and we responded to thousands of false alarms together, but he never lost his temper. Maybe he understands more about life than most. He laughs a lot. He likes to clown around, though I found out that he really is very shy. Walter is a terrific human being. He is putting in his retirement papers and I'm going to miss him.

Chapter 14

Chief of Operations (retired), New York City Fire Commissioner (retired) Augustus Beekman

I joined the fire department because I needed a job. I came out of the service in March of 1946, I took the civil service test, and by January of 1947 I was marching into 58 Engine at midnight. In those days you went directly to a firehouse before going to the training school. And since the job was on the three-platoon system, the day started at midnight.

I lived two blocks from 82 Engine, and at that time we were told to go to the nearest firehouse, where a fire fighter would look at the order and tell us where we were assigned and how to get there. So I walked into 82 Engine on Intervale Avenue and 169th Street in the Bronx. The fellow looked at the order and then he said to me, "What did you do?"

I said, "What did I do? What do you mean?"

He said, "You're going to 58 Engine. That's the busiest house in the city."

Engine 58 was in Harlem, on 115th Street at Lenox Avenue. It later moved to 114th Street, which was the house that had 26 Truck. They stayed there until I was promoted. Then they moved to 112th and Fifth, where they are now. When I first came on duty the captain happened to be working. He said, "Go to the rack, get a pair of boots that you think will fit you, get a coat, and try to get a helmet to fit you. If we go out and we have a fire stick close to me." That was my introduction. Thirty minutes later I was at my first all-hands fire on Seventh Avenue and 122nd Street in Manhattan.

It was, for me, enlightening and quite confusing and somewhat shocking because for the first time I found that fire fighting had to be done without any lights. In this case, the fire was blowing out of the windows on about the fourth floor, and there were no lights in the building. I was trying to assist in stretching hose in the hallway, and I didn't even know what "stretching hose" meant. I was told to stay outside as the company moved in on the fire floor. There were other probies working in the other companies. I recall a chief coming in from the Sixteenth Battalion and seeing us in the hall when the fire was inside the apartment. I can't repeat his language, but he wanted to know what kind of fakers we were. When the other men came out, they explained to the chief that we were all probies and had just gotten there so to speak.

After that first night I went home and told my mother, "Jeez, I think I may have made a mistake. It was rough." But it was not what the Fire Department would call a rough night. Of course 58 was the busiest engine company in the city at that time. They had about a thousand workers. The work in those days was all real work. There wasn't too much junk work. These were tenement fires where generally the smoke and the heat are going to meet you a floor or so below and you have to move up and into it.

When you walk into a new company they look at an order and your name is on it, and as of that minute you're a member of that company. Everyone wants the best for you, because doing your best is going to do the best for the company and the company can then maintain its reputation. All of us were young going in; I was twenty-three. I was raised without a father, so in addition to learning about fire fighting I also learned a lot about being a man from the members and the officers of 58.

The lady who was to become my wife visited me at the firehouse in the early days, and of course there were rules—like no woman can go past the house watch. So I was talking to her in front of the firehouse on 115th Street. The captain came down and he said to me, "Gus, bring your fiancée up to the office." He didn't feel that she should have to stand out on 115th Street. Now, that was a personal thing; it was not something he had to do. We didn't have a relationship; I was new in the company and they didn't know whether I was going to be a turkey or not.

There were things like that which guided you and were character-building. The firemen talked to you, not only about putting out fires but also about how to conduct yourself and about your credibility—in other words, they told you that your word is your bond.

Once I was in the fire service I became aware of the promotion structure. I felt that it was possible to make the Fire Department a career, not just a job. You could advance on your merit, and I made the decision relatively early to try to do so. At that time there was a black battalion chief in the job, and he was the reason I felt I could be promoted. Think back to 1946. In those days blacks had a better chance to make it in the civil service than in the private sector. I was now in the public sector, and I was in a department wherein the promotion process seemed to be as objective as it could be—and I still think it is—because it didn't involve your name or an evaluation. All you had to do was take the exam, and based on marks and seniority, a list of promotions was published. It was all out front; there was no subjectivity in it—no interviews where you might run into cultural bias or any of that. Seeing Wesley Williams and recognizing that this man had become a chief in 1938—and certainly the racial climate was not as good in 1938 as it was in 1947—I felt that if it was possible for a black man to do that in 1938, what was to stop those of us who were coming in now from doing the same thing?

But like everybody else, I played around for a couple of years. I was on the track team. I came in first or second in the two-mile run for the Fire Department and for the citywide meets. But after a couple of years of that and with the Delehanty Institute cranking up, I began to think about going to school. We all had the G.I. Bill, so I started to study.

When I was promoted to lieutenant I went to 11 Engine on East Houston Street on the Lower East Side. This, too, was another learning experience. Harlem was very intense with residential work, and of course I benefited from being with a number one company for an extended period of time. The mere fact that you were coming from 58 Engine gave you the halo effect. But the old-time chiefs were saying, "Well, you may be a Harlem hotshot, but down here you have to prove yourself." Not that anyone was putting any burdens on me, but that's the nature of the Fire Department. No matter what you've done in the past, this is where you are now and are you going to be able to cut the mustard here?

It was a different type of work down there. You have a lot more uncertainty when you start dealing with the kind of construction that's characteristic of the Bowery and Chrystie Street, where there are subcellars. Then, going west to Broadway, to Greene, to Mercer, it's heavy commercial. That area was a great learning experience which was to serve me in good stead later on when I became a chief.

You see, from that location we went to major fires, not only in Manhattan, but to Brooklyn as well. Because of their proximity to the Williamsburg Bridge, the Lower Manhattan companies also go to Brooklyn on fourth and fifth alarms, so that we were exposed to a lot of commercial fires. And that was helpful in that you would meet people who were battalion chiefs when you were a lieutenant. Later, when they became deputies, they knew you had been tested and that you could be depended upon, so it made your career a little easier as you advanced to the upper ranks.

I enjoyed my whole career, but if I had to pick one period of time I liked best it would be when I was a captain. As a captain you are the boss, and it's here that you can really be tested, because the company is a reflection of the captain. If the company is good generally it's because the captain is good. I went into 17 Engine and it was very enjoyable. Charlie Ryan was a lieutenant in 18 Truck at the time, so he and I worked together. We had a very young house, which meant that we had an opportunity to assist people in developing themselves and also to create a good company, which we did. One of the most enjoyable things is to see how the men progress. To feel that we had made some contribution to this, that we were good role models—Charlie, Ray Gimbler, myself, and the other fellows who were down there. We encouraged those men to study. We were not beating anyone over the head; we were simply giving them an example of how to conduct themselves within the department, as we had been taught.

But we really went through some tough fires in that area. At the Grand Street fire, for example, a company had gone into the cellar of the fire building. It was a commercial building, and that kind of fire always has an element of danger. The fire occurred in late afternoon and I was due to work that evening, though I generally got in early. When I came on duty somewhere around 5:15 a report came in that a company was trapped in the Grand Street fire. So I waited until the incoming platoon was all in, and we went over to the fire. Now this was winter, it was cold, there was snow on the ground. We went to relieve the crew that had been on duty. The trapped firemen still hadn't been recovered, so the day crew said that they would remain for a while. Well, "a while" stretched out to three hours. By now it was confirmed which companies were involved, and as we went through the evening it got down to the point where three men were still missing. There was no overtime in those days, but the off-duty men said, "Okay, we'll continue to work until such time as these individuals are recovered." The men were recovered, and the off-duty fire fighters still remained on duty. This fire was no place to be, and yet those men all insisted on remaining there. Finally about midnight, our company was told we could return to quarters. However, all of our hose was frozen stiff. This crew of off-duty men assisted us with getting the hose back on the rig and then went back to quarters with us to help change the hose before going home. That exemplifies the type of people we were working with and their lack of selfishness. I'm sure that would repeat itself in other companies, which tells you something about the character of the Fire Department and the men in the Fire Department and the reason why men remain past the twenty years when they could retire.

After I made deputy chief, I asked to work in Community Relations, because I felt that at that point in time I could serve the department better there than in Operations, which I eventually returned to. But this was during that period in the late sixties when the Fire Department and the community were in conflict—not conflict caused by the Fire Department. It was a period of social unrest and you had the racial tension in there. We had people in Community Relations who were sending out material asking the firemen not to strike back, not to react. But those people did not really understand the degree of pressure that the men were under. In other words, there was too much social science and not enough pragmatism of looking beyond what's happening to us. I thought that our number one priority was to take steps to protect ourselves, to take steps not to be a part of the confrontation. But at the same time we had to sort of hold this city together, and for fifteen years we really did battle. The units just responded tremendously.

When I got into Community Relations, I spoke to the captain of every company that served our urban centers. I saw them in my headquarters and then at their location. One of the satisfying things is to see the leadership capability of the men in this department, particularly the captains, and Matty Farrell was one. At that time Matty was the captain on 103 Truck in East New York, which was one of the really difficult areas to work, and yet he had everything under control, as did so many others.

Over all my years in the department, I only left one assignment, and that was in Queens. My dissatisfaction had nothing to do with Queens itself. I just wasn't in the heart of the action; therefore I didn't seem to be learning as much. It's just a different atmosphere, I guess I just wasn't the right man to be out there. I was wild to get back to Manhattan. It seems contradictory, because most people would say, "Well, if you're going to a place where there's less danger, less work, and it's fifteen minutes from home, you should feel good about it," but that's not what you're in the department for, once you're in long enough to recognize what the department is about.

Probably the telephone company fire was the most challenging one I ever went to. I was chief of operations at the time and so of course I went to major fires all over the place. However, it was the consensus of many of the staff chiefs that this was the most difficult fire that we had encountered in the course of our careers to that point.

It occurred in 1975 and somewhere around April. The fire started at night. Eddie Kane was the staff chief in charge of the fire that night. He was a very capable individual. But when the fire went to an outside attack, as the chief of operations, I responded. I got there at four o'clock in the morning and took command of the fire. I never got off my feet until six o'clock the following evening when we got the fire under control.

The problem with that fire was the uncertainty. We have

had bigger fires, but when you know what the situation is, you know what to do about it, so it's not a problem. This fire had started in a vault below grade level. It had gotten out of the vault into the cellar. While Kane was there he had accomplished pushing the fire back from the cellar into the vault. That vault, I guess, was about thirty feet wide and whatever the depth of the building was running down Thirteenth Street—maybe 200 or 300 feet long. The vault ran down that whole side of the building, and it was full of cables. The fire had been pushed back into the vault, as I said, and it appeared that we were going to hold the fire under control. As we got into the morning, the vault fire was out, there was no fire in the cellar, and whatever fire had been up on the first floor was contained. The chief was up on the third floor with some companies trying to prevent vertical extension through shafts. But the second floor had never been vented. When we ordered it to be vented from the outside, it developed fire conditions that were later pictured on the cover of *WNYF*. It turned out to be a fire whose characteristics we did not foresee, nor did the telephone company. So much so that the telephone company, I forget at what cost, ran a mock-up of the fire just as a learning process. As a result of that fire they changed the design characteristics of all telephone exchanges.

The problem with the fire was that the vault, the first floor, and the second floor were full of cables, with each wire individually wrapped with polyvinyl chloride insulation. Now, extending up through the building were these huge cylinders, which appeared to be twelve-by-twelve-foot building columns. However, they were all wire—not one mass, but all individual wires, all with wrappings. Then on the upper floors was the switching equipment, which looked like a giant toaster, and whatever wiring was needed to connect one set of equipment with another set of equipment. During the course of many hours on the second floor the heat had been breaking down this PVC and distilling a gas out into the air, so that the place was filled with fuel in vapor form and with tremendous heat. The only thing the fire didn't have was oxygen. When we vented the building to let the smoke and heat out, we provided the oxygen for the fire. The polyvinyl chloride started to burn, and from that point on it was a very difficult fire.

The telephone company engineers were there with the plans of the building. They told us there were voids in the outer walls, so we asked them where the voids ended. Did they end on the top floor? Did they go to the roof? They couldn't tell us. So there was a great deal of uncertainty with that fire, and consequently we felt a great deal of satisfaction when it was over, because we handled a new kind of fire, using our basic knowledge and our experience to work it through. Of course, there was plenty of help, since I had different borough commanders there.

We feel that we were successful in that the fire building never collapsed. However, that fire did generate some medical concern after a number of people who had been there came down with cancer. Whether the cancer was directly related to the fire has not as yet been determined, but certainly there has been a greater enforcement of the use of self-contained breathing equipment as a result, although that was a full-mask fire. We did not allow anyone in the building to operate without the mask on. However, there was much smoke in the street. Occasionally people changed air bottles in what they considered an area of safe refuge, but the gases in distilled form could still have been out there.

I was outside most of the time. When you reach a particular level, most of your work is directing a fire like that from the outside. But we also had to coordinate an attack from three directions inside. There were three good stairways in there, which became the marshaling areas from which we initiated our attack. The safety characteristic was such that at each of those posts we had someone of the borough command rank. We had deputy chiefs on the floor along with battalion chiefs and the companies. Normally the deputy chiefs direct from outside, but in a major fire you get the deputy chiefs inside to command those stairway positions with the battalion chiefs.

That fire went to a fifth alarm. However, instead of transmitting a sixth alarm, a seventh alarm, or a borough call, we would ask the dispatcher to send groups of engine companies and groups of ladder companies to relieve our firemen. I would estimate that if we had counted the total number of companies there, we would have found that we were well past the equivalent of an eight or nine alarm fire. But that total force was not working all at one time. The fire lasted fourteen hours, and we had to bring in fresh troops because we were exhausting the people who were working there.

BRAVING THE FLAMES 237

We evacuated a lot of people from the surrounding area. There was a hospital across the street and that also had to be evacuated.

That fire turned out to be a major problem for the phone company in that so many of the phones went out in that area. In fact, it's the only fire I know of whose fifth anniversary became the subject of a cocktail party held by the telephone company. All their people who were instrumental in putting that section back together after the fire were promoted. Lee Elmhurster, who had a city-wide title at the time, was advanced to head of state operations. The telephone company took a negative and turned it into a positive. They turned it into the miracle on Thirteenth Street. They restored telephone service in a week's time. We learned something from it about logistics from watching what a major corporation can do. While we were still fighting the fire, the telephone company recognized that they were going to have to do major repairs and so they started diverting equipment right then that they knew they were going to need. They brought workers in from out of town and put them up in hotels. It was really a tribute to American industry's ability to manage resources and produce results when a problem of that nature occurs.

To be a good fire fighter you have to be a team player. You can be taught to be able, but you must be willing, and you must accept the concept of team and group responsibility. Then as part of the evolutionary process you develop pride in what you are and what your organization is in terms of being professional. You learn to handle yourself in a way that will cause you and your group to be admired, not looked down on.

In my judgment, you cannot be a good fire fighter if you don't get into the deep end of the pool. If you do not go to the working companies you won't have an opportunity to use your craft, to hone your skills, to gain the confidence that is necessary for you to become a good fire fighter. There's no such thing as a born fire fighter. The first time you hit that heat and smoke, you might decide that God did not intend for your system to function in there. You can be taught to overcome that and in time gain confidence that you can handle yourself in this atmosphere as we had to back in those earlier days, because we didn't have breathing equipment.

Confidence is necessary if we are to look at a fire objectively. We see the people running out of the building and the firemen running in. If you're running in, either you're confident or you're crazy. Well, which is it? The Fire Department has had programs aimed at rotating people. They were resisted not so much by people in the slow areas but by the people in the busy areas who did not want to leave. There's a tremendous satisfaction in doing a job and in doing it well, and many men aren't willing to give up that satisfaction.

To be a good fire officer you have to recognize that you have more than one responsibility. You have a responsibility to your platoon and your company—in other words, to the group that you are a part of and that you supervise—but you also have a responsibility to the department. You have a responsibility to the citizens of New York, too, and very early on you have to determine that when varied responsibilities come in conflict, you must make sure that the primary responsibility with which you are charged is carried out. I've worked with many people who became union presidents, particularly the Uniformed Fire Officers Association, Ray Gimler, Davy McCormick, and others. We came from the same pool, in other words at some point we were working together as lieutenants, captains, and chiefs, our value systems are the same. However, our goals and objectives, as one group goes to management and one group goes to labor, at times are divergent. Now, that doesn't mean that we have to be in a nasty conflict. I recognize what the goals of the union are, they've done well for the Fire Department and for the city of New York, but at the same time when you take the oath of office as a fire fighter, or as a fire officer, you are swearing to protect the citizens of the city of New York and whatever those total responsibilities encompass you have a responsibility to do that.

I was chief of operations when we had a strike, and that was a responsibility. We only had three companies in service in the Bronx, three in Manhattan, and I think twelve in Brooklyn. That was the worst day in my life in the Fire Department.

First of all there had never been a strike before, so there was no way to know what percentage of the fire fighters would go on strike. The command level of the Fire Department, including uniform commanders, met with Mayor Lindsay the night before the strike. The mayor knew he would be questioned on the eleven o'clock news, and he was trying to find out if we expected the strike and, if there was a strike, what percentage of our men would go out. Our feeling was that the strike would not be at the hundred percent level. We really had no way of knowing—maybe twenty percent, maybe forty percent; we just didn't know. As it turned out, the strike was ninety percent effective. In the morning, of course, there was a lot of preparation, but there was no backup. Either we were going to have people who would not strike and stay with us, and we did have some probies, or it was going to be very difficult. The morning of the strike we got a call that the strike would not take place, and a half-hour after that we got a call that the strike was on. At that point we had to determine what companies had enough personnel—either probies or men who were not striking—to be in service.

We started out in a very shaky position. The officers were not on strike, of course, and as the day wore on, we tried to set up a mechanism wherein they would be able to at least respond and protect life without violating the guidelines that they had been given by their union, which was that the members could do a job required of an officer but not a job required of a fire fighter. Well, by bending these rules we were gradually able to get some companies back in service. They might not have been full companies, just someone to respond, to address the question of life loss. Now as the day wore on, the real worry was what would happen that night, because that's when the real problems usually start. Fortunately, the strike ended after five and a half hours, in midafternoon, which was just in time for men to get back on duty before the nighttime fire experience started. That night there was a fire in which four people lost their lives, but by then we had all companies back in service.

I was born in Harlem Hospital, and I was raised without a father. At one point I was sent to a Catholic child-care institution, where I received a very excellent education. I was taught by nuns—I was in effect raised by nuns and by the priests.

Although I was black in a country that had racial conflict, I didn't develop a racial animosity, because of this early experience. I was raised by white women who gave up their lives to serve black people. The Fire Department is a part of American society, and it has some problems. For example, in the earlier days when the first blacks came in, there were separate beds only for them and things like that. I didn't get hyper about them. But in the course of my career I was able to work problems out with people, since I was not always on the edge, even though I feel that tolerance is certainly important in our society. As a black, you're trying to function in this environment, and you must be able to move through it and not take every little situation as the result of racial prejudice. By the time I entered the Fire Department I knew that I was able to function, I knew that I was able to compete, I didn't have any inferiority complex as far as being able to take and pass exams along with my peer group and I think that was helpful.

On the job a number of people have influenced me. One was Matty McMahon. He was a division commander in the first division when I was a lieutenant in 11 and also when I was in 17, and he was a role model for many of us in terms of how you conduct yourself as an officer: being professional, certainly being knowledgeable, meeting your responsibilities, and doing all of that without worrying—not being a bad guy. If something went wrong, Matty McMahon would let you know it was wrong and in doing so he was training you. Matty's name is always one of the first ones to pop out, but certainly there were others. My first captain, Ralph Sneeden, is another example.

I was appointed commissioner in January of 1978. Koch organized search panels when he first came into office, which is not the normal way of selecting commissioners. He was elected in November 1977, and he had until January to identify people for the different positions. He had a panel for each major department. The search panel for fire commissioner was headed by Mike Shinn who was the president of Metropolitan Life. The six or seven members were people from various disciplines.

To be commissioner of the Fire Department in the city of New York if you were coming in cold I think might be exhilarating. Having served in various ranks, from fireman to chief of operations, certainly I recognized that being commissioner was a unique opportunity. I mean, not everyone gets a chance to become commissioner. It's a hardworking job; there's a lot of demands. But there's one problem with it. From fireman to chief of operations you are operating within the Fire Department, and within the Fire Department the majority of people operate on the same value system. Our personal relationships have a certain characteristic which makes it easier for us to deal with each other and with our work, because everybody knows where the other person is coming from and our reputations are out there already. In going to commissioner you're entering a different environment, one with which you are not totally familiar. I acknowledged this even when I made my acceptance speech after the mayor swore me in. In taking the job there's not so much apprehension, but you do question whether or not this is the wise thing to do, because now you're in the environment of city government politics, and value systems are not quite the same. There's more shifting sands. While you enjoy the work, you're not entirely comfortable in that position. No matter what the challenges were in the difficult period we went through from 1963 through 1978 with fires, with riots, and with the strike, we knew what we were going to do and how we were going to do it, and we knew we could depend on and have confidence in the people we were with. We all marched to the beat of the same drum. In the field of politics that's not the case. There are people out there marching to the beat of different drummers.

I prefer the Fire Department. In saying that, I don't mean exclusively the Fire Department, but that type of environment, where value systems are clearly defined and where generally people do not have ulterior motives. Where people will not say one thing to you and say something else to their constituents.

We had an incident in Brooklyn that illustrates this tendency in politicians. We were going to move a fire company from an old firehouse to a brand new house. It's difficult to close a firehouse, even if the companies are staying in the same neighborhood. We weren't leaving the community at all. We met with the local representatives, the City Council representative and the state assemblyman and other elected officials, to alleviate the fears that they had.

One politician asked me, "Are you sure you're familiar with our neighborhood?"

I said, "I'll tell you what I'll do. You pick the day and the time. I'll meet all of you at the firehouse and we'll have buns and coffee there—which we did—and we'll walk the streets and any problems that you're concerned with I'll address them."

Well, only one of the elected officials showed up. The one who spoke the loudest never showed up at all. The one who did come walked the streets with me for at least an hour. Then we came back to the firehouse and discussed the move. He seemed to accept the fact that we were acting rationally, that we weren't going to hurt the community. We couldn't build a new firehouse right next to the old one, and we were just centralizing one of the trucks within the same community.

Well, on the day that we closed the old firehouse, he was among the first protesters to arrive and get himself arrested. I'm not faulting him for it, but he's not the type of person that I am accustomed to. In his community if there was going to be opposition, then he had to be a leader of the opposition in public; he had to go through this process of getting arrested even though it was a charade. I wouldn't want to spend thirty years working in that kind of political environment; it's nonproductive and unnecessary.

In my thirty-one years as a uniformed member of the Fire Department and in my ten years as a uniformed command chief, I was faced with greater problems than I had during the three years I was commissioner. In fact, the most difficult task I had as commissioner was to speak at plaque dedications for fire fighters killed in the line of duty. It was one thing to speak at the annual memorial service where I was talking to the department. I think I was able to get my point across there, though we did have the widows and the children there. But I found it much more personal to go to the firehouse for a plaque dedication, because of my empathy for the fireman's family. I have a family, I've also served in the same position, and I know we're all vulnerable. What can I say to this wife, to the children? Yes, I can speak about the heroism, but then I have to try to get it into a context that will cause the family to feel satisfied that—although they've lost their husband, their brother, or their father—somehow his death is not a wasted death but a true contribution to the good of us all. That's a general way of putting it, but it's difficult. That's one of the things that I don't miss. It is a responsibility and one that I accepted willingly. It was just difficult to do it in such a way as to reach the people I was talking to with the message I wanted to give to them.

The fire service has done a lot for me. First of all it enabled me to raise my family the way I wanted to raise them. On a personal basis, it provided me with an opportunity for self-development in a number of areas. It increased my self-confidence; it provided enough challenges to satisfy me; it made me feel that at the end of my career my life hasn't been wasted; it made me a better person; and it made me more knowledgeable. The Fire Department helped me develop, and it also confirmed the early values that I was given. Those earliest value systems enabled me to function until they were strengthened and reinforced by the values that I inherited from people with whom I worked—and I am not talking about formal education. Some of the people I learned from in the New York City Fire Department were people who had not been to college but who had an inherent understanding of how human beings relate to one another. So a great deal of self-development and career development and certainly the opportunity to become the commissioner—all of these came to me from the fire service and from those who helped me earlier in my life. Little Flower Children Services, which is the institution that I was in, had the satisfaction of having a person whom they had helped as a child succeed to the point of becoming the Fire Commissioner of the City of New York.

Chapter 15

Assistant Chief Matthew J. Farrell *Manhattan Borough Commander*

When I switched over, in 1957, from the police to the Fire Department I found out, much to my shock, that we had to take turns cooking in the firehouse. That's one thing I didn't know anything about. I told my wife, "Gee, I have to cook a meal. What can I make for the fire fighters? They're going to be upset. I can't tell them to skip over the meal. Everyone takes their turn."

She said to me, "You can cook spaghetti. All you have to do is take a couple of packages, break it up, put it in hot water, stir it around, and throw it in a colander. You buy a couple of jars of sauce or you make it out of puree."

It seemed pretty simple, so I said, "Okay, fine."

Well, my turn came up to cook. I was in the house with a single engine company, but there was also a deputy chief in quarters. It was the Fifteenth Division. In fact, it was the division commander I happened to be working with that night, Mike Beilman. At any rate, I cooked two or three pounds of spaghetti. I don't recall the exact amount, but it was quite a bit, because we had the five fire fighters, the deputy chief, his aide, and I think somebody was working extra that night. So I was cooking for eight or nine fire fighters including the chief. I was doing fine until we got an alarm for a fire and we jumped on the apparatus and out we went. I forgot to shut off the flame under the spaghetti. When we came back in, I ran into the kitchen. I was horrified to see that the spaghetti had sunk to the bottom of the pot and it had congealed. They were all on the apparatus floor yelling to the kitchen, "When the hell is that meal going to be ready?"

So I dumped the spaghetti into the colander, and it all fell out in one large mass. It was the exact shape of the pot. Even the dents at the bottom of the aluminum pot were now in this mass of spaghetti. It was lying in the colander in a big blob and I was staring at it, with all the men yelling into the kitchen, "What are we eating? When are we eating?" Quite frankly I was terrified to tell these guys that there was no meal. We had a large commercial slicing machine that we used to slice cold cuts. I put the spaghetti on it like it was a ham, and I sliced it. Then I put the slices on the plates and covered them with sauce. After putting the salad and the Italian bread on the table, I called the guys in and just kept my fingers crossed in the hope that I would be able to get by. Well, I should have known better. Fire fighters are a pretty good judge of cooking. One by one they either just looked at it or they tasted it, spit it out, and dumped it into the garbage. Meals didn't cost much in those days; I think dinners were half a dollar a night. The men threw their money on the table. I was so embarrassed I said, "No, it's okay, you don't have to pay."

The guys said, "No, it was worth the half a dollar just to find out never to eat with you again."

That was the kind of comment I was getting. Now, this was only the fire fighters. I hadn't gotten to the chief yet, and I was even more scared of him because he was the division commander. He came down from his office and he sat at the table, took up his fork, and started to eat. He continued to eat. He didn't make a single comment. In fact, he ate everything on his plate. He said, "This is delicious, what was it?"

I said, "It was pasta, a new pasta dish."

He said, "Gee, that's great. Have you got any more?"

I had plenty more, I had about eight plates that nobody ate.

Needless to say I took quite a ribbing on that, and they told that story for some years. It was a couple of years before I could laugh at it myself. My wife thought it was hilarious. But I was relieved from cooking for several months after that.

Initially, I came into the fire service because, as Gilbert and Sullivan said, "A policeman's lot is not a happy one."

And it was something that I had wanted to do for a very long time since my father was a member of the department.

I remember my first fire quite well because of the unusual nature of the fire. It was in the East New York section of Brooklyn. I was in Engine Company 233. That's where I was appointed. My father had also been a fire fighter in 233 on Hull Street off of Broadway. We were the first due engine. A fire fighter from Rescue 2—Piela was his name—and a young baby died at this fire. So it was a very traumatic experience for me to go to my first fire and see a fire fighter and a young baby die.

A kerosene heater was the cause of it. In those days they were in common use, though extremely dangerous when not used properly. The fire got a good start, and when we got there it was rolling out the windows, heavy smoke condition. I was a novice and I wasn't used to the organized chaos, with lines being stretched, trucks putting up aerial ladders, rescue company coming in, the press of people on the stairs, the heavy smoke, and the screaming and yelling. I can recall the thought that ran through my mind, besides the feeling of panic from the conditions, the heat and the smoke—it was that the whole thing appeared to be complete chaos. Subsequently I found out that this is a novice view. There is a plan, there is movement, everyone has a job to do. They are doing it under terrible conditions. While you don't get used to everything, you do get used to a good portion of it. We were stretching a line up the stairs to the second floor. The flaming embers were dropping down on us, bouncing off our helmets and coats. Then the smoke started to come down and I couldn't breathe. It felt like somebody grabbed my windpipe and shut my air supply off. People were throwing up and screaming and yelling. I was lying on the stairs and guys were climbing over me. Glass was breaking. I still recall a very unusual smell—something I wish I'd never had to experience, but I did and every fire fighter gets to know it; it's the smell of a person's body burning. It's unique, hard to describe, but it's a very distinctive smell. You smell it one time and you never forget it.

After that first fire I thought I would go back to the police department, I really did. But at that time 233 Engine was in with the Fifteenth Division. There was a chief there, who subsequently became a deputy assistant chief before he retired, his name was Walter Woods. He called me in the office

and asked me how I was making out. I told him, "All right."
I was a little ashamed to tell him that I was upset by the fire
and the people dying. He told me to take a seat. This was a
senior man with thirty-five years in the job. I have that today;
he was an old guy like me. But he said, "Listen, everyone
goes through this thing." He had good perception and must
have realized, without me telling him, that I was very upset.
It wasn't like you see in the movies where everyone gets
saved and you can just romp through the place. People die at
fires. And fire fighters die at fires.

He told me, "Give it a chance, don't do anything rash.
Stay with the job; it'll get better when you get to know a little
more about how things work. We don't always lose people.
You're going to save people, and that's going to more than
make up for the people you lose." It was excellent advice,
which I followed much to the present.

I wasn't with 233 too long. Although I only had two years
on the job because of my police time (which was four and a
half years), I was able to take the lieutenants' exam—once I
got off probation—and I passed it. Again, thanks to the
assistance of the fellows in the firehouse; they had a terrific
study group there and they drew me into it. I wound up
getting made a lieutenant in 1961. All told I was in 233 about
four and a half years. But I would have to say that those were
probably four and a half of the happiest years I ever had,
because I was a fire fighter, and I was very actively responding to fires, and I hadn't yet had all the responsibilities that
come upon your shoulders when you become an officer. I like
to think back to what I call my carefree days. When I was
really working with the brothers and enjoying myself.

Then I went to Ladder Company 103, which was a very
busy truck company, and I spent four to five years there as a
lieutenant on Sheffield and Livonia in the East New York–
Brownsville section of Brooklyn. When I got made captain,
I came back to 103 Truck. At that time I think it was the
busiest firehouse in the world. We were doing somewhere
upward of 7,000 runs a year, and I would say you'd pick up
three, four, five working fires every single tour that you
worked. This lasted almost all through the 1960s and 1970s.

There were so many fires that most of the ones that stick
out in my mind unfortunately are the ones where we lost
children or babies. I don't know why, but—and I'm sure that

other fire fighters share this feeling with me—I must have been at maybe a hundred fires where adults died and, while I certainly feel bad about it, it doesn't stay with me too long. In my own case, at least, I would recover within a day or so, and it wouldn't really bother me too much. But for some reason—and I've discussed this with fire fighters over the years, and most agree with me—the ones where you lose little babies, infants, or small children stay with you for months and months. I'd wake up once in a while still dreaming about some kid we didn't save. We'd make the top floor and find him burned in a corner or in the closet or underneath the bathtub, or down in the air shaft after he fell, or down in the basement covered with debris.

I don't like to think of it, but my mind drifts back, I guess, unbidden at times, to the fires I had where we lost the children. I think of those as the bad ones. The good ones were the fourth and fifth alarms where nobody lost their life. We wound up putting the fires out—big fires, showy fires that made the newspapers. But those little ones where we lose the people, they don't make the papers at all. Those are the tough ones.

Then there were the riots that went on. The riots took place predominantly in East New York. It was East New York–Brownsville section, but the riots we had in the mid-1960s were all in East New York, and they were terrible times for the Fire Department. In fact in our own department I think very few people knew what was happening to the fire fighters in our area. But I was there and I can remember that well, too. We would go to a box and get shot at. I think one of the first indications that we had a riot was when we went to a box on Livonia Avenue and Barbey Street—I still remember the location. I don't know who it was, but somebody started to shoot at us. He was a bad shot, but needless to say we got out of there quick. Over the next couple of weeks we were constantly bombarded with cinder blocks thrown off the roofs of five-story buildings.

It sounds almost ludicrous to say this in 1988, but I remember one night as we were going down the block a whole mob of people boarded the apparatus, just jumped aboard. We pulled up to the box and we realized what they had done. In those days they would set a trap for us. They would pull a particular box knowing we would come into the block. They would push an old car or something out to stop us from going forward, then push something out behind us to hold us in the block. At that point they'd start throwing stuff off the roof at us. This one particular time they climbed on the apparatus and the firemen were literally beating them off the sides. It almost looked like people repelling pirates trying to board a ship. I turned around and saw the fellows swinging hooks and axes to keep them off.

The fellow driving was Tom Hores. Tom was an excellent fire fighter, probably one of the best chauffeurs on the job. He could handle the aerial like he was extending his fingertips—he could tap glass out with the end of it. People started throwing cans at us. They would take a tin can and with a beer can opener open it up all around so jagged pieces of metal would be sticking out, and then they'd put rocks in it. They would wear a glove and they would take that can and throw it with all their might. This thing would come at you with some speed, because of the rocks inside, and if it hit any portion of you it literally ran over your body, chewing up whatever was hit with the jagged metal. One of these cans hit Tom and laid open his whole face. The blood started pouring all over his lap and down his hands. He was having a hard time holding on to the steering wheel. But we couldn't stop. If we had stopped I think they would have killed us. So, much to his credit, Tom kept the apparatus going and we managed to get out of there. We went right to Brookdale Hospital and had him taken care of. I recall that he spent about four hours on the operating table that night. The can opened up his whole cheek, went through the interior of his mouth and literally cut his gums and his tongue. It was a deep, deep wound. I guess it could have been worse, he could have lost an eye, or he could have been killed. That type of occurrence was not that rare.

The other things they would do is open a hydrant and then drop flattened tin cans into the hydrant stream while directing the stream up at us. The cans would come at us with the speed of a projectile. And if one of those things caught you it would take your eye out.

Charlie Hooper, one of the fellows in the engine company, got his face and his chest slashed with a knife at one of the fires we went to. Mike Timmons was another fellow from 25 Engine; he was the MPO. They jumped out and threw an ash can right through the front of the apparatus windshield and he wound up getting glass in his eye. He retained his sight, but he had some damage. He subsequently was put out of the job because of that injury. Those were bad times, very bad times.

It seems hard to believe, but in the middle of this we were constantly going back and forth to fires and dropping people off at the hospital. Somebody else would jump up into the seat and we'd go off to the next fire. Then something else would happen and we'd go to the next fire and so forth and so on.

We had an excellent rapport with the police in the Seventy-fifth Precinct. They were very good; they really were. We ultimately wound up going out as a convoy. A radio car would go in front with two police officers, the engine would follow, then another radio car, and the ladder company would bring up the rear. When it got really bad, we'd have a patrolman actually sitting on the apparatus and these cops were carrying shotguns or rifles. It was not uncommon for a patrolman to shoot at the cornices on roofs from where they were dropping Molotov cocktails. We turned out one night and the cop almost got killed. He was sitting on our turntable, which has I'd guess quarter-inch diamond plate that is almost indestructible; it's really hard steel. Somebody threw a cinder block down. It missed the cop by about six inches, but it left a dent in the diamond plate. If they'd hit him he obviously would have been killed even though he had a riot helmet on.

As we drove down the block you'd see these guys on the roofs silhouetted against the sky. The police helicopters would fly by and direct the cops to what roofs to go up to. They'd find the stashes of Molotov cocktails, bricks, heavy cinder blocks, metal bars, and old fifteen-pound sash weights—if thrown from a four- or five-story roof, you can imagine the impact one of those weights would have.

This one particular cop must have gone through a fortune in bullets. He'd take his gun out and put a couple of rounds right up into the roof cornice. You'd see pieces of the cornice flying off as he hit them. Let me tell you, that cleared the roofs. I'm not sure if he was authorized to do that—today he would be an ex-cop, I guess—but in those days I can tell you that we appreciated it. There was no question that this guy meant business. But nobody got killed, as odd as it seems.

Mayor Lindsay and Fire Commissioner Robert Lowery came to the area to talk to the people in an attempt to quiet things down but there was just complete social unrest and we became the unwitting victims for some reason. The firemen could be called anyplace, were not armed, but did represent authority in the city and they took their anger out on us. To this day I can't really understand that, but we took a hell of a beating out there. And it took a lot of guts for the fellows just to go in and out of that place. When you came to work in those days you ran a gauntlet. It was not uncommon to come in and have your car pelted with rocks. You really felt you accomplished something when you finally got to work. And of course many, many times you'd come out in the morning after running all night long to fires and find out that your battery was gone or your window was punched out or your car seats were gone. I found my car completely stripped one day. There was no interior in the car. My wife and I still laugh about it. I had to sit on a wooden milk box to drive home.

They had a little trick in those days. Car batteries were always prime targets. They would take any battery. It could be the oldest battery in the world—four, five years old, not worth fifty cents. The fire fighters said, "Gee, what dumb people. They stole a five-year-old battery, and it's no good anyhow." What the fire fighters didn't know was they just took that battery and threw it away. They had no intention of using or selling it, but they would mark the car. They knew the car they took it from—a 1953 Chevy, say—and they knew we had to replace the battery. They did this to me so I know it's true. You'd go out to Sears or anyplace you could get something on time, because nobody had money in those days, we charged everything, and you'd put a new battery in. The night you came to work with that new battery they'd steal your new battery. Well, obviously, once we learned that, we found the stores that sold used batteries. You'd get your old battery stolen, you'd go out and buy another old one for a dollar and a half, two dollars, whatever you could find.

The fire fighters were absolutely fantastic. I think back, they were a little rough. These were not the kind of people you would invite up to a publishing party on Park Avenue. But they were good people—the best—and there were so many of them. One who comes to my mind passed away a few years ago. Unfortunately he retired and he didn't live too long afterward. He deserved to live a hundred years in retirement and happiness, but he didn't. His name was Henry Czubakowski. We called him Czubie. Henry spent some twenty or twenty-one years in 103 Truck. I don't know how that was possible, because it was the most arduous and demanding fire duty that you could imagine. I put perhaps four years in as a lieutenant and got out by getting promoted to captain. And I enjoyed my respite for two and a half years before I came back for maybe three more when I got out of there with another promotion. Henry stayed all this time. And he was there through all the bad years, all those heavy running years, and I never heard him complain. I guess he paid the price, because he died of cancer. I think it started out with lung cancer and it spread. I think all those fires that Henry went to over the years finally did him in. I'm smiling here as I'm thinking about Henry—he looked like he stepped out of Buchenwald or Auschwitz; you could count every rib in his body. I don't think he weighed 120 pounds soaking wet, but he was a great fire fighter and a fantastic fire officer—a legend in his own time.

Henry was a lieutenant in the company, and as a consequence he and I wouldn't go to fires together. I'd be working one tour when Henry was working another. But I do recall one summer afternoon I was working a day tour, which was nine in the morning until six in the evening, and Henry was my relief. In those days we were relieved anywhere between five and five-thirty. You spend ten, fifteen minutes reviewing what went on during the day: fires, accidents, missing tools, who was attacked recently, whose car was broken into, and so forth. I got a call about five o'clock from Henry and he said, "Matty, my car went on fire." He had an old bomb like the rest of us. I don't think I ever saw a brand-new car in my life during all those years in Brooklyn. He said, "I'll be a little late. Do you mind?"

I said, "Not at all, Henry, take your time. Do whatever you have to do and I'll be here when you come in."

We had a couple of more runs, and about six o'clock we came back. I went upstairs to wash up, and I heard somebody down on the apparatus floor yelling, "Chief in quarters!" That's an indication that it's an official visit. I knew all the chiefs in that area of Brooklyn, the deputy chiefs, the battalion chiefs. I'd gone to several thousand fires with most of them, and we had a good rapport so I didn't worry too much about it as I walked downstairs. I had on a T-shirt, a pair of blue watch pants, and black loafers. We wore loafers in those days because they were easier to get in and out of. You took your shoes off twenty-five to thirty-five times a day. You'd wear shoelaces out if you tied them that often.

But as I came halfway down the stairs I glanced over the railing and I saw a chief that I had never seen before. He was immaculate; he had on a brand-new white hat, the gold was shining, his shirt was starched, the collar was crisp, the pants were creased, the shoes were absolutely shining. I couldn't believe it, he was all spit and polish. I was thinking about going back up the stairs to get my shirt and tie when he spotted me. I figured, well, no sense in walking away. I might as well come down and explain to him what was going on. At any rate I walked over to him and I said, "I'm Lieutenant Farrell."

He said, "How would I know that? I don't see any emblem on you."

I said, "Well, Chief, we just came back from a run and I was washing up."

With that he started to walk around the apparatus. We had done about twenty runs that day. We had gone down to the junkyards, so we had mud and debris and fire residue and what have you all over the apparatus. We didn't stand on too much ceremony in those days. We came and went so often that we couldn't do too much cleaning. But he took exception to it. This was a covering chief. So I had to walk around the apparatus with him, and with each step he got a little more angry as he saw that the apparatus was dirty and that the men didn't come down immediately when they heard the yell, "Chief in quarters." They were upstairs going to the bathroom, washing, grabbing something to eat, what have you. It was change of tours, so it was a little more confusing. Some people were coming, some people were going. But of those that did come down, one looked worse than the other. One guy had a Mohawk haircut, one looked like a pirate, another looked like a samurai warrior. By the time we made one circuit of the apparatus he was absolutely fit to be tied. He started to read the riot act to me. This was a summer afternoon and the apparatus door was open. He had his back to the door and I was facing him, but as I looked out over his shoulder and into the street, I saw Henry's car pull up. Henry Czubakowski and he's covered with soot; he apparently did have some kind of a fire in his car. There was one little clean spot on the windshield where he had cleared the soot off with his hand. He climbs out of the car, and he's wearing shorts and sandals; that's all he has on. He looks like he just got out of a concentration camp and he's covered with soot. His hands are filthy all the way up to his elbows. There's soot all over his face. He comes running into the quarters and stands next to this chief who's standing there dressed immaculately in white. Well, this chief couldn't help but notice this apparition standing next to him. He did a quick sidestep. He didn't want Henry to touch him or get too near with the dirt. He looked like one of the derelicts that just got out of the gutter. The chief looked at him and asked, "Who the hell are you?"

Henry stood at attention, saluted, and said, "Lieutenant Czubakowski reporting for duty, sir."

And I still can remember the look on this chief's face. I almost felt sorry for him. He said, "*What?* Who the hell *are* you?"

I said, "Well that's what I wanted to explain to you, chief. There was a little accident and I'm not really the officer on duty."

He put both his hand up and said, "Wait a minute, I don't want to hear anything. Let me get the hell out of this nut house."

He got in his car and drove off and I never saw him again.

Henry looked at the disappearing chief's car and said, "What the hell's the matter with that guy?" Like there was something strange about the chief and nothing wrong with Henry. Well, I was laughing too hard to explain to Henry what it was all about.

When I went to Henry's wake I told his wife and three daughters that story. Although it was a very sad occasion, they laughed, because that was the Henry that we knew and loved and the Henry I'll always remember for the rest of my life.

And there were others. John Vigiano, a lieutenant in Rescue 2 today, was one of my fire fighters. John was a great fire fighter. He hung around with a fellow named Bill Trotta. The men called them the Katzenjammer Kids. John Vigiano and Billy Trotta were always up to something. They could go to fires all day and still had the surplus energy to devote to other endeavors.

Ray Simms was a fireman who was newly assigned to the company. Ray went on to become the president of the Ner Tamid Society (the Jewish fire fighters' organization). Ray is still on the job as a captain.

When Ray joined the company I gave him the locker that had belonged to the guy he was replacing.

Well we always had a couple of gallons of yellow safety paint around. The men would paint a four-inch yellow stripe across the face of their locker, let it dry and then with black paint letter their names on it—Jones, Smith, what have you. The locker I assigned to Ray Simms had the name Schneider across it, and it was very old. The yellow paint was smudged and dirty and "Schneider," although you could read it, was faded. You could see that it had been on there for quite a few years. Jack Schneider was one of the senior fire fighters in the company at the time he transferred. Well, Ray got his stuff together and the next day when he came in he decided to repaint the locker and put "Simms" on it. The first thing he did was paint over the whole thing with a yellow band of paint, which left just the faintest outline of "Schneider" on the thing, but you had to look very closely to see it. At any rate, Ray went home. Working that night, Vigiano and Trotta, the Katzenjammer Kids, saw what he had done. They got their paintbrush out—John is an accomplished artist by the way—and repainted the name "Schneider" on this yellow strip. They could see the outline, so that didn't take any skill at all. But—I still remember this like it was yesterday—they aged the yellow paint. They aged the name Schneider. I don't know how they did it. They put dust from the floor on it, or whatever the hell they did, and when I saw it a couple of hours later I would have bet you money that it was in the original condition. It looked like it had never been touched. When Ray came in for his tour the next day, these gentlemen were waiting for him, sitting on the bed idly talking about something or other, but within view of him. Ray walked up and looked at the locker and did a double take. He looked around, he checked, he went up and down the aisles looking at the other lockers, because he knew that he had painted his over. He didn't find any other locker without a name on it. That was his locker, right where he'd left it, but there was the name Schneider. He asked me did I know anything about it? I told him no and he couldn't believe it. He asked several people. No one knew anything about it. "That locker has been that way for years," they'd say. "It's Jack Schneider's; its always been that way." Well, within an hour or two they had Ray believing that he had not painted that locker. He *thought* he painted it, but he forgot—that's the truth. So he painted the thing again, and the Katzenjammer Kids went back and did the exact same thing over again. Well, Ray was taken in the first time, but they didn't take him in the second time. He came in the next day, he saw the locker, and he smartened up. Vigiano and Trotta's handiwork took a couple of hours, and they did this between runs and going to fires. It was just their way of relieving some of the tension. I always thought about that because of the tremendous amount of effort it required. Nothing was too much trouble for those two guys if the payoff was a good practical joke.

This'll give you an idea of the kind of weird, distorted, warped sense of humor these fellows had. There was a plumber named Walicki who was quite a character. He worked for the department as a civilian employee; he did all the plumbing for the Fire Department. He'd been in and out of our firehouse any number of times. We had a very old house there on Sheffield Avenue, and consequently we were forever bringing people in to do electrical work or plumbing. Well, the toilet in the bunkroom was broken, and Walicki came in to reset the bowl. If you know anything about plumbing, you know you have to be experienced to do this. It's not a job for an amateur. Walicki put in a lead bend, made the connections, put a rope of clay around it, poured the lead, and set this toilet bowl. Then he wiped the thing down. That job takes an experienced hand; it's a little bit tricky. Walicki was an old-timer, had been around for years, and he was forever telling us how good he was and how he never got leaks when he made joints. He was one of the few people around who could put a toilet bowl in and guarantee there'd be no leaks. When other plumbers did these jobs, if they were lucky, maybe one out of every four would leak, but Walicki had put fifty of them in and he never had a leak. He went on and on and on about what a good job he did. He made a mistake saying that, because he drew the attention of Vigiano and Trotta. They waited until he finished this whole job and said he was going out to get something to eat. He put a sign up, "Don't use the toilet," and he tied a rope around the bowl. I saw these two characters very carefully spill half a cup of water around the base of the toilet where Walicki had put the seal. For all the world it looked like the bowl had developed some kind of a leak. It hadn't, of course; it was probably a perfect seal. Walicki came back from lunch and took one look at the water and started cursing. "Damn it to hell, this is the first leak in five years. I can't believe it. Anybody touch that toilet bowl?" No, nobody touched that toilet. He broke the seal, removed the toilet bowl, and went all through this thing again, for maybe two hours. Then he went to make himself a cup of tea. Vigiano and Trotta ran back in and poured another half a cup of water around the base of the bowl. They were merciless. At any rate, unbeknownst to them, Walicki got his cup of tea very quickly, came back out, and caught them in the act. He chased them right out onto Sheffield Avenue and down to Livonia. There goes Vigiano, there goes Trotta, there goes the plumber, everybody's running. I had some talking to do to Walicki. He was going to turn them in to Chief of Department, but I calmed him down.

Thinking back on it now, I realize that some of these things that sound rather childish were actually a way of relieving tension and keeping our minds off the darker side of the job.

A crazy thought about that time: I have put in thirty-six years, all told—thirty-one and a half in the Fire Department and four and a half in the police. Many, many years have gone by, but my mind often wanders back to those early years, and it's very odd, but I find them to be one of the most satisfactory times of my life. Yet at the same time, those were tough years as far as hardship was concerned—staying out all night in terrible, terrible weather. It was not uncommon to come back in the winter and be so frozen that you literally could not get your coat off. You'd have to have hot water poured on yourself from the kettle to loosen up the latches on your fire clothing so you could remove it; you could stand the clothes up as if they were blocks of ice. There was no relief in those days. You would go from fire to fire and be so tired that you felt like somebody beat you with a baseball bat, with every bone in your body aching, walking around with a smoke headache—your head aches from the smoke. And, though you were all beat up, wet, cut, tired, you went home with a sense of satisfaction, a realization that you had done an excellent job. We literally kept the city from burning down in those days. If those fires, whether they were in individual buildings or in several buildings, had not been attended to so professionally by the fire fighters, we would have had whole blocks burning, and then we would have had whole sections of the city burning. I don't exaggerate when I say we could have had conflagrations and fire storms, but these guys prevented that from happening.

I think back and I say, "I should really say thank God I don't have to do that anymore." Yet, perverse as the way human nature is, I miss those days. I really do. There was a feeling of camaraderie and brotherhood among all the fire fighters. That's kind of hard to describe, and I really don't think you'll find it anyplace else. It was a unique situation. We were all tied together and we knew we were tied together. This is a life and death type of job, and we did it together. I take a lot of satisfaction out of knowing that I worked with all those good people over the years. Many of them are gone now, deceased, but they live in my mind, and when I think back those are the times I remember.

A strange thing about these memories is that we sort of bury the bad things and the good ones jump forward a little bit. I guess that's natural. It's good, too. If our minds didn't work that way, we'd become very depressed.

One story that comes to mind concerns John O'Rourke, who later became Chief of Department. John was captain of the 114 Truck, which at that time was a very prestigious truck company in Brooklyn—good spirit, good rapport. John was an excellent captain and fit in well with the fellows in 114. I was battalion chief back then, working at the Fortieth Battalion. One night we were making our twenty-fifth or twenty-eighth run. It was a freezing night, and it was starting to drizzle. We were answering our seventeenth or eighteenth false alarm—false alarms reached epidemic proportions in those days in the section around Third Avenue in Bay Ridge, Brooklyn. As I was winding the box, John came over to me and said, "You must really be happy being here."

I said, "Yes, this is my second favorite thing, to be out here."

He asked, "What's your first?"

"Being whipped with hot chains," I replied. John always told that story after that.

I was thinking about injuries and how lucky you can get.

Just because of a toss of the dice, so to speak, I had the good fortune to remain relatively healthy during all my time on the job. Sometimes I think how easily it could have been the other way. For example, one time I went to a third alarm at a toy factory on Pitkin Avenue in the East New York section of Brooklyn. This was in the wintertime. There were snowdrifts all over the place, and they turned out to be lifesavers, believe it or not. I was climbing a portable ladder that we had placed against a building. I got up near a window, and there was an explosion inside the building. I don't know for sure if it was lacquers, but I think that's what it may have been— volatile fluids they used for spraying. At any rate, the explosion blew the ladder off the building while I was standing on it. I flew over the apparatus with the ladder and landed in a snowbank. I was just kind of lying there in the snow, shocked that I suddenly wasn't up by the building anymore, but fortunately there was nothing wrong with me. I brushed myself off, picked my helmet up, put it back on, and went back to work and thought nothing of it. Another time a factory floor gave way during a fire, and I fell about fifteen feet and landed on a stack of cardboard cartons. In those two incidents, if you take away the snowbank and take away the cardboard cartons, you're looking at serious injury, if not death. I don't know what you call that—good fortune? God looking out for you? Whatever it is I've been pretty lucky. Of course I've had my share of minor injuries, fractures, burns, lacerations, contusions, and abrasions, too, but I survived them all.

Fire fighters enjoy a gallows humor, black humor, and people who are not familiar with the fire fighters often think it displays insensitivity. I can see how they can think this, but oddly, the people who should take the most offense are the ones who seem to enjoy it the most. I'll give you an example. I had a fire fighter in Brooklyn, Freddie Lacker, in 103 Truck. Freddie was my tiller man, a good fire fighter. He had a home workshop, and he considered himself an expert in the use of tools. He got careless one day with a table saw when he was working at home, and he cut his thumb off. He told us that his thumb bounced off his chest, and fell on the floor. He thought it was a piece of the expensive wood he was working with. He said, "Shit, there goes a good piece of wood." He felt no pain till he glanced down and realized he had cut his thumb off. He grabbed the thumb, put it in a towel, ran upstairs, called to his wife, Audrey, got in the car quick, and went to Syosset Hospital. The doctors sewed his thumb back on. Then they made an incision in his chest, pressed his hand close to his chest, and inserted the thumb right inside the incision. Your body is the best host, I guess. While the thumb is inside you, it's bathed by your own blood and it's kept warm. They stitch it up and bandage it so you can't move and you can't pull it out. Within a few days they can tell whether the reattachment will take.

The fellows in 103 went to visit Freddie while he was in the hospital feeling depressed, not sure if his thumb was going to take. They also brought him a fire fighter's glove with the thumb cut off. They bought him a book about wood-working. At the time, there was a movie out called *Cat Ballou*. In it Lee Marvin played a fellow who wore a tin nose, because some guy bit his nose off in a fight or something. These guys from 103 all wore tin noses when they visited Freddie. His wife was horrified. She thought this was a terrible thing. But Freddie laughed till the tears rolled down his face. He thought it was one of the funniest things. His brother Bobby was a fire fighter, too, and he also worked in 103. Bobby said that Freddie was going into a severe depression till the brothers came up with that stupid book, the four-fingered glove, and the tin noses. It really took him out of his depression.

In 1962 I covered as a lieutenant on a fireboat—the *Wagner*, which was then a brand-new boat. It was named after the mayor's wife, Susan Wagner. It was subsequently stationed by Gracie Mansion, the official residence of the New York City mayor, but at that particular time it was moored at Pier A, down at the Battery. The department had not yet accepted this particular fireboat. It was in a shake-down period. I was assigned to work my day tours down there. It was my first experience with the fireboats. The Fire Department had marine engineers looking at the *Wagner*'s engines and checking all the parts. I was making out requisitions, acting sort of like a clerk. The boat was moored at the pier with the bow facing out, the stern in toward the land. On the bow was a foam cannon, which was unique at the time. On a really hot day we all decided to go up to the Blarney Stone to have lunch. While we were on our lunch break, which perhaps was extended slightly that day due to the heat, some fellows from the marine shop came down to the boat. They wanted to make some modifications on the valve monitor, so they turned the boat around and put the bow toward the land, just the reverse of the way we had left it. Well, we came back from lunch—one of the wipers, the marine engineer, the pilot, and myself—and didn't get a good look at the boat on our way back to the pier, because she was moored next to this shed which we had to walk through. Lo and behold there's a red chief's car parked right opposite the gangway to the fireboat. I said, "I wonder who that is." I didn't have long to wonder. It was Assistant Chief of Department Frances Love. Now, Chief Love was quite well known in the department. He was not, however, known for his humor, or for being indulgent toward new lieutenants. At any rate, I no sooner stepped aboard when there was Chief Love standing on the deck. He asked me who I was and if I was the officer on the boat and where I had been and so forth. After I got through with his line of inquisition, he asked me if I was familiar with the new bow nozzle—the foam monitor.

I said, "Yes, I am."

He said, "Show it to me." So I immediately made a left turn and walked toward what had been the bow when I left for lunch. Needless to say we wound up at the stern of the fireboat. I stood there, he looked at me, I looked at him, he looked at the stern, I looked at the sea, he looked back at me. Since this was my first experience on a boat I couldn't tell whether I was on the stern or the bow, and somebody had stolen the goddamn monitor. After fumbling and stumbling around for a minute while the chief stood there shaking his head, I finally realized that somebody had turned the boat around. Then the chief took me down to the other end of the boat—the bow—and looked at the foam monitor. Finally, he left, but not before asking me how long I had served on the boats and I was still in one piece. But I learned a lesson from that incident: to always take a look at the boat before walking into the shed.

I had always worked in a land unit, and I was used to a very rapid turnout. By this I mean that from the time of the alarm to the time we got out that door it would often be less than a minute. You'd fly down that pole and into your boots, your turnout coat went on, and you'd hit the rig running. The door would be up and you'd be out. When I went to the boats

I expected the turnout to be somewhat similar. The first time I got an alarm I ran down the pier from the boat house, which is on the dock, jumped aboard the boat for fear that they would leave without me, and I was the only one standing there. Finally the screen door opened up and a fellow came out, looked up at the sky, looked down at the boat, walked to the gangway. I had forgotten that it took a relatively long time to get the boat under way. The men would take maybe twenty minutes to get into one of their assigned boxes.

I took quite a ribbing from the guys on the fireboat for rushing out, but inadvertently I kind of got even with them. I went back there in the freezing winter to cover one time. They were still kidding me. They remembered me running down to the boat in the summertime and being the first guy aboard. A signal came in for a third alarm at a box in Lower Manhattan, about a block and a half off the water. It was a boat box, which meant that the boat would go to the fire but would not be used unless the fire building was right on the water. Most of the chiefs in those days would invariably get a citywide radio report: "Marine company is in. Do you want their services?" Via the dispatcher, the chief would tell the boat to "Stand by," or would order the boat to return to its berth. That was common if it wasn't an actual marine fire. Well, we went to where the South Street Seaport is now, and before the men had a chance to tie up—mind you, now, this was twenty-seven years ago when I was young and agile—I jumped off the bow, landed on the pier, and ran down the block with the men on the fireboat shouting after me, "Where the hell are you going?" I reported to the deputy chief. He looked at me like I was a madman. "Where the hell did you come from?"

"Lieutenant Farrell from marine company so-and-so reporting."

This was the middle of winter, a January night when it's about eight degrees out. On the fireboat we had these large four-inch or four-and-a-half-inch hose lines that came off a huge reel on the bow. I volunteered to have one of them brought up to the foot of the fire building and have a manifold put on it, so the chief could take off as many lines as he wanted. I don't know whether he thought I was kidding him or whether he truly believed it, but he said, "Go ahead, son." I went back to the boat, taking a pumper with me. We got a length of roof rope and tied it onto the hose. Using the apparatus I stripped all the hose off the fireboat and took it down through the streets of lower Manhattan all the way to the fire building. We got the manifold on it, but it was never used. What did happen was that the hose froze to the ground in the water that was used on the fire, and the fellows in the marine company had to get off the boat and come down with their axes and literally hack and dig this huge block-and-a-half-long hose out of the ice. The hose was too stiff to roll up, so we had to carry it back in large pole-like sections and lay it on the boat. Well, if I thought I took a ribbing after my summer escapade, you should have heard them then. They sent my picture around the marine fleet with a message: "If you see this man, do not allow him aboard your boat." That was the last time they permitted me on the boats, by the way. I'm not sure if it was coincidental but that's what happened.

The fireboats provide a very necessary service. The department had quite a large fire fleet at one time. I think there were some ten fireboats in the New York City fleet. Their main function is to fight ship fires, which can be very scary and extremely difficult to fight. They're usually deep in the bowels of a ship, and the access to them is terrible, usually through very narrow passageways. The metal retains and radiates the heat. The hazards connected with explosions, unknown cargo, and so forth make these fires very, very dangerous. I did get to fight perhaps six ship fires in my time on the job, but oddly none of them occurred while I was assigned to a marine unit. I fought them either as a covering officer in one of the land units or as a battalion chief. I've had maybe two or three of them since I became a staff chief.

Every ship fire is a little bit odd in its own way. I can recall one in Brooklyn where nobody on the ship could speak English. They were talking a mile a minute, but nobody could understand them. They obviously had some very valuable information to tell us, but we couldn't make head or tail of what they were saying. We were there for some time before we got somebody who could speak their language. Then we found out what they were trying to tell us: their cargo was stored gases and insecticides—a hazardous cargo. You'll often run into a language problem on ships.

I stayed in Ladder Company 103 until 1969 when I got promoted to battalion chief. I went to Manhattan and spent two and a half years working the four Midtown battalions—

the Sixth, Seventh, Eighth and Ninth battalions. That was quite a change from the tenement fires I'd been used to as a fireman, a lieutenant, and a captain. I was very fortunate in those days that there was a group of very experienced older chiefs working in those battalions. Whenever I had problems they were extremely kind to me. They realized I lacked experience in high-rise buildings and in the type of occupancies you find in Manhattan. Jerry Collins comes to my mind—Jerry passed away some time ago. He was the commander in the Seventh Battalion. He promptly christened me "the tenement boy." After a short experience with Jerry I christened him "the fastest mouth in the West," because he had very quick wit and a fast mouth, and you could never get the best of him. I learned not to take him on, but for all his kidding, I never went to Jerry with a problem that he didn't give me a solution or at least put me in the right direction. I ran into Ed Lally in the Eighth and John Rice in the Ninth Battalion. The Sixth Battalion, in which I put quite a bit of time, over on Thirteenth Street behind where Luchow's used to be, became my second home in Manhattan. They had some of the finest firefighting chiefs I've ever seen—Fred White, Benny Ciranna, and Bill Delaney—and they were very generous in sharing their experiences with me.

When I came to Manhattan, Patty Conlisk was the deputy in the Third Division. I knew Patty from Brooklyn where I had worked with him in Brownsville. He called me into the office and he said to me, "Matty, I know you know all about tenements and I know that you can put a fire out in any building up to six or seven stories, but what are you going to do when you got a fire up at the fiftieth or sixtieth story of a high-rise building?"

I knew Patty was pulling my leg a little bit and so I said, "Well, I'll tell you what, Chief. I'll have them put the fire on the elevator and bring it down to the fifth floor, and then I'll put the damn thing out." He started laughing and that's the way we started out.

I had quite a few little fires in those days that threw me for a bit of a loop. I mean, one of the things about tenement fires, no matter how big they are, when you turned the corner you saw them. But now I was in an area where you walk into the lobby of the fire building and the people are walking around—no screaming, no yelling, no visible fire—and there is a fire going on in the forty-second or forty-third floor. It's as good a fire as you'd find in a tenement, but you wouldn't know about it because it isn't visible. That's when I found out how important the elevators were. I found out how important the communications were, too. In a high-rise fire, your company officers have to give you information. Where is the fire? Are there people trapped? Do you need any assistance? You learn to do things that you never had to do before—using standpipe phones and fire wardens' phones. It's a crash course and it's one of those things where you sink or swim.

I covered over in the Eighth Battalion when they had a fire on Fifth Avenue around Forty-eighth Street. It stuck in my mind because ten or twelve people died in that fire. The strange thing was that they died on the second floor. It was some kind of silk-screening or printing place, and the fire started in some combustible solvents. The people who worked there went out and waited for the elevator in a very narrow hallway adjacent to a doorway that would have taken them to the street and safety, but they bunched up in front of the elevator instead. And a ball of fire caught all these people and killed them. It was a very high loss of life, and it seemed so needless—two floors above the street.

I returned to Brooklyn, because there were no openings in Manhattan at that time. I wanted to stay in Manhattan. The traveling wasn't great for me, but I got to like it. I found it was a challenge, particularly in the Sixth Battalion. I liked the Sixth Battalion because they ran into the tenements on the Lower East Side and it kind of took me back to my old days in Brooklyn with the tenement fire fighters. They had some excellent fire fighters over there on the East Side. The Sixth also ran uptown so they had high-rises, too, and they had some piers. They had quite a good mixture of types of buildings. Also, the Sixth Battalion was busy. At that time it was probably the busiest of the Midtown battalions.

Anyway, I had an opportunity to go back to my old stamping ground in Brooklyn. Tom Murphy, my former battalion chief, was to be made a deputy. His spot was opening up in the Thirty-ninth Battalion, which is in East New York, on Conduit Boulevard and Liberty Avenue. I grabbed the opportunity. The job was only fifteen or twenty minutes from my house. I knew everybody in the company, I knew the area, and I had a high regard for the units down there. I went back to Brooklyn about 1971, and I stayed there until I was made deputy chief in 1976, at which time they put me in chains and took me back across the bridge to Manhattan, my second home.

This time I wound up in the First Division in Lower Manhattan, which was an extremely interesting area, and still is to this day. It's one of the three divisions I now have as Manhattan borough commander; my command area comprises the First, Third, and Fifth divisions, which cover lower Manhattan, Midtown, and Harlem. I was deputy in the First Division when Jack "Black Jack" Fogarty, my predecessor, was the borough commander of Manhattan. At any rate, I worked a couple of years in the First Division.

It was a great opportunity to learn more about high-rise fires. I had a second alarm in the World Trade Center, for example.

I had a few here and there that I thought perhaps I wouldn't be able to put out. One of them was on John Street. When we were fighting that fire, I had some of the best officers anyone could possibly have. In fact, I had a battalion chief working for me at that time named John J. O'Rourke. I had Jimmy McKenna from the First Battalion, and I had a couple of real tough engine and truck officers. But this fire was in a subcellar, and we could not gain access to that subcellar. It was under a shoe store, and the owner had all his stock down there. In Lower Manhattan subcellars are not uncommon. That is the way the buildings were built many, many years ago, and some of the most difficult fires that you could possibly have are in these subcellars. They are two stories below grade—and I mean two full stories. The only access you might have is through a manhole. You lift up the manhole cover and use a chute to provide some ventilation. The interior stairways leading to these subcellars are very, very narrow. You can imagine trying to make it down. It's like coming down a chimney after a fire has been lit.

We threw our best people into that subcellar fire. I had a captain of 55 Engine, Benny Esposito. He had been an officer in Brooklyn; our paths kept crossing. In the department there are twelve thousand fire fighters, but it's like a small town; everyone you run into you'll see again as time goes by. I knew Benny was an excellent officer. He gave it a crack. His men did the best they could, but they couldn't reach this subcellar fire. I got a rescue company that was noted for doing some of our tougher work, and they took a crack at it, but they couldn't get down there, either. I had a battalion chief in the back of the building with two truck companies trying to breach the floor. They couldn't do anything there. John O'Rourke had gone over to exposure two, the building on the left, to breach the cellar wall and come through there with a couple of hand lines. The wall was three or four feet thick. They couldn't do it. Well, it seemed to me like we were there six years or so. The Chief of Department at that time was Frank Cruthers, he came down the block and asked, "What the hell's going on? You've been down here for three hours with a multiple alarm assignment."

I said, "Very simple, Chief. We got a fire we can't put out."

I don't think he was prepared for that honesty. I think Frank, for one of the few times in his life, was taken aback. But subsequently we did get that fire out. But what happened at this fire is something fire fighters don't like—a waiting game. Sometimes when you can't make headway you have to sit back, hold the ground you got, see that the fire doesn't extend, and you're really on your way toward a win, especially if the fire's not going anyplace and there's no life hazard. Here we knew where the fire was; it was not extending to any other portion of the building. We had a foothold on the floor above. We were on the first floor and second floor, and we were down in the cellar. Eventually the fire would burn out from lack of oxygen or lack of fuel. In this case it burned up all of the available fuel. We eventually got a hand line down through the chutes. We worked the hand line down with the nozzle tied to a rope. We used that as sort of a portable distributor, and we got some water on the fire. I remember that incident because of the stubbornness of the fire and because we tried everything until we had just about run out of ideas. I can't remember another fire where I had so much talent on hand and we still couldn't put it out as quickly as we would have liked.

This sort of thing generates frustration. Fire fighters pride themselves on putting the fire out. They like to think they can get in anywhere and put any fire out. It creates a little doubt in your mind when you have to stand there for a long time—and I mean hours and hours. You have to reassure yourself that time is on your side, and not do anything foolish. One of the things that happens—it's a very weak moment—is that you get too frustrated and you allow your emotions to run roughshod over your objectivity. You're liable to make a couple of rash decisions and maybe put someone into a bit of a hazard that they wouldn't ordinarily be in. At this particular time, the very aggressive fire officers and fire fighters are all asking you to give them a chance—tie a rope around their feet and give them a nozzle and drop them into the manhole, or "Throw me down the stairs with a nozzle in my arm and when I land in the basement I'll get a shot at the fire"—and other very practical suggestions. So you have to fight off these guys who want to put the fire out. Generally a little experience comes in from the senior chiefs in the department. When you're a young officer you think they're a bit too conservative, but now that I look back, I realize that my chiefs were experienced and their advice was timely and good.

I've had a couple of high-rise fires that were very difficult. High-rise fires are hard because you can have trouble getting to the fire and because you sometimes have fire on several widely separated floors. I had three separate floors going in a high-rise at one time. This fire had gotten into the ventilating shaft. This building was over fifty stories; we had fire on the twentieth, on the thirty-second, and on the forty-fifth floor. Each fire was very serious in itself. Each floor would take an all-hands assignment: three engines, two ladder companies, and a battalion chief. So here we are in one building with three fires. It was really a contiguous fire that had spread from the original fire and wound up as three separate fire incidents. To fight this as three separate fires and still retain control over the whole thing, you have to put people above fires. For instance, I had to send men up to fight the fire on the thirty-second floor. They were now above the fire on the twentieth. Likewise with the fire on the forty-fifth floor; those firemen were exposed to the two fires below them. You have to be sure that you can control the fires on the lower floors so that you don't endanger the lives of the fire fighters up above. Yet you have to put those upper fires out in order to be able to make a good search. It's an axiom in the fire service that the most dangerous position is above the fire. Of course, that goes not only for fire fighters but civilians. If you're above a fire you're at risk, depending upon the conditions.

I had the Grand Central Station fire in 1985. We had

eighteen railway cars burning four levels below the ground. It was like taking a high-rise fire and laying it on its side. Under Grand Central we had zero visibility and a tremendous amount of heat. It was very debilitating. The masks ran out very quickly. We had a problem supplying masks to all our units. At first we couldn't tell exactly how many cars we had burning. The fire and smoke got into six or seven of the buildings above the tracks. There was heavy smoke coming out all the emergency exits. But we had a tremendous commitment there. We had special-called a lot of units on an individual basis. I believe we had the equivalent of a seven or eight alarm fire.

These railroad cars were pullmans, which are very, very large, and we had eighteen of them. This would be the equivalent of maybe twenty apartments burning in a large building. Imagine that much fire. Then stick it down four stories below ground. It caused a serious evacuation problem in some of the adjacent buildings, which were completely engulfed in smoke. We helped to evacuate the area. We had a severe problem with derelicts. A lot of homeless people live down there in the tunnels, and they were in all kinds of little crannies. When you get down below the ground in New York City there's all kinds of little rooms, cul-de-sacs, little spots alongside the tracks, shelves, and so forth. Six, seven hours after the fire we were still finding people in need of assistance. It was a long and arduous job.

The fire started in one of the cars. We think some derelicts started a cooking fire in one of the cars and it caught on to some of the upholstery, burned through the tile to the wooden floor of the car, and then spread fairly rapidly along the string of cars, from one to the other. It jumped across one portion of a track to another string of cars and then in a pretty short time became a very, very serious fire.

Initially we knew we had a fire, but we didn't know exactly where it was or how many cars we were dealing with. We had to be very, very careful with the fire fighters we were sending down there because, as I said, the visibility was zero, there was tremendous heat, and you can very easily get lost in those tunnels. Ventilation was very difficult. We opened up every place we could, including the emergency exits. We set up some fans to create a draft. We had to stop the trains, of course, and that caused a massive commuter foul-up. People were stuck on trains. We had electrical problems with live rails. We were trying to get the people who had controls to shut the power off so that our fire fighters wouldn't get electrocuted down there. Unfortunately it's the movement of the trains that keeps the air circulating down there. If you stop the trains, the ventilation stops. We had to set up lighting.

That kind of job always turns out to be a tremendous exercise in logistics and control. It's literally a job aside from the fire fighting to get the apparatus in, to get all the equipment and supplies that are needed, to provide fresh air bottles, to arrange for relief for the units. To have emergency service stand by to give emergency medical aid and treatment for the injuries that the men sustain. To exercise head counts and controls, to see that every unit that goes in comes out. We could easily lose somebody under those conditions.

At the same time we had fire commissioners there, the Mayor was there and all the media, and they all wanted to know what was going on. That was one of the things I wanted to know—what the hell was going on.

Bob Cantillo was a battalion chief down there. He's a good chief and he was one of the people who did an excellent job. Some of those fellows spent literally hours down in that tunnel. I made two trips down there. I went down the first time to get an idea what the conditions were like, after John O'Rourke, who's the Chief of the Department, came in. Later on, I made another trip through the place to see the damage that had been sustained. The tremendous amount of heat created spalling of the concrete, and large pieces were falling into the tunnel. It was a mess down there for quite a while. We had some water problems, too. We had to drop extra lines down there. The poor visibility prevented us from finding things that we could have used. The fire fighters went right by some of the ladders that went up to the street. It was dark. When I say dark, if you could picture yourself in a closet with absolutely no light at all, where you literally could put your hand in front of your face and not see it, that was the condition that you would run into in portions of that tunnel. Now add heat and add the equipment the fire fighters are wearing: breathing apparatus, coat, helmet, boots, tools. Now imagine climbing down ladders or walking down five or six stairways into this black area where you hit the smoke, and then start walking through the tunnel. You can see how easily fatigued, confused, and disoriented you could become. That was one of the more challenging fires that we had.

We were there the better part of a day. We must have spent seven or eight hours fighting the fire before we finally could declare it under control. The firemen had to go from car to car and put the fire out in each one. Then overhauling those cars was very difficult because of the confined space and because they have Lexan panels in the windows. You hit them with an ax and the damn ax bounces off.

Another one that comes to mind is the Con Ed fire that we had when John Hart was the Chief of Department. I was one of the many chiefs who helped fight it.

There was a fire in the Garment District, two floors below grade in a transformer vault. We had difficulty getting close to that fire because it was a roaring inferno. There was a shaft adjacent to the area that supplied a natural run of air in the fire. It was literally being force-fed oxygen so that this thing burned with a heat that was unbelievable. It cracked the first floor, which was two floors above the fire and perhaps 150 to 200 feet away from it. It looked like that first floor might cave in. And this was remote from the fire, so it gives you some idea of the heat that was being transmitted.

When I first went down there, the winds in those narrow hallways, as we approached the area of the fire, were almost hurricane force. Your coat would pull out from your body. One of the fire fighters had a cup of coffee. He dropped the cup and it was sucked immediately down the entire length of this hallway into the fire and was gone. A small person, weighing 100 pounds or less, would literally have been blown away. It was like working in a wind tunnel. We had several options. We tried foam. I think it was partially successful although the oil that spilled on top managed to relight. We never could get a good solid blanket on it. The Rescue Companies tried with the hand lines and eventually we did get down with hand lines and put that fire out. There are some fires that you just can't approach; this was one of them. It was a very bad fire and it was one that again required patience and waiting. As I said, John Hart was the Chief of Department. Harry Truman used to say, "The buck stops here." Well, that day the buck stopped at Hart. Everybody was looking at the Chief of the Department. "What do you want to do now, Chief?" He had all kinds of suggestions, from using inert nitrogen gas to flooding the cellars with water. Eventually through patience we worked some hand lines down, managed to ventilate the fire, relieved people on the lines, got fresh masks, and set up secondary command posts. Finally we got a foothold. We held on, consolidated, brought more units in, and resupplied them. It was something like taking a hill in a war, where you keep moving up and you eventually get there, but it's slow going. Fires are not all easy. But if they were all easy our work wouldn't be that much of a challenge.

I have been blessed and this is no credit to me, I do think it's good luck, but in all my years of fire fighting—I've been an officer for twenty-seven years, and I've been chief for almost twenty years—I've never lost a fire fighter in any of the thousands of fires I've gone to. It's happened to some friends of mine and it kind of leaves a mark on you for the rest of your life. I've had tragedy strike very close to me, though. I've lost a number of good friends in the job. I worked with a fellow in Brooklyn, Frank Smith, who was a lieutenant in 236 Engine. Frank was also a neighbor of mine and a fellow parishioner—we went to the same mass on Sundays. Frank was a good officer and he loved the department. In East New York one day, they had a good fire going. He tried to make it up the stairs to the fire on the second floor; he died of a heart attack. I came in that evening and the fellows told me that Frank had died that day. I couldn't believe it. I can see him now smoking his pipe and laughing. He loved a good gag. He loved the fire fighters. Here it is many, many years later and I still think about him. Some of these people don't seem like they're gone to me, because I can think back in my mind and I can see them. I can see Czubie standing there with the chief that day almost like it was yesterday. To me it seems like he's alive. I can see Frank sitting in the kitchen smoking his pipe and laughing at someone's anecdotes.

I have been at numerous fires, a lot more than I wish I had to admit to, where children died, and every single one of those fires to me has been very tragic, because a very young life was shut off—a potential lost. I always wonder what those kids could have been. When I was a battalion chief in Brooklyn someone dropped a cigarette on a bed. A baby was lying among all the bedding and clothes that had been thrown on this bed. While the adults were in the kitchen drinking, the baby burned to death two rooms away. I had to restrain a couple of firemen that night. They wanted to beat the hell out of the people who were drinking—not that it would have meant anything, because those people didn't know where the hell they were. The damage was just to the bed. The baby was incinerated on that bed. It was maybe two or three months old when it died.

We tend to think about the people we lose, but I'll tell you we save a hell of a lot more than we lose. For every person I ever saw lost at a fire I would say we probably saved a couple of hundred people. I saw some excellent rescues in my time, and I think being associated with people who can perform at that level is satisfying. By the way, I think the Fire Department is probably one of the most misunderstood agencies in the city. I really don't think the average person on the street fully understands the work that the Fire Department performs. I mean, people are well aware that we ride through the streets in our red fire engines and that we put fires out. But to say that's all we do is like saying a doctor works with sick people and that's the full extent of what a doctor does. This lack of understanding is probably our own fault. We haven't really gone out of our way to let the people in the communities know what kind of work we do. Nevertheless, fire fighters have always been highly thought of by the people in the city. By and large we are thought to be one of the premier agencies of the city and I think that reputation is well deserved. We work very hard at what we do, and it's not just a job to us. I think the day the Fire Department becomes just a job, a place you go just to get paid, that's the day we're going to fall off.

My father was on the job for thirty-three years. I am coming up to thirty-six years. My brother Charlie put twenty-two years in. My son Richard has about five years, and my other son, John, has about three years in. That's a total of ninety-nine years for us. This year the Farrells will pass the hundred-year mark. My father died a couple years ago, but I know he'd be very proud of that. I know I am. My brother Charlie got injured in the job. He's out on disability, but I know Charlie is very proud of the work our family has done. And I'm sure my two sons are. It's something that I think that anybody would be proud of. There are days when I feel it's time for me to get out of the job and let my two sons carry on. This is a young man's job. We have some guys out there with a lot of years in, and they still perform. They probably have too much pride to tell you, but it gets tougher and tougher every single day when you're out there trying to fight fires.

Would I do it over again? Yes, I would. Would I make any changes? I doubt it. I'd probably do what I did before. Got a lot of good memories, I'll tell you that, and I'm taking those into retirement with me. I miss the people who are gone, but I can still laugh about the good times we had. I just hope my sons get as much enjoyment out of their careers as I got out of mine. It's time to "take up."

STANDARD ALARM ASSIGNMENTS

Box 020 Location: City Hall

Alarm	Engines	Ladders	Special Units*	Chiefs
1	6, 7, 10	1, 10		B1
2	4, 55, 24,	9	R1, ST1, FC	B4, D1
3	15, 33, 17, 28	15	MW, MK	
4	18, 5, 3, 16	6		
5	1, 34, 65, 224	20		

*R1: Rescue Company 1
ST1: Satellite 1 (carries large hoses, foam, and a monitor)
FC: Field Communications
MW: Maxi-water system (a high pressure pumper)
MK: Mask Service (provides additional fresh air bottles)

   The numerical designation for each assigned company, at each level of alarm, is given above. For example, on the first alarm Engine 6, Engine 7, and Engine 10 will be sent along with Ladder 1, Ladder 10, and the First Battalion (a battalion chief and his aide). If the first arriving companies find that an actual fire is occurring, they will give the 1075 radio signal to tell the dispatcher to send all of the units in the first alarm assignment and to start the rescue on its way to the fire. On the second alarm, an additional battalion chief is sent along with the division (a deputy chief and his aide). At any point in the fire, other units may be special-called to the scene, including the floodlight unit, if it is a night operation.

GLOSSARY

AERIAL A hydraulically powered ladder mounted on a truck.

ALL-HANDS A fire in which the entire first alarm assignment is working.

APPARATUS Another term for fire trucks.

APPARATUS FLOOR The ground floor of a firehouse where the trucks are kept.

APRON The sloping part of the driveway in front of a firehouse.

BACKDRAFT The sudden in-rush of air to a fire that has consumed the available oxygen, but retains heat and fuel.

BATTALION A group of engines and ladder trucks that cover a particular geographical area. A battalion is commanded by a battalion chief.

BOROUGH CALL—A fire that has gone above a fifth alarm assignment.

BOTTLE The compressed air cylinder for the self-contained breathing apparatus.

BOX One of 16,000 alarm devices on the city streets. Every alarm is assigned the number of the nearest box.

BREACH To make a hole in a wall.

BUCKET A three man basket at the top end of the hydraulic boom of a tower ladder.

BUFF A devotee of fire operations. To buff a fire is to watch it being fought.

BULKHEAD A small structure on a roof which provides access to the interior stairs.

CAN A two-and-one-half-gallon water-filled fire extinguisher.

CHIEF OF DEPARTMENT The highest civil service rank in the FDNY. He commands the uniformed force.

CLASS I The highest level of heroism award in the FDNY.

COCKLOFT The space between a ceiling and the roof or the floor above.

COMPANY The firefighters assigned to each ladder truck, engine, rescue, or fireboat. Each company is commanded by a captain and three lieutenants, and has approximately twenty-five firemen assigned to it.

COVERING Working (often in another unit) in place of the assigned officer.

ENGINE The apparatus that carries the hose lines and pumps water.

ERS BOX A part of the Emergency Reporting System that allows two-way communication between the person in the street and the fire alarm dispatchers.

EXPOSURES The area extending from one of four sides of a building. Exposure one is the front of the building. Exposure two is the left side (if you are facing the front). Exposure three is the rear, and exposure four is the right side.

FIRE PATROL Units that respond to fires to perform salvage work. They are funded by the insurance underwriters.

FIRE TRIANGLE Heat, fuel, and oxygen—the three components of fire.

FIRST DUE The first assigned truck or engine company to a particular location.

FOAM The generic term for a variety of smothering agents that look like soapsuds when applied.

FRONT PIECE   A leather device with the fire fighter's rank and unit on it that is affixed to the helmet.

HALLIGAN TOOL   An all-purpose steel prying tool invented by Huey Halligan, a former member of the FDNY.

HAND LINE   Fire hose that is literally moved into the fire by hand.

HOOK   A six-, ten-, or twenty-foot pole with a pointed metal tip and a short hook several inches below.

HOSE STRAP   A two-foot length of rope with a loop on one end and a metal hook on the other. It is used to secure a hose line to a fixed object so it does not fall back down a stairwell or off a roof.

HOUSE LINE   A hose line that is preconnected to a building's stand pipe system and is usually located in the stairwells.

HOUSE WATCH   An office on the apparatus floor near the front of the firehouse. When a company is in quarters, this office is manned by the fire fighter who has the watch. The person on house watch answers the phones and monitors the teleprinter. It is his job to turn the company out if an alarm is received.

HURST TOOL   Also known as "the jaws of life," it is a hydraulic cutting and wedging device manufactured by Hurst, but it also has become the generic term for similar devices by other manufacturers.

INTERCHANGE   A system whereby slow and busy companies are sent to cover each other's firehouses. It was initiated to give the men in the busy companies a rest.

IRONS   The forcible-entry tools, particularly the ax and the Halligan tool.

KNOB   The nozzle of a hose.

LADDER PIPE   A high-pressure nozzle mounted on the top of an aerial ladder, but controlled from the ground.

LINE   In most instances it is the shortened version of hose line, as in, "We moved the (hose) line in." A search line, however, is a length of rope which is anchored at one end so that you can find your way back to its origin in zero visibility.

MASK A self-contained breathing apparatus that consists of a face piece, regulator, air tank, and backpack. The masks currently in service with the FDNY are manufactured by Scott.

MPO The motor pump operator, who drives the engine and runs the pump to supply water to the hose lines.

MULTIVERSAL A high-volume nozzle. Because of its weight and the pressure that develops it is set in place before being charged. The Stang is another brand of high-pressure nozzle.

OVERHAULING The manual pulling down of ceilings and the opening up of walls, floors, and window frames to expose hidden pockets of fire.

OVM Outside vent man, one of the positions assigned to a member of a ladder company.

PLATOON A way of dividing the work force to provide twenty-four-hour coverage. The old three-platoon system had a day, evening, and night shift. Currently the FDNY uses a two-platoon system, where the day shift is from 9:00 A.M. to 6:00 P.M. and the night shift is from 6:00 P.M. to 9:00 A.M.

POLE The brass pole on which firemen slide down to quickly get to the apparatus floor. The opening in an upper floor through which the pole passes is called the pole hole.

PROBIE Probationary fire fighter—e.g., a beginning fire fighter, also known as a Johnny.

RAILROAD FLAT A long, narrow apartment, usually two to a floor in a tenement or row frame building.

SPECIAL CALL When a chief requests the dispatcher to send him a particular type of apparatus, e.g., "Send me an additional truck company," or "send another rescue company."

STOKES BASKET A wire basket that is used as a stretcher.

TAKE A BLOW To get a breath of fresh air or to take a rest.

TAKE UP FDNY jargon meaning to go. The implication is that after a fire you gather up your hose lines and tools before leaving.

TAPS   When the bell system was in effect, companies could communicate with the dispatchers by tapping on a telegraph key.

TAXPAYER   A row of stores one story high, though occasionally a taxpayer will have a second story of offices.

1075   The radio signal given by the first arriving unit if there is any indication that a working fire exists. This signal tells the dispatcher to fill out the first alarm assignment and start a rescue company on its way.

TILLER   The rear steering position on a tractor-trailer type of aerial ladder.

TOWER LADDER   A type of truck that has a bucket attached to the end of a telescoping hydraulically powered boom. This device is erroneously called a "cherry picker" by the press.

TRUCKIES   The members, i.e. fire fighters assigned to a ladder truck company.

V PATTERN   Burn marks in the shape of a V. Since fire burns up and out, by locating the apex of the triangle you can determine the fire's point of origin.

WNYF   The magazine of the New York Fire Department. It began publication in 1946 and is now issued quarterly.

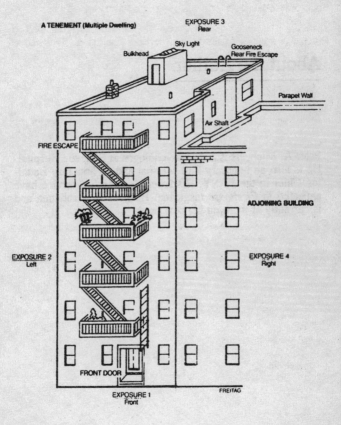

A TENEMENT (Multiple Dwelling)

EXPOSURE 3
Rear

Bulkhead

Sky Light

Gooseneck
Rear Fire Escape

Parapet Wall

Air Shaft

FIRE ESCAPE

ADJOINING BUILDING

EXPOSURE 2
Left

EXPOSURE 4
Right

FRONT DOOR

FREITAG

EXPOSURE 1
Front

About the Author

Peter A. Micheels is a staff psychologist at Bellevue Hospital. He is also an honorary Fire Marshal and an honorary Battalion Chief in the FDNY. His articles on the fire service have appeared in *Firehouse* magazine. He lives in Manhattan and is currently at work on his next book.